Living in the Sweet Spot

"I've always been interested in how to perform better—for myself and now for our players. Performance at the highest level is always a challenge. This book provides some excellent practical ideas of how to achieve and sustain high levels of performance from the psychological perspective."

— Jason Garrett
head coach, Dallas Cowboys

"This book provides an exceptional grasp of the scientific research in the area of sport psychology/performance excellence. The material is presented in a practical manner that will be extremely beneficial for anyone who wants to perform when the pressure is on. This book is a must read."

— Ken Ravizza
author of *Heads-Up Baseball: Playing the Game One Pitch at a Time* and a world-renowned peak performance consultant

"*Living in the Sweet Spot* is an invaluable companion for any performing artist. The interesting and inspiring narrative along with numerous practical tools designed to achieve optimal performance will help artists complement their daily practice with mind-based strategies. Most importantly, the book addresses the importance of getting in touch with what drives us all: passion and enjoyment."

— Christine Vitale
professional violinist and optimal performance coach

"In my best races, the X factor was positive mindset—love the craft, love the chance to be pushed to the limit. This book is not only a great exploration of the psychology of success, but also a real training tool for extreme performers seeking to be at their best when it counts."

— Michelle Guerette
two-time Olympian, 2008 single-scull Olympic silver medalist

"In Karate, the expression '*Nana korobi ya-oki*' means 'fall down seven, get up eight.' This represents your 'Indomitable Spirit or Winning Attitude.' The ideas in this book are the same as those that have given me strength and a competitive edge throughout my years in football and karate, where 'living in the sweet spot' means no limits and no final destination, but still maintaining benchmarks and high standards. In other words, it is our attitude that shapes the forces in our lives."

— Andre Tippett
Pro Football Hall of Fame 2008 inductee and
Uechi-Ryu Karate Godan/5th, Shihan (Master Instructor)

Living in the
Sweet Spot

Preparing for Performance in Sport and Life

A M Y L . B A L T Z E L L

Fitness Information Technology

A Division of the International Center for Performance Excellence
262 Coliseum, WVU-CPASS ▪ P O Box 6116
Morgantown, WV 26506-6116

Library of Congress Card Catalog Number: 2010935126

ISBN: 978-1-935412-09-0

Production Editor: Matt Brann
Cover Design: 40 West Studios
Typesetter: 40 West Studios
Copyeditor: Berkeley Bentley
Proofreader: Geoffrey Fuller
Indexer: Geoffrey Fuller
Printed by Thomson-Shore

Cover image: © Kerry Kay-Smith | Dreamstime.com

10 9 8 7 6 5 4 3 2 1

Fitness Information Technology
A Division of the International Center for Performance Excellence
West Virginia University
262 Coliseum, WVU-CPASS
PO Box 6116
Morgantown, WV 26506-6116
800.477.4348 (toll free)
304.293.6888 (phone)
304.293.6658 (fax)
Email: fitcustomerservice@mail.wvu.edu
Website: www.fitinfotech.com

I'd like to dedicate this book to my husband, John McCarthy, my children—Shayna, Luke, and Zoey—and to my parents.

— AB

Contents

PART I: THE BUILDING BLOCKS OF A CHAMPION APPROACH

PART II: PREPARING FOR PERFORMANCE OR COMPETITION

PART III: THE DAY OF PERFORMANCE

Acknowledgments

A special thank you is owed to Cathy O'Connor, who has gone beyond anyone could ever ask for. I am humbled by her generous and brilliant editing and mentorship.

I thank my husband, John McCarthy, for his tireless and kind support of all that I do. I thank my sister and brother, Laura and Mark, for their encouragement and love. Thank you Bronwyn Malicoat, Katie Kilty, and Linda Flaherty for your steady friendships. And I appreciate the support and space that my kids—Shayna, Luke, and Zoey—gave me through the many early morning sessions and weekends that it took me to write this book. I thank my college coach, Pat Callahan, who believed in me and helped me learn how to get the best out of myself.

Thank you Linda Sargent for believing in me and getting me moving. Thank you to Karen Levy, freelance book editor, who guided me through the many hurdles of the book publishing world. And, of course, thank you to Steven Pope, director of Fitness Information Technology, who believed in this project from the start. I appreciate all of the hard work of Matt Brann, my editor at Fitness Information Technology. And finally, I am grateful to Phil Simms' generosity in writing such a powerful, heartfelt foreword.

To my academic world: Thank you to the leadership in Boston University's School of Education. A special thank you to Charlie Glenn for the sabbatical to write. Thank you to my past co-authors and collaborators: John Yeager, Richard Ginsburg, and Steve Durant. Thank you, past department chair, Shanley Allan, for your frequent encouragement. Thank you to Karen Bohlin's steadfast belief and support in my work. And thanks to Adam Naylor, who has been a wonderful colleague.

I would like to thank all of the athletes, musicians, parents, teachers, and coaches with whom I have worked. Through their stories, they have helped me understand what it takes psychologically to get the best out of ourselves.

Foreword

I wish I had this book in the early days of my career playing quarterback for the New York Giants. Let me give you a prime example why. There would be games in which, if I threw an interception during the first possession, I would go sit on the bench after the interception and stress over the mistake. I would think to myself, "I can't make another mistake the rest of this game." And when games started that way, I was never able to overcome that interception and have tremendous days. A lot of the games would turn out OK, but very seldom would I have really good performances.

On the other hand, there were games in which, if I threw an interception during the first possession, I would go to the sideline and I wouldn't stress over that mistake. In fact, I would tell my teammates, "I don't know, I might throw four interceptions today. All I know is I'm going to be aggressive and I'm just going to let it go." When I had that mindset during games, it would generally lead to great performances. Following those games, Coach Bill Parcells would say to me after the game, "Simms, you were aggressive and daring. That's how I want my quarterback to be."

As I look back, I realize just how powerful your mind can be when it comes to athletic performance. But I didn't have a book like *Living in the Sweet Spot* to help me develop consistency in using my mind to help produce great performances.

Sometimes we do get properly focused. A great example is my Super Bowl XXI MVP game, when I completed 22 of 25 passes in a victory over the Denver Broncos. Early in my career I had read many accounts of quarterbacks saying that the Super Bowl game was so big that they could not settle down until the second quarter of the game. They had a difficult time remembering and focusing on the plays that they ran during the first quarter. And as I read those accounts I recall thinking, "If I ever get a chance to play in the Super Bowl, I am not going to waste 25% of that game just trying to settle down."

In the two weeks leading up to that game in January 1987, I thought to myself many times, "I am not worried about the outcome. I am going to be aggressive and confident in my thinking." I remember thinking, "I am not afraid to fail." Having that mindset just kept me loose and confident leading up to and through the entire game. As I look back over my career, I have often thought, "Why didn't I approach more games like that, or really, why didn't I approach *all* my games like that?"

Since my retirement, I have studied sports from the physical and mental standpoint, which I now understand much better than I did during my playing days. I realize the approach you take in training and playing the actual sporting event can be made more productive and can absolutely be made more enjoyable. This, obviously, is going to lead to a higher rate of success. After reading *Living in the Sweet Spot,* when I hear somebody say "the sport is 50% mental and 50% physical" I won't just think, "Wow—that is just another dumb cliché." I realize that, in fact, it is the truth. By not knowing that earlier, I kept myself from having more success. I should have and could have enjoyed my experiences even more.

In reading this book, I particularly enjoyed reading the accounts of the athletes who thought they were not achieving enough. They thought the only way they could achieve success was to physically and mentally put themselves through misery—the old "paying the price" adage. What I learned in this book is that if you focus on the positives and what actually brings you joy, it will change your perspective, and maybe most importantly, give you more energy. Everyone, not just athletes, can benefit from reading *Living in the Sweet Spot*—we can learn how to accept ourselves, our endeavors, our sport, or our profession. Our thoughts and perceptions really have a lot to do with performance levels, outcomes, and just being able to enjoy what we're doing. It's true what I heard growing up—so many things in the athletic world mirror what goes on in your life off the field, no matter if you are a housewife, a business person, or a brain surgeon.

I always say this to kids and to people in general, and it's one of the things I found so true and enjoyable as I read the accounts and Amy Baltzell's solutions: **It's not always about winning.**

The sad thing is, some athletes actually believe that it's only about winning and about having championships to validate their careers. I played 15 years in the NFL, started four years in college, and played all through high school and grade school, so I have a lot of experiences to choose from. But one of the best moments in my entire athletic career, when I remember feeling absolutely satisfied with how I played, did not come after a thrilling victory. It was the last game of the 1993 regular season and we were playing the Dallas Cowboys. I thought to myself, "Whoever wins this game will probably go on to win the Super Bowl." We lost in overtime.

I remember walking into the locker room when the game was over, sitting down, and not having a single thought of sadness or remorse. Instead, I was thinking about what an accomplishment it was to take an above average team, play against one of the best teams I ever played against in my career, take them into overtime, and just play the best we could possibly play. It made me realize that it truly is about just doing your best. And with that comes deep, deep satisfaction.

As I wrote in the introduction to this foreword, I wish I would have had this book during the early days of my playing career. After reading it and knowing how much it can help athletes enjoy their sport while becoming better performers, it would be crazy for any of today's athletes not to read *Living in the Sweet Spot*. Reading this book will put you in a better frame of mind and will result in more enjoyable and successful performances.

Phil Simms,
CBS Sports lead NFL analyst
Former New York Giants quarterback
Super Bowl XXI MVP

Preface

Living in the Sweet Spot: Preparing for Performance in Sport and Life provides the knowledge, inspiration, and tools needed to be truly ready when your big race day, game day, or your big moment shows up. All of us are looking for ways to ensure that we will do our thing well, so that we can achieve success. We are looking for an edge to help us do our best when the results could influence our reputation, self-esteem, pride, future opportunities, teammates' views, coaches' opinions, scholarship offerings, or our chances of making a team, getting chosen for an orchestra, or landing the job we've always wanted.

Anyone trying to achieve success spends countless hours preparing for big performance moments. There are people cutting albums, earning college scholarships, dancing, singing, speaking, or playing for world-class orchestras who are phenomenal at what they do. Yet many of these same performers find themselves working very hard while at the same time feeling unfulfilled, burned out, and/or short of their desired mark of excellence. You may be one of these performers who feels that they could be even better but don't know how to get there. You too may work intensely hard and find yourself feeling like you could be better and could get more satisfaction out of what you are doing.

From the novice to the professional performer, we have high standards for our achievement. We live in a world that highly values succeeding, winning, and even dominating. We are expected to push ourselves and thrive in whatever we do. Yet most of us have not been given the parallel psychological education or training to learn how to truly get the most out of ourselves in a way that is fulfilling while also setting us up for our best performance. (I certainly did not, even as an Olympian.) Most of us have not been given the psychological-emotional skills to cope with the intense demand of pushing to achieve.

This is the book that I wish that I had had as a young, aspiring elite athlete, a rower who qualified for the Olympics. Twenty years ago, I didn't know that I had a choice in how I felt, what I thought, or how I performed on a given day. I believed that socially, emotionally, and mentally planning for competition was a waste of time. I believed that trying one's hardest, physically, was all that mattered. I had no idea how to handle my fears of not making a team or my angst over wanting to be one of the best and fearing that I would not be. I know now that I could have been faster and I could have enjoyed the ride much more. My life's work is committed to helping others perform better and be open to enjoying the process more (which actually helps greatly with performance, but more on that later).

Not knowing how to get into a positive, constructive, focused state of mind for training and performance is an epidemic. I have worked with hundreds of athletes and musicians who have lost their love for doing their thing. Many have totally lost perspective on the skills and abilities for which they have worked so hard. Many have no idea what they can psychologically lean on when the pressure is on and when they feel like they are losing control. But many of these same performers learned how to regain a sense of control. They learned how to be more focused on what truly helped them both perform to the best of their abilities and (perhaps most importantly) to draw satisfaction from what they were doing.

If you are open to thinking differently while you are still standing before the peak of your athletic or performance career, I write this book for you. It is possible to be fully and consistently engaged while competing. It is possible to enjoy competing, to want to be there. It is possible to love your daily training.

However, be forewarned. Changing your psychological approach to performance is truly challenging. Making even slight adjustments to your psychological-emotional approach to training and performing is not for the faint of heart. Creating a champion mindset and approach to competing is possible, but it takes hard work (sometimes harder than the physical preparation). It takes honest self-reflection and a willingness to take stock of how you think and feel. It takes effort to shift thoughts and feelings and to be willing to absorb information, even critical information in a positive, constructive way. Sometimes, it even means truly accepting negative emotions, presssing on, and doing your thing (though you can learn to lessen the sting of the negativity).

How is this book designed? *Living in the Sweet Spot: Preparing for Performance in Sport and Life* is divided into three sections. Section I (*The Building Blocks of a Champion Approach*) addresses a critical piece that is often missing in the performer's preparation for big moments. This section encourages you to consider what is already good—your strengths and the good of what is already occurring in your daily living and training. Also emphasized in this section is how to set yourself up to experience positive emotions in the weeks and months before a key performance. In the world of achievement, we often ignore or dismiss the value of positive emotion. Other essentials to creating a solid psychological/performance foundation include considering the importance of wisely using our willpower and developing a habit of learning (versus chronically judging ourselves).

Section II (*Preparing Mentally for Competition*) more specifically focuses on factors that will help you become socially, emotionally, and cognitively competition-ready. This section includes chapters on how to enhance your sense of engagement while competing, how to cope effectively with negative emotions, and how to let in the best of teammates and coaches, as well as the use of imagery and goal setting for the day of competition.

Section III (*The Day of Performance*) focuses on helping you get ready for the actual day of performance. Specific strategies are provided that enhance effective focus and minimize the potential adverse effects of negative thinking or aversive emotions on the day of competition or performance. These chapters address empowered thinking, thriving emotionally on game day, and methods of purposefully shifting one's motivational orientation just prior to and during competition (*motivational flexibility*). The last chapter focuses on helping you develop a plan and choose what you will actually do to help prepare psychologically for the big day.

This book is for you if you are looking for specific ways to give yourself the best shot at optimizing performance on the day of an important performance. I give to you the best of what I know from my own experience as an Olympian and professional athlete, and from what I've learned over the last decade as a sport psychologist and professor of sport psychology. I provide you with case examples, key theories, and the best from the research world. I also have carefully designed exercises to help you tailor the ideas presented such that you can integrate them into your own training and key performance moments. Welcome and read on.

PART I
THE BUILDING BLOCKS OF A CHAMPION APPROACH

1

What Is Living in the Sweet Spot?

Achievement and Happiness

"I raced the best race of my life.
I lost, yet I was so happy."
—World champion rower

"My first audition I was terrified. I could not walk
straight. I decided after that that no matter what
happened, that I would not be afraid. I won't care
about mistakes. I won't care about not being selected.
I would never be afraid like that again."
—Current Boston Symphony Orchestra musician

If you could wave your magic wand and create one thing, what would it be? If you could put aside your fears, your self-judgments, your current life constraints, the demands and desires of others—what do you want? I'm guessing that you already know what you want to achieve. You may want to make a particular team or group. You may want a college scholarship or a spot on the U.S. Team. Once you know what you want to achieve, the most important question is, What will help you achieve your goal? I'm sure that you ask yourself this a lot. "What will help me get there? What do I need to do to give myself an edge?"

We know that the right physical, technical, and strategic training are essential for achievement. So what else is there? The following example highlights what I've seen missing in top athletes and musicians over the past decade. A few years ago I worked with a nationally ranked 12-year-old gymnast—I'll call her Hannah. She was flown in from another country to work with me for the weekend. Her main reason for coming to see me was that she wanted help overcoming her fear of doing back flips on the balance beam. This young athlete was living in a sports academy and training approximately six hours each day. As we explored options to help her with her fear of doing back flips, I asked her what she loved about doing her sport. She abruptly responded, "I don't like gymnastics." She went on to say, "I only want to get over my fear of doing back flips … I just want to make my National Team." Hannah was doing everything possible that would behaviorally contribute to her becoming one of the top gymnasts in her country. She was giving all that she could physically, technically, and in terms of hours spent on the mat, balance beam, and high bars. She was dedicating her life energy, yet she was coming up short. She was uninspired and emotionally flat. What else was there for her to do?

Hannah's biggest shot at improving her performance was to tap into her love and enjoyment of some aspect of gymnastics. She had become so focused on achieving a significant mark of success that she had totally lost touch with what got her involved with the sport in the first place. That weekend we made some good progress in re-engaging her with what she enjoyed about the sport. We created strategies for her to create positive intentions for her back flips. We created specific imagery scripts for how she would like to be moving and *feeling* emotionally. We worked on integrating the parts of what she loved back into her awareness as she practiced.

Hannah is not alone in her exclusive focus on success at the cost of her love of what she was doing. I have seen hundreds of athletes and performers—many scholarship collegiate athletes, elite athletes, Olympic hopefuls, and classical musicians—who also do not prioritize their own happiness and enjoyment in the process of trying to optimize performance. Most high achievers are willing to forgo their own immediate happiness in exchange for trying to fast track themselves to achievement. And, sadly, some, like Hannah, totally lose touch with the joy of it—why they began in the first place.

As an elite athlete, during the peak of my career, I had no interest or concern for my fleeting moments of pleasure, joy, love, or passion. I was more interested in forcing myself to do my best each day, thinking that this was giving me my best chance of attaining success. If I was physically or emotionally intensely uncomfortable, I figured that this was simply the cost of success. If I were entertaining negative thoughts or fears, I figured that the aversive feelings were just part of the territory. I also thought that positive emotions were distractions that made me too emotionally soft. Yet I learned the hard way that this does not work. And I have since observed hundreds of high-level performers employ this force-it-and-be-miserable approach that leads to lower levels of performance, burnout, or withdrawal from participation.

I have spent the past 25 years trying to determine what psychological habits, approaches, and tools contribute most powerfully to best performance. First I looked for what would lead to top achievement for myself as an athlete. And then, for the past decade, as a sport psychology consultant and professor, I have worked hard to unpack the magic that allows some to thrive, regardless of their circumstances. I have come to realize the power of positive emotion, positive intentions, and the importance of mitigating negative emotions (such as fear and dread), especially when these are paired with the power of sport psychology mental skills.

Essentially, the missing piece in training and performance for many of us has been the role of our positive emotion and ultimately the role of nurturing our own happiness in the effort to become our best possible performing self. Often we don't think of happiness and achievement working together. Yes, we do think about how winning will provide us with a powerful sense of happiness and joy. We know that such emotions are nice when they happen. But we don't often prioritize feeling good while training or performing. To many performers it is a novel idea to consider the fact that nurturing your positive emotions—ultimately your personal happiness—could give you an edge over your competitors.

So what does happiness have to do with achievement? Happiness has to do with *the how* of your pursuit. It has to do with what you pay attention to in practice and performance. Many of us were never taught the value of positive emotion—how passion, authentic interest, and presence can help us leverage our ability to do our best. The irony is that many of us can get better (very quickly) when we hook into our love for doing our thing.

Consider *the how* or the process of (then) young oboist Keisuke Wakao. Keisuke immigrated from Japan to the United States to pursue his dream of making a world-class orchestra. He spent his childhood preparing for such an opportunity. In his first tryout for a premier orchestra in the US he recalls wanting more than anything to be selected, and feeling unexpectedly terrified. He recalls feeling emotionally overwhelmed: "I felt like I was struck in the chest as I walked into the performance hall. I couldn't walk straight. I couldn't think. I couldn't play." He had practiced for 20 years for this chance, and he was blocked by an overwhelming sense of fear.

Keisuke's moment-to-moment experience during this audition was miserable. Essentially, his negative, fear-based emotions got in the way of him playing well. Though he was a highly skilled musician, he failed. What was missing for him at this audition? Though well prepared technically, Keisuke was missing an ability to tune in to doing his thing well—and enjoying it—regardless of who was watching or evaluating his performance. How you think and feel while training and getting ready for such performances is at the core of this book. The focus of this book is about how to create and use your habit of positive emotion and focus to prepare for such high-pressure performance moments so you can thrive under pressure.

BUT FIRST, WHAT IS THE *SWEET SPOT?*

Many of the guides we have available to us are *either* about how to achieve *or* how to be happy. The message seems to be that you either choose to pursue happiness or achievement. Living in the sweet spot is about blowing up the myth that you must choose between being happy and being successful. This approach gives you the best chance of both. It is hard to fully achieve—to thrive—without intentionally making the pursuit a personally interesting, engaging, and (often) enjoyable pursuit. Living and performing in the sweet spot lies at the intersection of achievement and happiness. To live and perform in the sweet spot we must simultaneously value achievement *and* happiness. The sweet spot exists where you are both giving yourself the best shot at personal achievement and leveraging what it takes to maintain and nurture your own personal happiness while striving toward your goals.

In clarifying what I mean by *living in the sweet spot,* I will start with what it is *not.* It is not about always being successful (compared to others). It does not mean that you will always win. It does not mean that you always feel positive emotions. It is not about always making a lot of money, or being physically perfect, or dominating others in whatever you wish to find success. It's not just living in a dream world of effortlessness. Living and staying in the sweet spot is not easy. It's not just feeling sensations of joy and happiness. It is not the same as the message of the recent phenomenon The Secret, which promises great success with only wishing for it to be so.

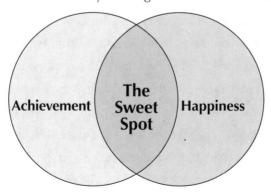

Figure 1.1: The Sweet Spot

So how can we recognize the sweet spot? A *physical* experience of the sweet spot in sport—say in tennis—is when you hit the ball just right with the racquet. When you hit the ball in the sweet spot, you instantly know that the shot was hit just right. It just feels right. This physical experience of the sweet spot is the same for softball and baseball—hitting the ball just right with just the right part of the bat. You know that you could never hit the ball better for that given moment. Hitting a ball in the sweet spot requires focus and effort. It probably cannot happen unless you are fully present, doing all that you can do in the moment to play or perform your best. Physically, hitting the sweet spot can seem elusive. You can't always hit it. But this book is about what it takes to give yourself your best shot of hitting the sweet spot more frequently with focus, determination, and hard work.

When I *visually* consider the sweet spot, I often imagine a dog chasing a ball. The dog doesn't care what others think because she is highly energized in the moment to do what she is doing. The dog is totally focused and seems to be experiencing pure joy while chasing the ball. And if the dog can't find the ball after jumping and diving after it, the dog will just wag her tail contently, waiting for another chance to live such an engaged, joyful moment. Whether a young puppy or a three-legged old dog, dogs' intensity, joy, and sense of contentment are evident.

Psychologically living in the sweet spot requires putting your full effort into your training, thinking, and feeling in ways that are authentic and attuned to the situation. It means living, training, and performing moment to moment in ways that truly feel right to you. And when we live like this, we get true satisfaction from our daily effort. Living and performing this way takes significant, purposeful effort—in what you do, feel, and think. Living in the sweet spot is truly being engaged with what you care about. It means gleaning quiet, intense satisfaction from your efforts during and after success and failure. It is also about providing yourself with the best chance of achieving success in the external world.

Living in the sweet spot includes doing all that you can to learn and improve in your discipline of choice. But this high commitment is not enough.

Recall Hannah the gymnast. She was highly committed yet found herself in a fear state with nothing on which to lean. The question is not whether or not you are committed, but whether or not you are able to maintain a priority of doing your thing—because you want to for your own reasons. For example, this means running because you truly enjoy running or value the benefits that you get from running—not because someone else expects you to run well. Training and performing in the sweet spot means not only are you hard working but you also are able to hook into the love of what you do.

When your happiness serves your goals, you also are challenging yourself to think and feel in the most productive ways possible. Clearly this takes attention and great effort. Let's return to Keisuke Wakao, the oboist. How did he get over his great disappointment of missing out on one of only a few opportunities to achieve his goal of being a core member of a premier orchestra? He made a decision to prioritize his joy. He decided that no matter what, he would never let himself be afraid again. He decided that, "It didn't matter anymore if I made mistakes. It didn't matter any more if they might not like my sound. It didn't matter any more if they didn't select me. I would never allow myself to feel such fear again! In fact, I decided it didn't matter how others sounded. It didn't matter how good they were. What mattered was that I shine. What matters is that I enjoy what I do and shine! If I don't enjoy it, it is not worth it." Keisuke later earned a spot on the Boston Symphony Orchestra as an assistant oboist when he was 26-years old. (Most musicians don't enjoy such success until well into their 30s, if at all.)

Keisuke decided to value his own happiness above all. This shift to maintaining his love for playing his music and determination to be someone that shines was powerful. He says, "I wanted to be the type of musician that shines. I wanted to be so good that when I made a mistake they [the listener] would say, 'Oh, he made a mistake!' That is a beautiful part of the music!" So he chose to value *both* his own happiness and achievement. He became determined to live and perform in the sweet spot. He aspires to be the best and at the same time, to shine with love and joy for doing his thing.

One of the core requirements of living in the sweet spot is developing the ability to focus one's thoughts in empowering ways. It took great mental effort for Keisuke to shift how he was thinking. After 20 years of training, he decided to think differently. He became determined to only play his instruments with love and passion. He decided that how he felt inside trumped all marks of success of others' evaluation of him. This is a hard shift to make and is quite uncommon. Without honest self-reflection and valuing our own internal experience, we can default to valuing above all how we compare to others.

Living in the sweet spot allows you to glean a sense of satisfaction and fulfillment from your endeavors whether you win or lose. Yet, without clarity and determination, losses can serve as a source of devastation. I recently spoke with a young man, Shawn, who was discussing a key moment in his high school sport days. In fact, it was one of the last games he played. He was recalling a game when he was pitching against another athlete who was considered to have been quite good, equal in ability to Shawn. Shawn recalls coming up to the plate (at the top of the ninth inning) and the count being three balls and two strikes. His batting record against this rival pitcher was .500. Shawn swung and missed. He struck out. The game remained tied.

Shawn then pitched the bottom of the ninth inning. And as fate would have it, his rival pitcher was up to bat. The count returned again to three balls and two strikes. This time the story was different. His rival pitcher connected hard and solidly with the ball and sent the ball over the fence. Shawn's team lost, and it was one of his very last games as an outstanding high school athlete. Shawn made the comment, "It was crushing. One of us had to be crushed, and it was me that day." I asked Shawn, "Did you train hard? Did you love playing? Did you play to the best that you could?" Shawn's response was, "Of course. I loved to play. I lived to play."

At this point I asked him, "Was it really necessary to be crushed? Yes, for the moment it was disappointing. But if you did all that you could, you enjoyed what you were doing, and you played up to your potential, didn't you, too, deserve to enjoy a sense of satisfaction and fulfillment?" Shawn was living in and performing in the sweet spot while he was playing baseball in high school. At the very end of his high school career he allowed himself to be bumped out of the sweet spot. He allowed his unhappiness at a comparison with a rival to get in the way of appreciating his own abilities.

Living in the sweet spot takes effort: it requires getting clear on what you value and working hard to achieve your goals—and valuing this. It can be easy to get caught up in how we compare to others. We all do this. But living in the sweet spot requires that we gain (and regain) our perspective on valuing what we can control.

Living in the sweet spot takes effort: we must become consistently aware of the thoughts, feelings, and actions that are serving our life—and become aware of those that are not. And living in this space takes courage: courage to make changes that are needed to allow you to thrive. It requires a commitment to your own thriving and well-being. When you are living in the sweet spot you are attuned to making choices and focusing your effort in ways that consistently allow you to thrive. And when we get out of this groove (and we will), living in the sweet spot means making an effort to get back—to get realigned with making choices that help us think and live in the most positive, empowered way.

HOW DO WE NUDGE OURSELVES INTO THE SWEET SPOT?

All of us at times can find ourselves spiraling downward. The trick is not to avoid these episodes—we simply can't; we are human. We can, however, learn to catch these moments and turn them around progressively more quickly. Living in the sweet spot is not just about feeling passionate, joyful, energized, and having consistently positive thoughts. Living in the sweet spot is about learning to be honestly aware of our thoughts and emotions—and learning when to either *flow* with naturally occurring thoughts and emotions or when to challenge ourselves to *change* our attitude, perspective, or focus.

Living in the sweet spot also means allowing in and honoring our emotional responses to life—allowing in the pain and joy—and honoring the feelings with thoughtful reflection. It means that we have the option to return to living in a grateful, present space whenever we choose. It means surrounding ourselves with people who we feel comfortable with—and setting limits and boundaries on activities and relationships that are not currently working for us in a kind, compassionate way. Living in the sweet spot is ultimately about *giving yourself the best chance of achieving success,* whether that be in sport or in other areas of performance, business, or relationships. Living in the sweet spot is idiosyncratic; our sweet spots are unique to each of us. Only we know for certain when we are living in it.

I have worked with many performers who only need to work in one specific place in their training to get themselves back to living and performing in the sweet spot. I worked with an Olympic hopeful rower—I'll call her Kate—who seemed poised to make the next U.S. National Team. Kate was the fastest athlete in her training group. Kate loved training and had a very optimistic view of her chances of making the U.S. National Team. She seemed to have a good working relationship with her teammates and coach. Overall, she was upbeat and positive about her training. But she was out of sorts when I first met her.

When Kate came into my office for our first session, she quickly informed me that she had read every book in sport psychology that was on the shelves. Kate said that she had tried everything. She had tried using visualization. She had set long-term and short-term goals. She had tried deep breathing. She had tried meditation. She had posted affirmation statements on her bathroom mirror. She had written notes on her hand. She had pasted notes on her boat. After Kate completed her long list of what she had tried, she then announced that I was her last ditch effort and that she was just hoping beyond hope that there was something magical that I could provide that the books could not.

I made no promises. I started with having Kate tell me what a typical race or a typical practice felt like to her. I suspected that she had some habits of thinking, feeling, or behaving that were getting in her way. I asked her to talk me through the typical practice and race and take her time describing the thoughts and feelings that she had throughout each. She began with the early morning alarm, through her coffee, and into warming up and practicing. She told me both her practice and race experience as if none of it was of concern. She told the story in a way that indicated to me that she was certain that nothing unusual would surface. She had thought carefully about it, and nothing she did, from her perspective, could get in the way of her doing her best when training or racing. Well, something did show up.

There was one problem. When it came down to important races she ran an internal audiotape in her head that went something like this:

> I'm ahead. I'm way out. Oh no! I'm out in front again. Now I wonder how long it will take them to catch me. I wonder when in the race someone will pass me. I can see someone starting to make a move on me. I wonder how long it will take her to get me?

Kate could get away with this way of thinking, most of the time. She had an edge on the other athletes physiologically (she had extraordinary fitness and strength), yet her negative thinking was beginning to catch up with her as her teammates were progressively getting stronger and fitter.

For Kate to nudge herself back into the sweet spot, she had to become aware both of what was and was not working. She had to admit that she had habituated herself to saying very destructive, uninspiring self-statements in the first quarter of all of her races. (This was the case for Kate; it might be possible that those exact same thoughts would inspire another performer to push harder.) But without the awareness of what she was doing that was destructive to her performance, Kate had no hope of getting back to that place of training in the sweet spot. When we are honest with how we are thinking and feeling, we then have a good shot at nudging ourselves back to training and performing when it feels right.

What did it take for Kate to change? She had to intentionally think about what thoughts to have when those expected doubts would charge into her mind as she pulled ahead of the pack. All of the affirmations, images, and goals were for naught if Kate could not also contend with the intense negative thinking each time she pulled ahead of all of her competitors. It took us developing a phrase for Kate to think as she was racing. It sounds so simple, yet it was a hard shift for Kate. She had to challenge her belief that they would catch her once she pulled ahead. She had to trust her body. She had to trust her technique. Though she had plenty of evidence that she could stay ahead (she often did anyway), she had to overcome her greatest critic—herself. Kate also learned to infuse positive emotions into the race experience and to hold positive intentions for the quality of her race experience and outcomes.

Though Kate had already achieved international success, this athlete was able to take great strides in both her racing speed and her enjoyment of her sport through learning to implement empowered thinking in key moments of her racing and training. This type of shifting is possible for all of us; we must be willing to consider the moments when what we are thinking, what we are feeling, or what we are doing no longer serve us. This book will provide you many opportunities to consider the areas in the psychology of your own training and performance where you could nudge yourself back into your sweet spot of living and training.

I use the word *nudge*, but sometimes it takes extraordinary mental effort to move away from destructive patterns of thinking, feeling, or doing. Coming up with and implementing a plan to think, feel, or do differently, and in a more empowered way, can take great effort. To do this we must be willing to challenge our own thinking, actions, and decisions in our effort to live in the sweet spot and to become better at something. In our society we think a lot about the simple, measurable, tangible outcome. Did you win? Did you make the team? Did you get the scholarship? We tend to respect someone if they hit some mark of success. Yet there is more to it than just the goal achieved. Living in the sweet spot is about *how* we achieved the goal. When we can essentially both enjoy what we are doing and set ourselves up to have the best chance of external success—then we are living and performing in the sweet spot. We will tend to be more successful, more often, and will actually appreciate and enjoy what we are doing.

I was a successful, gold-medal winning athlete but kept coming up short—on the inside. I looked the part. I acted the part. I had learned how to be successful, to make my mark wherever I focused my energy. Yet the satisfaction and self-acceptance was all too fleeting. The sense of fulfillment on a daily basis was glaringly absent. A win or a success would last only a day or two—at best a few weeks. I luckily stumbled onto sport psychology along the way. Fifteen years ago this was the only discipline that I knew of, in academia, where I could learn about what it took psychologically to be consistently successful. And more recently the new field of positive psychology has emerged; this field focuses on what makes people happy. The answers for how to thrive and how to be both externally successful and enjoy the process are now available to us.

The intention of this book is to inspire self-awareness and to provide strategies that you can tailor to your own training, so that you can empower yourself to begin living in the sweet spot. You also will see new ways to expand and strengthen positive emotions or passions that you already have for your performance domain of choice, to keep the habit of living and performing in the sweet spot stronger. Once you see this opportunity, you may have to work very hard on how you think, what you do, or how you respond to your emotions, but you will discover what it is that will help move you into living and performing in your sweet spot.

By suspending harsh self-judgment and personally valuing your focus and effort, you will get powerful outcomes. Those powerful outcomes may be personal best performances. They may be winning performances. They may be insights about why you didn't get a win. But they will be powerful in some good way. The balance of this book is about providing information that will inspire you to strive toward living in the sweet spot. I draw on theory and research from sport psychology and positive psychology, and from my experience as both an elite athlete and practicing performance psychologist. Each chapter is a stand-alone chapter that introduces an idea or tool that will help you nudge yourself back into the habit of living and performing in the sweet spot.

2

Self-Awareness and Your Strengths

Learning How Your Strengths Can Impact Your Performance

"For weeks before Nationals I can't sleep. I worry about my times. I'm afraid that my taper won't work."
—Top junior swimmer

For the past 15 years, I have helped professional athletes, Olympic hopefuls, other elite athletes, and musicians optimize performance. I have been struck by the fact that many of them feel unsettled, or even intensely anxious, about upcoming performances. Many top performers lack confidence in their ability to do their best in performance. Whether they are starters, full-scholarship athletes, or national team members, an understanding of how to mentally prepare for competition or performance is missing.

We can be lulled into thinking that the top performers *should* know how to prepare mentally for competition. There is no doubt that most elite or professional athletes are unusually gifted in their ability to physically perform.

Most top musicians or other non-athlete performers are gifted in their fields as well. Yet most of these top performers, elite or not, have not had the opportunity to learn about the core psychological skills and strategies that will help them consistently perform to the best of their unique abilities—given the pressures of *game day,* whatever game day might mean in their fields.

The purpose of this book is to help you learn about and use a number of techniques to help you prepare for your moments of high pressured performance, whatever those may be. In this chapter, we identify ways in which a standard approach to training and performance preparation can backfire. We will also begin to provide specific, self-empowered strategies that can lead to better performance. The strategies that are provided will help give you a better chance to succeed at what really matters to you. In addition, with these same strategies, you will be able to find more satisfaction in your daily training.

THAT LAST 2%: IMPORTANT, BUT NOT ENOUGH!

We were all taught in school, in sport, and in work settings to focus on what is wrong so we can fix it. We think about how we could have said something in a more effective way, how we could have tried harder, or how we could have remained steadier under pressure. Our coaches tell us what is wrong with our swing, our stroke, and our effort. Our parents tell us how we should act more appropriately and more respectfully. They are clearly trying to help us!

We have been bombarded with what is wrong in an effort to help us get better, to reach subsequently higher levels of success. We are supposed to learn from this critique what needs to be fixed. Awareness of what needs to be improved is good. It helps us get better, and we certainly need feedback on how to get better. Certainly a "good job, good effort" response at every turn would lead us only to mediocrity. We need to know specifically how to improve, day by day.

This habit of consistently focusing on any factor that needs improvement related to best performance is certainly necessary to reach one's potential.

Most of us have mastered the first 98% of what we need to learn in our performance realm to be great at what we do. The remaining 2% is what stands between us and our highest levels of performance. However, in this chapter I will argue that the *exclusive* focus on what is wrong and what needs to be improved (the 2%), combined with a chronic lack of attention to what has and is going right (the 98%), can eventually undermine our confidence and can actually hurt performance.

Henry, a world champion many times over, exemplifies how focusing on only what is wrong can end so badly—focusing on that last 2% had led him away from what he most desired. Henry graduated from one of the best colleges in the country. After incurring an injury from which it would take six months to fully recover, Henry literally lost the will to live. Henry came to work with me just a month after he had been standing on a bridge, ready to jump to his death. Any reflection on Henry's accomplishments left him empty-eyed and unresponsive. During one of our first sport psychology consulting sessions together, I asked Henry, "Given all that you have achieved, what are you proud of? What do you respect about yourself as an athlete?" Henry had no answer, so we sat in a painful silence. Finally, he said, "I just can't think about that. I keep thinking about how I'm not on my game. I need to figure out what's wrong with me."

We did need to help Henry figure out how to mentally refocus on his training and performance. Yet, the issue at hand was much more profound than just thinking about how to refocus his technique and effort. It quickly became apparent to me that Henry was unable to focus on any of the good about himself as an athlete (or human being). He had completely lost perspective. He could only focus on what—in the moment—was wrong with his ability to perform. He believed that he was only as good as his last practice or game, which represented his value of himself as both a performer and human being. If he was successful, he was worth something. If he wasn't successful when competing, he was a worthless human being. He lost sight of his good, of the 98% that was already well in place.

On the one hand, many people would argue that this mindset had helped Henry and had contributed to Henry's national and international status. It had certainly driven him to train hard. However, focusing on the 2% that he needed to improve had also become a significant source of psychological pain in his life when he could not live up to his own expectations. Henry was not able to draw strength or confidence from his long list of accomplishments (the other 98%). He was therefore lacking access to a rich source of inspiration and strength that he himself had put together. He had no idea how to adjust his mindset to a more constructive approach.

Henry represents a somewhat extreme case of what can result when what I call the last 2% *blinders* take over. As a sport psychologist, I have seen that this challenge has become epidemic in competitive athletes and high-level performers. The trend in sport experience is to transition from love of participation to a total focus on what went wrong and how it must get better. I've seen this over and over in classical musicians as well. This mental approach can give rise to significant fears and anxiety about success on the day of performance. Over the past 15 years, I have worked with hundreds of athletes who were fearful and uncertain come game day. Performers become exclusively focused on what could be improved, become terrified of not living up to expectations, and totally lose touch with what they can authentically rely upon when the pressure is on.

Athletes have a great deal in common with those striving for high levels of performance in other areas including medicine, academia, business, and the arts, among others. Many of us are challenged with the 2% *blinders*. Most people who are predominantly successful in their lives have created a very strong habit of ignoring the 98% that they've mastered, focusing instead on that last 2% of what is wrong. This makes sense: they are looking at what needs to be improved so they can achieve even more. Professional musicians will review passages of music and think about how they could have expressed the emotion of a difficult phrase better; the professional boxer will think about how to better present himself in the media; the sprinter will consider how to do a better kick on the last half lap of the race; a golfer will focus on perfecting the eight-foot putt; and a public speaker will consider how she could have altered her speech to elicit more insight, humor, or engagement. This focus on the last 2% of what still needs to be improved is an essential, core habit for those driven to excel.

Yet there is a great risk if you get in the habit of exclusively ruminating over how you could have been better and how you must improve. You can lose your emotional awareness of the skills, abilities, and accomplishments that you have already developed and achieved. You can lose sight of the things you can be proud of, and more importantly, what you can rely upon right here, right now, in your particular performance realm. Put simply, you can lose faith in yourself if you only look to what is wrong. And this exclusive focus can lead you to lose your nerve in key performance moments. You can lose your ability to perform your best when it counts because in focusing only on that last 2%, you may fail to build your core faith and belief in your own abilities.

The what's-wrong-and-how-do-I-fix-it attitude can be extremely helpful in helping us improve, persevere, and accomplish, but there is a significant downside to this approach. If we only focus on what is wrong, we psychologically wear ourselves out. We don't learn to buoy ourselves. We do actually need to work on what's wrong, but if this is all we do, it can be deadly to our souls and to our performance abilities.

WHAT IS THE ALTERNATIVE?

Surprisingly, one key component of making ourselves mentally ready for competition begins with our strengths. Specifically, it is learning to acknowledge and strengthen our belief in our personal strengths. We all have strengths. But many of us have not been encouraged to notice what good we bring with us. Though we are expected to be confident and successful in all aspects of our lives, we are not trained to honestly take stock and acknowledge our strengths. We all want to achieve, we want approval from those around us, and we want to be good at whatever we do. In this chapter, I discuss how we can develop awareness of our strengths in ways that will actually improve performance at critical moments.

Being good or excellent at your craft is critical to top performance, but it is not enough. You must also believe in your developed skills and abilities when you are in high-pressure moments of performance. The academic sport world refers to the belief in one's ability to successfully accomplish a task as *self-efficacy*. Self-efficacy, a concept developed by Albert Bandura (an intellectual giant in the field of psychology), is integral to an athlete being ready to perform. It is a belief that you can be successful at a particular task, in a particular situation. It is not enough, like Henry, to be a multiple-time world champion.

Henry was one of the best in the world in his sport, yet he did not believe in his ability to perform well at his next event. Why? He lacked self-efficacy. Why did he lack this? I hypothesize that he lacked self-efficacy because his mind was full of only self-criticism and self-judgment. His mind was filled with the examples that demonstrated small moments when he came up short, when he wasn't demonstrating perfection in a particular movement or execution of skill, paired with being temporarily slower than his top competitors due to injury. His chronic critique of his training and performance left no space for him to acknowledge the good—the 98% of his focus, persistence, and intensity that was excellent. After his injury, when he could no longer rely on the wins to confirm that he was worth something, his confidence crumbled.

What is the solution to this loss of confidence? We must develop a belief in ourselves independent of successes in comparison to others. Certainly, how we stack up to others matters. However, it cannot get in the way of understanding and respecting our strengths and acknowledging our progress. If we can believe in the skills and abilities that we have developed to date, and if we can use this belief as a resource during performance, then we give ourselves the best shot to do the very best with what we've got.

According to Bandura, developing our belief in ourselves for pivotal *performance moments* is dependent upon spending some of our time focusing on what has already gone well and how we can envision things going well into the future. This idea lies in stark contrast to the focus on that last 2%— the 2% that could go wrong or that has gone wrong in the past. Instead, we learn to focus on what could go right, or what has gone right in the past. Eventually, you will be able to concurrently hold on mentally to what might go wrong (the 2%) and what will go right (the 98%).

In his seminal book, *Self-Efficacy: The Exercise of Control* (1997), Bandura recommends that to build one's self-efficacy, the performer should nurture his or her *success thoughts*. Bandura is essentially encouraging performers to fill their minds with evidence of both past success and possible future success. This is the focus on the 98% of what is already good, of what has already been accomplished. To do this, he recommends that they reflect on four major areas.

*1. Reflect on: **When you performed well.*** Think about when you (individually or with a team) played well at some particular point in a game. Take a moment to consider practice sessions over the past month. Fill your mind with aspects of the practice that went well. Think about particular moments when you were executing a skill, strategy, or your physical movement in just the way that you'd always like to be able to do it. Bandura calls this reflecting on *performance accomplishment*.

*2. Reflect on: **Positive comments about your performance.*** Think about specific encouragement or positive feedback from others. Recall when a coach, teacher, or teammate noticed what you were doing well. Remember how it felt to receive the compliment. Sometimes we give ourselves positive verbal feedback: remember a moment when you had a positive, supportive statement float through your head in response to some event. Consider the time when you actually thought something positive or constructive about what you did or could do. Bandura calls this increasing your success thoughts through *verbal persuasion*.

*3. Reflect on: **An excellent example.*** Think about a teammate or competitor who executes a particular skill or move that you'd like to do just like they do. Imagine them doing this move. Now imagine you doing the move, just like they do. Think about paying attention to another person succeeding in the same way you would like to succeed and then seeing yourself having the same success. Bandura calls this increasing your success thoughts through *modeling.*

4. Reflect on: How you have managed emotional energy. Recall a time when you were under emotional control when competing. Think about moments in an event when you were performing at your very best. Recall how you felt, the emotions that were surging through your system. Remember what you may have been saying to yourself or what a coach, teammate, colleague, or teacher was saying to you. Remember the energy in your physical body. How did it feel and how did you apply the energy? Bandura refers to this as you *managing arousal and emotion.*

Thinking about past and future success, hearing positive statements from others, and observing someone similar to yourself achieving success can all serve to strengthen your belief in your ability to achieve a particular task. You can learn to strengthen your sense of competency. Just as muscles and nerves reorganize into more effectively performing routines through constant practice, our minds can reorganize into an effective support system for our sense of confidence in our competency as performers.

In the rest of this chapter, you will work through exercises that will help you use these and other strategies to build a sense of your base of strengths. Some involve filling in charts. Others involve talking to a friend or writing about a past event.

YOUR 98%: FOCUSING ON WHAT IS RIGHT ABOUT YOU

It can be helpful to acknowledge what is good about ourselves, what we respect about ourselves. With this, we can begin to put a name to what can help us persevere and thrive when we are challenged. When we focus on our strengths, we help ourselves both achieve and enhance our sense of happiness. But how do we get to the point of being able to rely on our sense of accomplishment and strength?

Using your strengths begins with considering what is good about yourself as a performer and reflecting upon it. This step can be awkward. Though many of us yearn to be good at what we do, wish for acknowledgment, and hope for the respect of others, we tend to be quite hard on ourselves. Often our minds are filled with what has gone wrong, how we could have done better, why we are not good enough, how others are better than us, and worries about how things might not turn out just the way we hope in the near and far future. Some of us have been explicitly trained not to praise ourselves or focus on our strengths, for fear of becoming complacent or conceited. Sometimes, parents or coaches have trained us to believe that if we are feeling good about something we did, we are heading for an inevitable fall.

Some people, on the other hand, have been trained to report that they are fantastic, no matter what. I met with an undergraduate once who attended one of the top universities in the world. She began the conversation with how truly impressive she was in all respects. She had gone to an international school in secondary school; she'd been the top academically and a tremendously gifted athlete. In appearance, she was slim, beautiful, well dressed, and seemed to have everything going for her. Yet about 15 minutes into the conversation, she began talking about her drug rehabilitation experience, her concerns of getting back into shape to play on a collegiate athletic team, and her worries about what others thought of her. She was so worried about judgments from others that each day she took a taxi that dropped her a few miles from her campus so that she was assured no one would recognize her as she went on her daily runs to get into shape.

We have a lot of pressure on us from all around to pretend we are completely together, to present an image that we have it all under control. Yet the truth is that all of us struggle in some way, some of the time. Our confidence will waver. Fear of how we might perform poorly can seize us and not let go. When we are stretched during a high-pressure moment, knowing that we can rely upon ourselves to stay steady and focused is essential for performance. When we know what our strengths are, we can then lean on them when we need to. The belief in yourself must be grounded on the solid base of your real accomplishments or well-developed character strengths on which you can rely.

Take some time to fill in Exercise 2.1. Completing this exercise is a great first step in learning to recognize what has gone well and what is already good about your ability to control your emotions, direct your focus, or even to recognize a habit that you may have created such as that of courage (doing what you need to do, even in the face of fear). It can be hard, but very liberating, to begin noticing what is already good and right about you in your performance world.

WHAT YOU RESPECT ABOUT YOURSELF AS A PERFORMER

Often when I work with groups of athletes or musicians, I use an exercise to help them clarify what they can count on when things get tough mentally, socially, or physically when practicing or competing. I ask them to write down 10 things that they respect about themselves as an athlete and performer. In

Exercise 2.1. Your 98%: Focusing on what is right about you

Performance situations	What did it look like and feel like when it went well?
When I performed well	
Positive comments about my performance from someone else or myself	
An excellent example: How someone else like me performed well	
A time when I managed my emotional energy well	

Exercise 2.2, I encourage you to do the same. Write down 10 things you respect about yourself as a performer.

What might you respect about your abilities or attitudes when training or performing? You can write in the space below, or better yet, take out a note card or piece of paper that you can later carry with you or put in a safe place to look at occasionally. It doesn't matter if what you are considering sounds impressive to others or not. I've had athletes write things like

- *I give it 100%*
- *I'm coachable*
- *I love what I do*
- *I'm a good teammate*

What really matters in this exercise is that you believe that what you write is *true*.

Only you know what you respect about yourself. The right answers are within you. No one else really knows what you value about what you can do—be it your physical abilities, love of the sport, commitment to the sport, training effort, mental attitude, or contributions as a team member. I've found that thinking of one or two things that are good about yourself is easy for most performers. The challenge comes after the first few things that you respect about yourself are recorded. Though we all want respect from those around

Exercise 2.2. Top 10 things that you respect about yourself as a performer

1.	6.
2.	7.
3.	8.
4.	9.
5.	10.

us, we spend little or no time considering what it is that we respect about ourselves. Are you hard working? Caring? Determined? Compassionate? Kind? Joyful? Are you able to savor the moment? Are you grateful? Do you do your best? Are you good under pressure? Do you practice with 100% effort?

Taking the time to think about yourself in a positive, honest, and authentic way is a great way to begin considering the strengths about yourself upon which you can rely when things get tough, or when you have a true opportunity to stretch your limits and thrive. It may feel boastful or arrogant to reflect upon your strengths, yet we need to know what we can rely upon when things get tough. This exercise is perhaps not something to talk about with most others (in fact, I encourage you not to), but it definitely is one that is important to seriously consider. It can be invaluable to have a quiet understanding of what you can rely upon when things get tough mentally or physically.

The strengths that you've thought of reflect some things in your unique package of good. With purposeful awareness of your strengths, you may continue to have new insights into what you respect about yourself as a performer. These will be sources of strength that you can draw upon when things get tough—and they always do.

WHEN YOU WERE CHALLENGED, WHAT DID YOU RELY UPON?

It is important to be clear as to *who you are being* when you are at your best and performing. When you get clear on the strengths that you exhibit when it really matters, you can create a plan to consciously rely upon these strengths the next time you are in high-pressure moments.

This line of thinking is inspired by two studies that I conducted about how elite rowers effectively (and ineffectively) coped with competitive pressure. Many trained for years—up to two decades—to get a few chances to make the US or Olympic teams. In the two studies, I interviewed 38 elite rowers; they were either on the US/Olympic rowing team or they were training at one of the few training centers across the country. As part of the study, I asked them to tell me about a time in their elite rowing experience when they coped well with competitive pressure. All 38 athletes selected a time when they were either competing in a race to make the US team or when they were actually racing at the World Championships or the Olympic Games. In all 38 episodes, the athletes reported that they wanted very much to be successful (of course). And they were all faced with the possibility of not achieving their goal—of either not making the US or Olympic team or of not winning a medal.

All of the athletes conceptualized the time that they *coped best* as when they were able to compete to the best of their ability, physically and psychologically. Their coping approach was independent of whether they ended up achieving the outcome they had hoped for (just like performing in the sweet spot). Among all of the athletes, the following characteristics were mentioned most often as demonstrating their effective coping:

- *Focused and Engaged:* These athletes demonstrated the ability to stay focused on what would help them succeed. They were able to primarily focus on how to row effectively—how to connect, apply their power in each stroke, and follow their race plan.

- *Accepting:* These athletes demonstrated the ability to accept the possibility of failure while not focusing on failure. They focused on how to perform their best, moment to moment.

- *Determined:* These athletes were determined to do their best, no matter what the outcome of their race.

- *Present:* The athletes were able to stay in tune with the signals from their bodies to make sure that they were most effectively applying pressure on their blades to make the boat go as fast as possible.

How were these athletes able to summon these features of effective coping? These states of mind—*focused, present, accepting,* and *determined*—are all crucial components of effective performance in high-pressure situations. How did these athletes get to those states? We can speculate that they may have drawn on a variety of their key strengths to help them achieve these four crucial states of mind.

Everyone is different, so everyone has a unique set of strengths upon which they can draw. Some of the athletes may have been able to stay focused because of their *love for the sport*. Others may have drawn on their personal strength of *courage*. Courage is defined as having the ability to face both internal fears (how I'll feel when I have to face the challenge) and external fears (e.g., the fear of being hurt, humiliated, or embarrassed). Others may have been supported by *trust in their training*. They took heart in knowing that they had done all that they could do to prepare, and that they could do no more. This helped them accept whatever would come and fully engage in doing their best. And finally, other athletes may have been able to draw their strength from the *loyalty and commitment of their families and friends*. They were willing to push themselves physically and psychologically to the extreme to honor those they loved.

We know that this is what we all want when performing, to be *focused, present, accepting,* and *determined.* The question is, what can you rely upon within yourself to help you get there more frequently? Consider the achievement arena that is most important to you. Think of a time when you were greatly challenged, and yet you handled the situation to the best of your ability. What factors about your mental approach helped you get through the situation? Was it courage? Clear focus? Compassion? Were you able to maintain perspective? In Exercise 2.3, make a note of the event that you just identified. Next, note a few strengths that you relied upon during this event. And, finally, consider the connection between the strength that you used (say, determination) and how this strength ultimately affected your performance.

We all have different combinations of strengths that we can rely upon. Sometimes, it can be hard to identify our strengths. We are unaccustomed to naming, either in our minds or out loud, what is good about ourselves. I've found it helpful when working with my students and clients to ask them to consider the list of virtues (compiled by Chris Peterson and Martin Seligman)

Exercise 2.3. Your strengths under pressure

The event	Your strengths that you relied upon	Outcome of your behavior/thoughts
Achieving a personal best time in a marathon	e.g., Determination	*"I was able to push the moments when I felt like giving up and stay consistent in my pace."*
Your Event:		
1.		
1.		

and character strengths, *human good,* to begin thinking about the personal strengths that they value in themselves.

VIRTUE AND SIGNATURE STRENGTHS

Peterson and Seligman, two leaders in the positive psychology movement, spent three years considering what was good about people around the world. They considered the factors that are universally respected, valued, and hoped for as humans develop. They considered the essential *ingredients of the good* in people, their character strengths. They did a fantastic job compiling a universal list of *good* that can emerge in all of us. These are qualities of humans that tend to contribute to living a good life and often include helping move toward both achievement and happiness.

Peterson and Seligman started with a short list of overarching themes of good in which they indentified a list of *virtues* (there are six: *wisdom and knowledge, courage, humanity, justice, temperance,* and *transcendence*). Within each of the virtues, they also provided a list of 24 dimensions of the virtues, which they titled *character strengths.* These character strengths are intended to represent human behavior when we are at our best. We all have a unique blend of the character strengths, with some being strong and habituated (considered our *signature strengths* by Peterson and Seligman) and others lying dormant within us.

The first important step involves acknowledging our strengths and then becoming aware of the fact that we all have different strengths. We have different sources of power that help us strive and achieve. The challenge is that we often take our own strengths for granted. We can easily slip into the illusion that if it is easy for me, then it must not be very important or highly valued. "Of course I try hard. I'm persistent. Who isn't?" Or, "Of course I am willing to help a teammate or competitor who is struggling. There's nothing special about that." We often think that what we do that is good, kind, right, or courageous is just what anyone else would do. And when we ignore our strengths, we also tend to ignore the 98% of us as performers that is good. When we focus only on what is wrong and what needs to be improved, we tend to put on our 2% blinders, which will ultimately weaken our ability to perform when it counts.

In my positive psychology classes, I always have students fill out the signature strengths inventory developed by Peterson and Seligman. (I recommend visiting their website at www.authentichappiness.sas.upenn.edu/Default.aspx and fill out their signature strengths inventory to assess your strengths.) My students often report feeling surprised that a test can identify their good (that the test fairly assessed their strengths). They also report feeling embarrassed that they had to report what was good about them. But they ultimately acknowledge (often with surprise) that the inventory does accurately identify their strengths. I often have them ask three trusted friends to write down or tell them verbally what their strengths are. This, too, can be an awkward, but very affirming, exercise. This feedback can help you begin to name the strengths that you can rely upon, particularly when preparing for the pivotal moments of pressured performance.

SELF-REGULATION IN HIGH-PRESSURE MOMENTS: A KEY STRENGTH

Self-regulation (also referred to as *moderation* and *self-control*) is one of the strengths that we must all develop, strengthen, and sustain in order to perform to the best of our ability when faced with high-expectancy conditions. At high-pressure moments, we all need to be able to have our thoughts, emotions, and behaviors under our control. Peterson and Seligman refer to the ability to control or temper oneself as the signature strength of *self-regulation*. Aristotle refers to the same idea as self-control or moderation. Self-regulation is essentially being able to regulate what you feel and do and to be disciplined about this.

Just for a moment, assess your ability to regulate your thoughts, emotions, and actions when performing. It can be helpful to get a snapshot of where you stand in these broad categories. It will give you a sense of your current psychological ability to regulate your emotions and behaviors. In this assessment I'd like you to take off your 2% blinders. Consider both the 98% of what is already good and where you might be able to improve, your 2% opportunity of change. Assess yourself on a scale of 1 to 10, in which 1 equals being close to out of control (e.g., breaking tennis rackets when you lose a point) and 10 equals being at ease and fully focused (e.g., when you get passed in a race you remain calm). The chart in Exercise 2.4 will give you a sense of what aspects of mental training you might want to focus on to help you strengthen your habit of self-regulation for key moments of performance.

Exercise 2.4. Snapshot of your self-regulation in high-pressure moments

Examples of high pressure performance moments	My current level of self-regulation Scale: from 1 (low) to 10 (high) (circle one number)
Emotionally (How effectively I minimize the negative and expand on the positive)	1 2 3 4 5 6 7 8 9 10
Mentally (How effectively I focus my thoughts)	1 2 3 4 5 6 7 8 9 10
Physically (How effectively I focus my physical energy)	1 2 3 4 5 6 7 8 9 10

USING YOUR STRENGTHS:
STRENGTHEN YOUR HABIT OF SELF-REGULATION

I'd like you to consider an upcoming challenge in which you'd like to more ef-fectively self-regulate your attention, thoughts, emotions, or behaviors. Using the chart in Exercise 2.5, or just through reflection, identify the upcoming chal-lenge. Next, think about the strengths that you already have well developed.

For the event, think about how you could specifically call upon your strengths to help you have better self-control over your thoughts, emotions, or behaviors. In the example below, I've used the challenge of *fearing* that you will not perform your best at an upcoming event. The goal is to have more control over the intrusive rushes of negative thoughts and make good use of the sometimes too-intense surges of adrenaline. With this control, you will be able to more fully focus on the task at hand.

But the question remains, what are the strengths that you can rely upon in this moment to help you more effectively control or guide your thoughts and

Exercise 2.5. Using your strengths: Strengthen your habit of self-regulation

The upcoming event/challenge	Your strength	How-to call upon your strength	Moderation/self-regulation strengthens
E.g., Fear of not performing my best in giving a talk to a big audience	Perseverance	"I'm prepared. I'll try my hardest no matter what."	Focus shifts from fear of future outcome to putting all effort into the task at hand
E.g., Fear of not performing my best in a basketball game	Perspective	"I know that I'll be ok, no matter what happens in competition."	Focus shifts from fear of future outcome to performing effectively
Your upcoming event			

feelings? Once you have this, come up with a short phrase that will help you call upon your strength when it counts. Sometimes this is all that it will take to overcome distracting thoughts and emotions. Build awareness and create a clear, simple plan to make a potentially significant shift in how you handle your distractions and ultimately perform.

Consider the phrase that you just developed for the category, How To Call Upon Your Strength. You can plan to bring that phrase to mind whenever you experience negative thoughts about your upcoming performance. Noticing and paying attention to your strengths can be a great source of confidence and set you up to have a stronger mental approach as you prepare to perform.

3

Positive Emotional Experience

**Strengthening Your Resources
Through Nurturing Positive Emotions**

*"I never realized how good I feel sometimes when
I run. Since I've been paying attention more, I've
begun noticing some stretches when I feel really
light and the running feels totally effortless."*

—5-K Masters racer

Why bother creating, noticing, or enhancing positive emotions? Until recently, positive emotions were considered to be fleeting, unpredictable feel-good experiences (as noted by Barbara Fredrickson—a world leader in the study of positive emotions). Why emphasize positive emotions if they aren't going to help with performance? You might think, "If something doesn't help me run faster, jump higher, or score more goals, I'm not interested." Though we all want happiness and enjoyment in our lives, we tend to undervalue the importance of positive emotions in the performance realm.

There has been little to no emphasis placed on the added value of positive emotions in the performance arena. Though it may be assumed that we all love to do our thing, few leaders are helping us nurture that love.

How often does your coach or teacher say, "Make sure that you enjoy practice! Make sure that when you leave practice, you pay attention to the good in your life. I want you to spend time with people who believe in you and bring out your good; I want you to make sure that you laugh, enjoy yourself, and do things that just bring you a sense of joy. Hey, no matter what, make sure that you are having fun!"

Conversations about positive emotion and conversations about performance usually do not take place at the same time. We don't think that the lovely, fleeting positive emotions—things like joy, contentment, interest, and love—will help us perform. In fact, many high-level performers may think of such positive emotions as sources of weakness. Though we all want happiness and we all want to be successful, we often don't think of the ideas as interdependent. Yet joy and best performance often are interdependent.

Chris, a full-scholarship soccer player, is a great example of being intense and self-critical on and off the field. Without knowing it, she was blocking all positive emotions and suffering accordingly. She came to work with me because she was miserable. When she came to my office, she wanted me to help her talk with her coach so she could quit the team. I would help her quit if she really wanted to, but first I had to get a sense of how badly she was feeling and then help her consider the pros and cons of quitting.

Chris turned out to be an intense, serious athlete. As she talked about playing soccer, it seemed as though she felt that playing soccer was a life or death matter. Of course being serious, focused, and determined are essential ingredients to becoming successful. Yet when we are 100% deadly serious about our training and performance, it tends to pull us out of our sweet spot . Chris had on her 2% blinders. She was only focused on her weaknesses and fears.

I asked Chris to tell me on a scale of 1 to 10 how poorly she was feeling, with 1 meaning that she was so miserable that she didn't want to get out of bed and 10 meaning that she was in a state of nirvana and delighted to be alive and doing what she was doing.

Chris said, "I'm a 2 out of 10." She had a hard time sleeping and felt a lot of anxiety when she went to practice. She was chronically aware of competing for the spot of goalie against Jen, an underclassman. Chris's total focus was on how the other coaches coached Jen. She ruminated over who would get to start and watched for every indication, from how Jen performed in practice to her coaches' facial expressions to Jen's saves and misses in the goal.

We explored the pros and cons of Chris both leaving and staying on the team. We explored all the reasons why Chris could possibly like being on the team (the 98% of what was already right), like the many friends that she'd made, getting to travel, having a place to remain fit, and simply to be playing outside. We also discussed the current challenges of feeling so uncomfortable emotionally. She decided that, even though she was feeling anxious and angry about her starting position hanging in the balance, she would stay with the team until the end of the season; then she would quit.

I suggested that Chris make the experience as positive as possible for the time that she had left on the team. She agreed that this would be a good approach for her. We could have spent endless hours deeply exploring all the signs and reasons that made Chris miserable. Instead, we did the exact opposite.

We spent a number of hours together helping her consider the aspects of soccer that she loved and what she could focus on during practice to help her both notice what was going well and what she could control to make small improvements. Every time Chris began dwelling on Jen (her competition), we created a plan to think back and review something that she had recently done well. For example, when she found herself comparing herself to Jen, she'd review in her imagination an excellent save (blocking a shot from going into the goal) that she'd made in a practice. If a save was her focus, I'd encourage her to think about why the save went well and what she did to make the good save.

Chris definitely struggled at first with noticing what was good. She had developed a strongly ingrained habit of focusing on what was wrong, what her weaknesses were, and how she'd feel if she got beaten out of the top spot. Her 2% blinders were strong. With determination Chris focused on what was good, what she could control, and how she'd like to perform. As she focused on what was going right and what she was doing to influence this, Chris's emotional experience began to slowly shift. Instead of feeling anxious in practice, she became more interested in practices and more engaged in an effort to make improvements. She began to feel more satisfied with her efforts. She began to take more risks in trying to block low-percentage saves. She was feeling more confident, courageous, and creative.

At the end of the season, I asked Chris how she was feeling about soccer on the scale from 1 to 10. She said, "Eight!" She had decided that she no longer wanted to quit and had regained her love for the sport. She ended up sharing the starting goalie position with her teammate Jen that season.

THE VALUE OF POSITIVE EMOTIONS IN SUPPORTING PERFORMANCE

Exciting new research has explored the importance of positive emotion. Fredrickson has conducted dozens of studies that support her Broaden and Build Theory of Positive Emotion. She is interested in learning the value of positive emotions. Her theory suggests that experiencing positive emotions such as joy, contentment, interest, and love makes us more aware and present to the options in our immediate experience. Instead of functioning on automatic pilot, when we feel surges of positive emotions we tend to notice more options for how we can interact with and respond to the world around us. With positive emotions, we tend to be more present and creative.

Fredrickson refers to the broadening of in-the-moment responses as people's momentary thought-action repertoires. When we are feeling good, we tend to be more engaged and persist longer in whatever we are doing. We are more open to learning and our intuition and creativity increase. Our choices of what to do in the moment also broaden. We simply want to be doing what we are doing more when we are experiencing positive emotions. During such episodes, we are learning more, pushing harder, and building up our reserves to draw on when things get tough, such as high-pressure performance. We can reserve our execution of willpower for times when we really need it. Because when we are feeling surges of positive emotions, we want to be doing what we are doing. We do not need to use our reserve of willpower to make ourselves *just do it.*

The more often we experience positive emotional states, the more we build our enduring personal resources (physical, social, intellectual, and psychological). This means that in the future, we'll have stronger personal resources to rely upon when things get tough. So when the challenges hit—and they will—we will be more resilient and able to handle them. And this directly relates to preparing for our big moments. We need to build our personal resources to get ready for the times when we are faced with high expectations and highly skilled competitors.

C.B. Sands is an eight-time member of the U.S. National Rowing Team and a two-time World Champion gold medalist. In her life, she has struggled through literally thousands of days of practice in all kinds of weather and had times when she felt enthusiastic or exhausted, sick or well. I wanted to ask her how she felt about this issue of using positive emotions in practice to build toward successful high-pressure performance. In a recent interview with me, C.B. discussed her daily mental approach to training. I asked her if she thought that her daily mental attitude toward training affected her ability to be ready for performance when it really counted. C.B.'s first response gave a clue toward her longevity in the sport. "I would find it very difficult to be really good at something, to succeed, and not to be able to enjoy the process. I loved being at the boathouse. I loved being on the water. It was interesting and fun. I learned so much."

Not everyone would respond this way! And to some of us, C.B.'s attitude might seem completely unrealistic. Didn't she experience the same difficulty that most athletes do? C.B.'s further discussion revealed that she was well aware of the reality of the difficulty of practice. She said, "There are days when it is not good. You question your ability to achieve that goal, the light in the distance." C.B. certainly recognizes that it is not possible to maintain pure optimism and gratitude for training every moment. So how did she maintain a sense of joy and appreciation for her daily training?

C.B. noted that one key action is noticing the positive. This helps to generate the positive emotions during practice. But what if nothing positive is happening? What if you are in the middle of a tough practice, not feeling inspired, and only feeling the struggle? Then, C.B. says, if noticing the positive isn't happening, you must purposefully generate the appreciation for the day. She emphasized that "you have to make the day-to-day enjoyable." She gave the example of training alone. She recounted that often she had to train by herself. Even when she was in the middle of the river, alone, and had a lot of hard training to do, she would think to herself, "This is awesome. It is ten o'clock in the morning, and I'm in the middle of the river basin. This is incredible to be here right now." C.B. chose to reflect on her love of the sport. Therefore, her appreciation of her training on a daily basis became part of how she thought and how she approached training.

Interestingly, C.B. said she had never talked about this and had never received training to work on her positive emotions about practice. She had developed her sense of the importance of a positive mindset on her own, and she had just taken it for granted that other top performers experienced the same approach to training. She realized she might be wrong about this one day when she went to watch the U.S. Olympic team trials (a series of races to select the Olympic team) after she had retired from sport. She went up to one of the athletes that made the team and congratulated him. She was shocked by a comment that he made. He said, "Forty six more days until it is over and I can move on." C.B. remembers almost not understanding what the athlete meant. "I was shocked that anyone would be counting off the days until the Olympics were over. I would think 46 more days to enjoy this." She couldn't imagine not enjoying doing her thing. It is, of course, possible to be successful and not be training and performing in the sweet spot. The cost of this is not enjoying what you are doing and risking the possibility that you could have been even better.

HOW CAN WE WORK ON GENERATING POSITIVE EMOTIONS?

How does building these resources work? Have you ever had an experience when you were very interested in something? Recently, I began playing the ukulele. I found myself spending hours learning the chords and practicing little melodies. While I was practicing, I found that I felt intensely interested and intermittently joyful. These emotion states definitely facilitated much longer practice sessions than would have been the case if I were just dutifully practicing something that held little interest for me. I spent more time with an intensified focus of attention on learning the chords, melodies, and techniques of subtle hand shifts.

Strangely, the idea that positive emotion encourages us to want to continue has been ignored in the performance realm. When we want to, when we enjoy, we are not only more present and engaged in the moment, but we are also strengthening ourselves for future challenges. My positive experience as a novice in the music world is similar to what we all felt when we first started in our respective performance fields. Generally, when people invest a significant amount of time over a number of years in a performance area, it is because, at the start, they loved doing the activity. This love could be attributed to being in a particular environment, with particular types of people, or simply being involved in the activity itself.

But what happens over time? Over time, when we develop more refined levels of expertise, we can lose track of our core passion and get distracted by expectations of performance, perfectionism, or achieving specific external goals. As I get better at playing the ukulele, I find myself thinking about how far I am from perfection, about all the things I can't do. This happens to many people as they progress in their sport, craft, or job. If not careful, we will all put on the 2% blinders and just focus on what needs to be improved. And worse yet, we will nudge ourselves out of the sweet spot—we may still achieve success but will do so with a lack of enthusiasm and fulfillment. If we allow ourselves to be nudged out of the sweet spot, we withhold what we are ultimately all pursuing—our own happiness. At the same time we also nudge ourselves away from being able to do the very best we can with what we've got.

NOTICING THE GOOD

Many athletes and high-level performers do not value noticing, expanding, or creating positive emotions in their daily training. They do not see the value of positive emotion as it directly pertains to performance. Though most of us start with the joy and love for doing our thing, we end up serious (sometimes deadly serious) and focused on expecting top results and focusing on what is not right. We strap on our 2% blinders.

The value of positive emotions was absent in my 10-year quest to make the U.S. Olympic team. I did, at times, enjoy what I was doing, but this oc-curred randomly. I never purposefully tried to create the good, in terms of having things feel good physically or emotionally. I was always going for more power, more fitness, and more speed. I didn't understand that with joy these aspects of performance can be strengthened much more rapidly.

In fact, I believed that my anger and anxiety was the fuel that I needed to help me optimize performance. To me at that time, positive emotion meant that I was losing focus. I thought that I needed to be intense and focused 24/7. For a long time, I believed that positive emotions made you too soft, too at ease. I've learned how wrong I was. I now have plenty of evidence from my decade-plus practice as a sport and positive psychologist that learning to notice, enhance, and create positive emotion in training and performance is one of the keys to being able to succeed under even the most intense levels of expectations to perform. Essentially, positive emotions help you strengthen personal resources, which you then can draw upon when things get tough. And positive emotions help call up resources when you are under great de-mand to perform in the moment.

A great place to start with strengthening positive emotions is to first start paying attention to the positive emotions that are already naturally showing up in your training and off-training life. The irony is that often they show up and we miss them! We miss the opportunity to experience them because we are so focused on some hope or fear. The idea is to consider what is already good, now. Notice when you have a surge of joy, interest, excitement, or passion.

In the positive psychology world, there is a wonderful, simple exercise that is used by both researchers and practitioners to help people begin to tune into what is good in their lives. The exercise has been one that Martin Seligman used both in his research and has shared with people around the world. The exercise is to, at the end of the day, write down (or say to yourself) three things that are good that happened today. After you've written down the three good things, next you can consider why they happened to you. You are encouraged to consider what was good about you that helped create the three good things to happen.

For example, if your coach makes a comment about you making an improvement in a particular aspect in a routine, you could note this as a good thing. The next step is more important than noting the good. The next step is to note why it happened to you. Was it your effort, attitude, or determination that allowed you to make a jump in your skill or ability? What was it about you that helped create or manifest that good? If a good friend stops by to say hi, why did this happen to you? Have you been a good, reliable friend? If you survived a challenging workout (the good thing), what was it about your abilities that got you through?

Take a moment to notice any good that has happened to you and why it happened to you. What about you helped elicit the good? Yes, I know that sometimes the good is random luck (e.g., I found a $5 bill on the ground in the park). But often we do help cause much of the good that happens to us. Even if you did find the $5, it may be because you were present to what was occurring around you instead of focused on why you made some mistake or fretted about your fears about an upcoming event. So in this example, you found the money because you were present. Another typical good thing that can happen is that your coach notices an improvement. Why did this happen to you? It may have happened because you are coachable and trying your best to integrate your coach's feedback into your practice. Let at least one good thing pass through your mind, and then ask why the good happened to you.

Notice how you feel after you try this. Do you notice a slight surge in any positive emotions? The positive emotion could be a subtle to intense range of feelings such as contentment, love, joy, or interest. The three-good-things exercise is a great way to begin to notice the good that is occurring in your life.

NOTICING THE GOOD IN YOUR PERFORMANCE REALM

The next step, specific to performance, is to notice what was good about your training today. What did you do well? Consider what it was about your character, attitude, skills, abilities, or mindset that allowed you to enjoy this good. The three good things don't have to be big or significant. In fact, the biggest challenge is to notice the small good things that happen, the good that usually goes unnoticed. Herein lies a gold mine of potential surges of positive emotion that will serve you well as you look to expand awareness of the good that is already occurring in your training and performances.

This exercise is to help you think about what already has gone well. Often, we neglect to think about what has gone well. When we do this, we are neglecting a number of things. First, we are missing out on the good feelings that are well-earned. We are also missing out on a chance to build our awareness of our strengths and skills. This is an essential part of effective training. We recognize things are good. We learn to both consciously and unconsciously begin to rely on what feels right, so when high-pressure performance moments arise, we know what to rely upon. Noticing the good is a very simple and powerful way to strengthen our ability to perform well.

Consider a small child learning to engage in the social world. When he says "please" or "thank you," the mother quickly affirms and notices the good of the child learning to be respectful. After about 20 (to 220) times of noting the good of saying "thank you," the child begins to say "thank you" automatically. It is a habit that he no longer needs to think about: saying "thank you" after someone does something nice becomes just what he does.

Similarly, if you notice the good in your effort, determination, mindset, particular skill, or strategy—if you notice it *enough*—you will begin to enact the good effortlessly. Consider the example of a tennis player noticing how good it feels to make a particular shot. I am not talking about the enjoyment that comes from making a shot and winning the point, which of course is good, too. I am talking about how it feels while taking the stroke. I am talking about noticing the physical movement of the body and what works. Noticing this and celebrating this internally is a way to create the physical habits

Exercise 3.1. Three good things that happened in practice/training

The good	Why it happened to you Your attitude, mindset, character, commitment, etc.
e.g., I hit six free-throws in a row.	I followed my pre-shot routine. I made sure to take a breath before each shot and visualize the ball going in the basket.
I enjoyed my lift today.	I was thinking about getting stronger (instead of comparing myself to my teammates).
1st Good thing:	Why it happened to me:
2nd Good thing:	Why it happened to me:
3rd Good thing:	Why it happened to me:

that you would like to reinforce. That way, when the pressure is on, you have paid close attention to how you do want to physically move and feel during performance.

Like all change, paying attention to the good in your training requires purposeful focus. You must keep your attention on this to make a real-life change. And if you do, you will train yourself to make your best effort and technique into your default mode. But this takes time and practice in terms of noticing the good. And each time you notice what went right, what is good, you also are increasing the frequency that you experience positive emotion.

POSITIVE EMOTION IN PERFORMANCE: DOES IT TAKE AWAY FROM OR GIVE YOU YOUR EDGE?

You may wonder why you'd spend any of your time and energy creating positive emotions in your performance realm. For many elite athletes, if someone recommends that they spend precious time trying to create positive energy and emotions, they may assume they are being encouraged to lose their edge. But I've argued in this chapter that there is a great deal of evidence that positive emotions enhance performance, not undermine it.

Nevertheless, there are times when feeling good and enjoying what you are doing *will* make you lose your edge. The key to recognizing these times is noticing what you are focusing on and what you are drawing from to create the positive emotion. The next example illustrates how seeking positive emotion can have negative outcomes.

I worked with Tim, a young full scholarship baseball player. He was mandated to work with me because he had tested positive for drug use. Essentially, he loved socializing and smoking marijuana. He loved having fun and, for him, marijuana was a source of positive emotion. Tim authentically enjoyed feeling positive emotions in his system, as we all do. The problem was that the fun that he had was primarily driven by smoking pot multiple times each day. Tim ultimately chose between his drug habit and sport. Unfortunately, he chose drugs.

This is an extreme example of an activity that seemingly brings good emotions, yet that is ultimately destructive. There are endless possibilities of distractions that could create positive emotion and, indeed, soften you up and wear down your edge. The types of positive emotion I'm talking about nurturing are those related directly to training, performance, or your chosen work. These positive emotions are achieved through you performing some type of intentional, effortful activity that contributes to your overall well-being in some neutral or positive way. These include activities to help you psychologically recover from training or points of focus that help you improve your ability to perform.

And, of course, training is not always fun. It just can't be. There are chunks of time in our training or practice that we must push ourselves and be physically, socially, and/or psychologically uncomfortable (all the way to sometimes being in pain). Though we can't always experience the fleeting feel-good moments of positive emotion in training, we do need to make way for it some of the time. Essential good comes from learning to create the positive emotions of joy, interest, and love within the training of our sport or performance realm itself.

One day, I found myself sitting with Bret. He was a highly talented basketball player who was spending a lot of time on the bench and causing some trouble for the team. The coaches had great hopes for Bret when they recruited him, but quickly became disenchanted. Bret showed a lack of effort in practice and used his quick wit to taunt teammates. When he rode the bench during games, he made his sour attitude known. Bret was sent to work with me because of his bad attitude.

After talking with Bret for a while, it turned out that he was intensely frustrated with his lack of playing time. He was struggling with the negative attitude that the coaches displayed toward him. He was feeling depressed. The main issue at hand for him was that he couldn't sleep. When he would lie down to sleep, he would begin ruminating over his feeling that the coaches had lied to him when he was recruited, that he was better than the guys in the starting lineup, and that he was embarrassed because he wasn't starting.

In my intervention with him, I worked toward helping him feel more empowered and engaged in practice. I wanted to help him learn to enjoy what he was doing again. With the boost in positive emotion, I hoped that many of the other issues would dissolve or be resolved. I asked Bret, "When did you last truly enjoy playing basketball?" When Bret began to remember his time playing in high school, his attitude totally changed. He recalled loving his teammates, truly enjoying playing the game, and the many creative moves that he used to make on the court. He spent considerable time recounting how good it had been (and, in contrast, how bad it was now).

Once this memory was strong in his mind, we focused on how he could re-create this type of enjoyment in his current practice. So I went to the place where he was most uncomfortable in practice with the intention of helping him transform those moments. I asked him to talk about the part of practice that was most difficult for him. He said that it was the drills. "We always to do the same, stupid, boring drills." I asked him to think about a time in high school when he did similar drills, but actually enjoyed them. His facial expression and demeanor immediately changed.

He talked about how he could attempt to once again be creative with his passes in practice. He was willing to try to do his creative moves during practice the next day during the (dreadful) drills. What happened? Bret began to immediately enjoy practice again. His sleeping problems disappeared. Within about six weeks he was in the starting lineup. This example is a great real-life example of how important it is to be aware of the importance of positive emotion and to learn to create and expand it in practice.

The key is knowing yourself and trusting what will most help you in terms of preparing for performance. In one of my studies, I interviewed a U.S. National Team rower about how he coped with competitive pressure. Specifically, I asked him how he dealt with the pressures of performance just before he raced. I was surprised to hear that he purposefully did a lot of socializing. He spent time talking with other competitors, laughing, and making jokes. In my green wisdom, I thought that he was purposefully avoiding preparing to race and that this would hurt his performance. It turned out that this young athlete went on to make another half dozen U.S. National Rowing teams.

More experienced now, I can understand that he wasn't avoiding preparing to race. Instead, he was purposefully generating positive emotions. It may have been that this is just what he needed to properly prepare for the grueling six- to seven-minute sprint that rowing requires. Perhaps for this athlete, creating an upbeat, light atmosphere and feeling loved were just what he needed prior to focusing on drawing out every ounce of his strength and willpower to be successful (for more on this specific topic, see Chapter 4).

In the following chart in Exercise 3.2, consider thinking about how you'd like to ideally feel when you are practicing. You could narrowly first only consider the tasks related to performing well in your performance domain. You may consider other areas, related to performance, that you know will help prepare you to perform well (like the athlete above did by socializing in his

Exercise 3.2. Choosing a positive emotion to enhance

The event	Positive feeling	Creating a positive feeling	Image
e.g., Practice	Engaged	"I'll allow myself to play and get creative."	"I recall myself fully engaged in a recent performance."
	Passionate	"I'll spend a minute before I start remembering when I loved it most."	"I imagine a time in a recent performance when I was feeling intense passion for performing."
Your event:	Your feeling:	1.	1.

effort to best prepare for racing). And then consider a phrase that you could say to yourself in that moment or an image that you could bring up to help create and sustain the emotion while practicing or training (more on these later). Enhancing positive emotions can sharpen your edge as long as the intention is focused on using them to help you ultimately train or practice best.

Once you have figured out one area during practice that you could notice, create, or strengthen a positive emotion, make a plan to try it soon. These ideas work as long as you actually put them into practice.

There is no question that there is a place for positive emotions in our lives. We need them in our relationships, when we interact with the world and with ourselves. At the minimum, generating positive emotions within ourselves can be a way to help us get through or recover from a tough training bout or long practice session. We need to learn to recover both physically and psychologically from training. A great way to do this is to have the goal of creating and expanding positive emotions and experiences outside of training. There are

Exercise 3.3. Positive emotion boosters

Activity	Things that will provide a positive emotional boost...
Things that I enjoy doing	1. 2. 3.
Noticing the good in others	Who? When?
Imagine enjoying your upcoming practice	What would it look like? Sound like? Feel like?
Best moments in practice or performance	Practice: What would it look like? Sound like? Feel like? Performance: What would it look like? Sound like? Feel like?

many ideas that you can try. I would only encourage you to try some of the following suggestions that seem to make sense to you in which you can easily imagine the effort resulting in a boost of positive emotion.

The first suggestion is to make a short list of things that you enjoy doing. It could be playing a musical instrument, knitting, reading a particular magazine, reading a certain type of book, or listening to particular music. After you make your list, using the chart in Exercise 3.3, try making sure that you incorporate one or a few of these into your daily routine. Some performers are excellent at integrating seemingly unimportant, personally meaningful activities into their lives, but others are not, mostly because they don't see the value in spending their time and energy on something other than their training or practicing. You will be surprised at how much of a generation of positive emotions will result from simply adding to your life one small activity that you truly enjoy.

I worked with a collegiate softball player, Mia, during a winter intersession a few years ago. Mia was feeling great pressure from her coach and team to put in extra hours to bring up the level of performance of the team. Overall, Mia was glad to be playing softball, but found her daily training more physically and psychologically challenging than she had expected. I asked Mia if there were other outlets in her life that were calming and regenerating. Mia immediately began talking about her love of playing the violin. She said that she just didn't have time to play. And then, after a short pause, she decided to bring her violin back to campus and to play a little each day. It turned out that playing her music was a great source of comfort and relaxation for Mia.

You also can consider purposefully noticing the good in those around you, including both in those who are close to you and in strangers. You can also extend this awareness of the good around you and make a conscious effort to be purposefully kind to someone who works with the public (e.g., a toll booth attendant, a waitress, or a janitor). Positive, authentic connection with others, whether with an old friend or briefly with someone who may only be in your life for a few minutes, can contribute to a positive state of mind and emotional thriving.

For a more practical activity that will generate positive emotions and help you strengthen your default performance of your best abilities, try to imagine enjoying an upcoming practice. Consider what it would actually look like, feel like, and sound like if you were fully engaged and savoring your practice session (instead of just trying to get through). You also could recall a few of your recent training bouts. It doesn't matter how far back in time you need to go to remember how you felt physically and emotionally when you were having a great practice. It may have just been a few seconds in a performance. Do your best to slow down, in your mind's eye, your re-imagination of the best part of the practice. Allow yourself to re-experience the positive emotion that comes from having a great segment in training.

Can we increase our sense of positivity? Can we increase our experiences of gratitude, love, joy, serenity, and hope? Is it really possible to generate these positive emotions and, concurrently, aspire to be as good as we possibly can? Yes, but ironically, to nudge ourselves into the sweet spot it can take some hard work. It is not easy to think about what is good about a practice when a teammate was just rude, or a coach spoke to you harshly. It is not easy to consider the good when the lactic acid is building up in your muscles. It is not easy to shift to what you love about what you are doing when you might face getting cut from a team or not chosen.

But purposefully focusing on the good is worth it. There are many opportunities throughout the day to purposefully focus on what is good in our lives. We have almost a moment-to-moment opportunity to choose what we do with our energy, where we focus our attention, when we choose to have perspective on the good that surrounds us all, all of the time. We can choose to act out of obligation, guilt, and duty. Or we can choose to act out of love, gratitude, acceptance, and joy. When we focus on noticing, creating, and extending positive emotions in our training, we are giving ourselves the chance to truly excel. We are giving ourselves a chance to be inspired.

At the minimum, we need positive emotions to help us regain our willpower and determination, as I will explain in Chapter 4. If we spend all of our training and practice bouts forcing ourselves through the two- or three-hour session, then we tend to literally drain our life energy. We can force our way for a long time. But when we do this, it will slowly eat away at our life energy unless we learn to regenerate with positive emotions, either inside or outside of training.

An important place to start is knowing what brings you joy while training and performing. The most successful athletes and performers with whom I have worked have learned how to be present to the aspects of their sport or performance arena that they love. We must know what resonates with us and how to get back to our center, and we must know our strengths. We must be able to focus our attention on the good. We can learn to stop being the victims of our own fears or expectations of others, and positive emotions are essential to this process. When we are in a state of joy, we don't care what others expect of us. When we are in a state of joy, fear dissolves.

4

Small Changes

Optimizing Willpower

"I just don't feel like going into the practice hall for the next six hours. I'm feeling uninspired and exhausted."

—Fully funded graduate student in music (with great promise of playing professionally in an orchestra)

We often are well aware of just what we need to do to ultimately perform better. It may include eating better or getting along better with our family, teammates, or friends. We might know that we need more sleep. We might know that we need to spend more time, or less time, on doing what is fun for us. We might know that we have to answer the questions that are piling up in our e-mail account. We might know that we need to say yes to our early morning training session and no to a late-night party.

The famous Nike swoop in the current marketing world states that you should "just do it." If you pause and think about what you want to accomplish, generally you know what lies at the top of your short list of next-step actions that you need to take to accomplish your goals. But why don't we always do what we know we should do to help us improve and prepare for performance? If we "just did it," we'd be more physically, emotionally, and technically prepared. We'd chip away at being steadier in the face of emotional turmoil. We'd trust ourselves and make the difficult decisions regarding what we do with our time, how to deal with the emotional bullies in our lives, and how to pursue our daily goals. When we are honest with ourselves, we know what we need to do to ultimately prepare for upcoming key moments.

Richard McCarthy's dream was to become a helicopter pilot for the U.S. Marines. He had one problem. He was not prepared for the academic aspect of Marine flight school. Many of his classmates had already graduated from the Naval Academy or already had their pilot's license. He had little training in mathematics. Richard had to learn, quickly, about time-distance navigation. He had to get up to speed on mathematical equations about things like how to climb to altitude and about the pace of fuel burn. The one change he had to make was to study—and to study hard. The studying was a small part of the challenge.

Unlike many candidates, Richard was able to take on the many psychological and physical challenges that seem almost inhumane. He was able to go without food for three to four days and hit exceptionally high scores on critical thinking tests. He was able to endure the water survival tests such as the hero dunker. He recalls, "They'd put you in something like a trash can, blindfold you [the dunker was weighted and would sink] and then see if you could get out. There were Navy Seals there to help you—but they didn't tell us that." He liked the physical and psychological challenges. And he loved the flying. "Flying formation of aircrafts is so much fun. The acrobatics felt like a day off."

The academic portion of the training remained the most difficult part for Richard. He recalls, "I was terrified of failing." But he did something about it. He made one change. He began to study extra. "I studied every waking moment that I had free. I had to do the problems over and over again." His basic strategy was, "I'd do a problem and then reward myself with a wedge of orange … I didn't want to drive a tank or be a motor transport guy, which would have happened if I had failed." Richard was ultimately able to complete flight school, become an aviator U.S. Marine Corps, and fly helicopters at war in Operation Desert Storm.

Richard could have gotten a tutor, meditated to calm his nerves, imagined himself being successful in the myriad of tests, made sure to sleep the right amount (when possible), eat the right amount, or exercise consistently throughout this stressful time. He could have gotten a counselor. This just begins the list of the many changes that Richard could have made. All of these changes would have contributed toward his ability to make it through Marine flight school. Yet, for Richard to try to do all of these changes at once would have been overwhelming. None of us can eat more healthfully, rest more, use imagery consistently, meditate daily, follow through on our daily goals, and improve our relationship with that key person in our lives who is driving us crazy! We can't change everything all at once. But why not?

WHAT DOES WILLPOWER HAVE TO DO WITH IT?

Willpower is a key factor in helping us make important changes in our lives. And willpower limits what we are able to do on a daily basis. It is incredible how hard it can be sometimes for us to do even one extra thing that we know is important and good for us. Consider reaching up your hand at night to turn off your light. Why does this seem like a simple action sometimes and so difficult other times? Why is it that sometimes we can push ourselves physically hard and our attention is easy to control? And why is it that at other times, it feels virtually impossible to get us to put out that necessary extra effort? And when we can put out that extra effort, why does it sometimes feel like that effort is draining us to the core? Our ability to control our impulses and do what is best for our training can be inconsistent. Why can we sometimes get ourselves to run a little faster in training runs, drink the extra water, or eat the lean, fiber-rich food? Why can't we *consistently* get ourselves to do what we know that we "should" do? It can feel so frustrating when we just can't get ourselves to do what we know would serve us best in our training and preparation for performance.

There seems to be a limit to how much we can control our thoughts, our actions, and our reactions. How can we get more control over ourselves? How can we get ourselves to practice more, practice with clearer focus, and keep at bay negative and self-destructive thoughts? How can we get ourselves to take in the good information from our teachers and coaches (and let go of the rest)? How can we gain better control of our negative reactions to losing? How can we better focus our minds on making positive improvements in technique when we've just made a terrible error or mistake while performing?

If you've ever been inconsistent in your ability to make yourself think something or do something, there is a very real way to explain what is happening and how to better deal with it. Recent research (by Roy Baumeister and others) in the area of *willpower* certainly helps shed light on why we sometimes can make ourselves do something and other times cannot. Many people think of willpower only in terms of making themselves do something that they don't want to do. Many think that we use willpower only when we're on a diet or running an extra lap. But current research conceptualizes willpower in a far more encompassing sense. According to Baumeister, willpower is the energy we use in any *volitional* activity. A volitional activity happens when you think something or do something consciously and purposefully. Any time you are choosing from a range of options of what to think or do you are engaged in volitional activity. So we are essentially engaged in volitional activity every waking hour of the day. And we are using willpower all that time.

According to this view, it takes willpower energy to decide whether or not to buy a car, make a salad, take a trip, decide who to date, choose to keep running or lifting even when exhausted, or make a plan to train three hours every day. Whether we are making decisions, planning, or trying to directly control our behavior or carry out a plan, we are using willpower. But sometimes, particularly for activities that are challenging, we seem to run out of willpower more quickly.

Baumeister conducted a series of studies that provides insight into why sometimes we can get ourselves to think, do, or say what we want to do (or what we know is the best choice for ourselves) and other times we cannot. His studies indicate that our willpower is a limited resource. We cannot continuously tap into our willpower to make ourselves do what we want ourselves to do. Once we put our willpower to work, like making ourselves work out when we don't feel like it or controlling our temper when we don't feel like it, we temporarily diminish our willpower's strength for the day.

One critical point in the findings from the research is that once we make or force ourselves to do something that we don't feel like doing in the moment, we tend to be less able to execute our willpower for the next choice. It becomes progressively harder to make ourselves do things that go against the easier choice in the moment for that given day.

In this view, using our willpower functions similarly to that of doing any muscular strength work. For example, we feel our strongest during our first set of push-ups or sit-ups. However, as we keep doing more sets of push-ups, we feel a progressive depletion of our muscular strength until we cannot do one more push-up. It isn't a matter of being strong or not; at some point, everyone's muscles tire and must be given a break. The same is true of willpower, even if we have developed a strong ability to get ourselves to push through— particularly when we don't feel like it. At some point, we can't keep forcing ourselves to choose the most effective thought, action, or behavior. We have our limits. We must choose carefully what we use our willpower for, because it is a limited resource.

The truth is that we may only have so much energy, literally, on which we can draw each day. In a recent study, Matthew T. Galliot and colleagues determined that our ability to use willpower relies, interestingly, on our glucose stores. When we use our willpower, our glucose stores dip below optimal levels. Once you've used up your glucose stores, generally your willpower access declines temporarily until glucose stores are replenished. We need to carefully choose how we use our energy so that we can invest ourselves in that which matters most to us. The good news is that our willpower strengthens like muscles strengthen. The more we put our willpower to use, the stronger it will become over time.

This leads to the all-important question of how we replenish our willpower once it has been used up for the day. Baumeister's research indicates that there are two keys to regenerating our willpower: rest and experiencing positive emotions. The need for physical rest seems self-evident. When we feel physical exhaustion, we need to rest our physical bodies. Yet I have found with highly competitive athletes and performers that more than physical rest is required after a hard training bout or performance to be fully ready for practice the next day. Often, we will be self-critical of what we did not do perfectly. We will consider, at length, comments made by our teachers, coaches, teammates, or other performers around us. In order to fully replenish our energy, it is necessary to find a sense of ease or contentment between bouts of training.

We need to fully recover not only physically, but emotionally as well. This is consistent with Baumeister's second finding: the second key to regenerating our willpower is experiencing positive emotion. We can build on the contents of Chapter 3 in thinking about how to do this. To rebuild our willpower, we need to foster a sense of contentment, joy, love, interest, or a sense of peace. What do you do to help yourself recover from intense training or high-level performance? Do you read novels, knit, shop, or watch movies? Do you cook? Do you paint or play guitar? It is important to recover both physically and emotionally from your training.

In retrospect, it is amazing that in my experiences as an Olympic athlete and a professional sailor on the America's Cup team, I never once had a coach mention the importance of *emotional* recovery. All elite athletes understand the value of physical rest and diet, but very few, in my experience, know how crucial emotional rest is. Actively seeking positive emotion is not only pleasant, but is essential to buoy yourself. Otherwise, you might not be able to push when you need it. Your willpower will not fully regenerate without it. Without adequate emotional recovery and without experiencing positive emotions, I simply could not bounce back and be fully prepared to dig in again.

An equally important idea is to consider exactly where and how you use up your willpower. I'll never forget a comment that my Olympic team coach, who was from Germany, made when I was training for the 1992 Olympic rowing team. During one practice, he said, "Amy, every day is not a race. Don't push so hard!" At the time I took this comment as a great compliment. I thought that I had met the highest standards. But as I look back on this moment, I realize that he was emphasizing that I was not choosing wisely in terms of how I used my willpower. Though I am certain that I was strengthening my willpower during those years of intense training, I also am certain that I needlessly drained my willpower energy tank. I tapped into it too often and too deeply. And then, for moments in important competitions when I really needed it, I would sometimes come up short in my ability to dig in and push. Sometimes I had nothing left to dig into.

ENERGY SOURCES AND ENERGY DRAINS

We need to more thoughtfully use our life energy in training, in time away from training, and in preparing for competition. When pursuing goals, we tend to overestimate the amount of energy and willpower we have per day to invest both physically and emotionally in our goals. Overuse of your energy can result in exhaustion, burnout, and reduced commitment.

One way to think about your energy use is to think about the sources that give you energy and to think of the life experiences that drain you. You may get energized by an endless variety of activities such as hanging out with friends, cooking, reading, watching movies, dancing, doing yoga, knitting, or talking with new acquaintances. Your life energy may be drained by worrying about what others think, training too hard (like doing too many extra lifts or runs), spending time with "close" friends who are negative and critical, worrying about how you will perform, or comparing yourself to competitors.

There is no list of volitional activities (purposeful thinking and acting) that will bring emotional recovery and enjoyment to everyone; it really matters what the activity means to you. For example, going to a party could be highly energizing for you. But for someone else, it could take all of their willpower to get through a party! We are all different. It is a matter of knowing what does and doesn't work for you.

In Exercise 4.1 consider three activities that contribute to your overall life energy and three that drain you. For the ones that drain you, consider an action you can take—or a thought that you could think—that would reduce the negative impact of the experience.

Considering the sources of positive energy and also what can drain your energy can be a wonderful awareness exercise. If we want to give ourselves the best chance to optimize performance for the high-intensity performance moments, the key is to make sure that we make the best use of each day between now and then.

We cannot blindly throw ourselves into our training to be effective. To be

Exercise 4.1. Energy sources and energy drains

My sources of life energy e.g., walking on the beach, going to the movies, talking with a best friend	
1.	
2.	
3.	

Things that drain me of life energy	Action or thought that I could take to minimize the drain
1.	1.
2.	2.
3.	3.

wise about training, we must think carefully about how we use our energy and the times when we must use our willpower to keep going. An essential aspect of using our energy wisely is to consider the factors and activities that are authentic sources of positive emotion for us. No willpower is necessary when we are feeling surges of strong interest, joy, and contentment. The more we can integrate positive emotion into our daily training and daily lives the better we will perform.

SMALL CHANGES, BIG IMPACT

Your willpower definitely plays a part in what you can change. We have limitless possibility and a limit to what we can do each day. The key is focusing in on the small changes that you can make in your life that can help most, in addition to all that you are currently doing. You could also think of them as adjustments. We all have to carefully select what we choose to improve or change, because we only have so much willpower to use up, even for our current demand. To make a change, we must carefully choose what potential change could have the biggest impact on our ability to optimize performance when it counts. And if we choose wisely, small changes can set off a positive ripple effect in our lives. Small changes—in what we do, think, or in psychological approaches—can have a big future effect.

Barbara Fredrickson is the current leader in the study of positive emotion. In her 2005 study, she discusses the effect of how a small change in positive emotion felt in the moment can have a big effect on one's future resources. She supports this line of thinking with the idea of a *linear dynamic system.* A good example is the way that weather forecasters think about changes in weather patterns. She notes that "the hallmark feature ... known as *sensitive dependence on initial conditions,* is often conveyed as the butterfly effect: As in weather forecasting, seemingly trivial inputs—like the flap of a butterfly's wings in one location—can disproportionately determine later conditions elsewhere." In other words, a small change upstream can result in big effects downstream.

As you read this line, your life contains many *initial conditions* that you could change in small ways to improve your performance life in major ways. For example, if you have the habit of going through the motions in training, you have the opportunity now to make a radical change in how you approach practice. A significant change in the future could be produced by a very small change today. You could decide today to fully focus on the feel of the motion as you practice a move. If you are a musician, you could fully focus on the emotion that you'd like to express during one specific challenging segment of music. If you have difficulty with a particular person who could impact your ability to perform, like a competitor or your coach, you could decide today to stop speaking or thinking critically of that person. Just for today, you could stop directing your energy toward the negative and nudge it toward the positive. Such small, unexpected changes in your regular patterns of thinking or behaving could potentially have a significant impact on your ability to optimize performance in the future. As this takes hold, you will find it easier to nudge yourself back into the sweet spot and will stay there longer.

Vanessa Trien, lead singer of *Vanessa and the Jumping Monkeys*, remembers writing her first song. She was living and learning how to play the guitar in Costa Rica. She was inspired by the Latin American music that she was hearing and learning. She recalls, "I sat down and was inspired to write my first song. It was a magical moment. … I felt in awe that I could write a composition, where I could express who I am. It caught me by surprise. … I had a million other things I could be doing. I huddled over my guitar. I sat for hours. When I felt it was finished, it was one of the biggest accomplishments of my life. I went from the start of writing a song to the finish. The song was entirely out of my own imagination. It was a kind of poetry that I could write that suited me."

Vanessa had not imagined writing her own music until this moment. Though she had studied the piano for more than a decade as a child, she had not entertained the idea of becoming a songwriter. With writing her first song, her initial conditions shifted. A new possibility for her future was seeded.

Now, 20 years later, she has had a successful career as both a folk singer and, most currently, leads a band focused on children's music. She has recorded three CDs and plays for sold-out crowds of parents and children.

Is there any way to prove that a small difference in the present can have a big impact into the future? In one study of positive emotion, Deborah Danner and colleagues analyzed the mental attitude of 180 22-year old women in the 1930s, who were on their way to becoming nuns. The researchers analyzed 180 handwritten autobiographies of these newly anointed Notre Dame nuns. The nuns had been asked to write a brief one-page reflection about their life and what brought them to the convent. Sixty years later, the researchers carefully analyzed the essays. The researchers were interested in the varied emotional content of the essays.

Line by line, the researchers counted the number of *positively toned* emotions expressed in the autobiographical reflections. What did they mean by positively toned emotions? Here is an example. One essay considered high in positive emotion content read, "The past year... has been a happy one ... I look forward with eager joy to receiving the Holy Habit..." The essays were broken into three groups: the top quartile (the top 25%, those that had expressed the most positively toned emotions), the middle 50%, and the bottom quartile (25%, those who had expressed the least number of positively toned emotions).

The findings were quite surprising. The nuns who exhibited the highest frequency (top 25%) of positively toned emotions in their letters lived almost 10 (9.4, to be precise) years longer on average than the nuns whose essays contained the fewest positively toned emotions. This study suggests that differences in emotional attitude or state, at a young age, can impact one's longevity: Some of the nuns' positive interpretations or attitudes toward their lives may have been the key to their longevity 60 years later.

In this book, I suggest possible shifts in what you do or how you think that could potentially make big differences in your performance. I encourage you to try the things that seem to resonate with you. You can't change everything, but even one key change can make a radically positive difference. In my practice, I have found that when performers make small, key changes in their approach to dealing with a performance challenge, they often experience a big impact on future performance.

Each of us is a complex system. As individuals, we are composed of many interdependent systems. Some of our major systems include our emotions, our will, our thoughts, our meter of right and wrong, our spiritual plane, our interactions with others, and our physical systems.

I am asking you to consider the many systems within your own life. All of the systems impact one another. For example, if you begin to exercise after a long hiatus, you may experience a triggering of positive thoughts about the new possibilities of your body and how you emotionally feel. This may trigger emotions of pride and joy. You may be more inspired shortly after the start of a consistent exercise routine to pick up the phone and set a date to meet up with a friend with whom you have long had a falling out. Your moral system may be triggered, feeling that it is the right thing to do to sort out the trouble with the friend. You may experience your courage as you place the call. Next, you might be perceived, by others, as someone of good moral character for reaching out to the old friend. Eventually, you may end up with an unexpected job offer, a date invitation, a desire to return to church, or you may get put in the starting lineup. One small constructive change in the system can have a ripple effect in your life in many unexpected and positive ways.

WHICH SMALL CHANGE WILL HAVE THE IMPACT WE ARE SEEKING?

What can we do to make the difference? First, we have to consider what we can change. A great thing to consider is our volitional (intentional) activities. We have control over these activities: what we think about, what decisions we make, what we commit to achieving, how we plan, and what actions we actually take. This is the go-to place to make change. But what should we pay attention to? What small change now could make the biggest difference in the future to heighten our experience of happiness and achievement? As a sport psychologist, I always recommend keeping it as simple as possible. We have the willpower issue to contend with, we have limited resources in making change. The more simple and clear your target, the better shot you have at actually making a positive change.

I realize that most athletes are already training a few too many hours a day, most musicians are practicing many hours a day, and in the workforce you are already working 40- or 50-plus hours or more per week. Anyone reading this is already pushing hard. The question is, what is the one small change that can catapult your performance upward?

I have worked with hundreds of athletes who have made the decision to think *one* different thought during a specific, planned-for moment in competition. In most cases, this one different thought created a positive snowball effect in a good direction of confidence, present focus, and excellent performance. And that is what we were looking for, a simple, clear way to significantly improve their ability to perform and compete.

One year I worked with a collegiate lacrosse team on various sport psychology issues and on that team I met Jane, a player who was having a very difficult time in practice. She kept dropping the ball each time her teammates passed it to her. Her increasing habit of dropping the ball was happening in both practice and games. For lacrosse, a few dropped balls in a game can make the difference between a win and a loss. Once, when I was working with the entire team, Jane initiated discussion around her continually dropping the ball when she was receiving a pass. I asked Jane what she was thinking about as she was running with her stick out, which indicates she is open and can receive a pass.

Jane said she would think, "Don't drop it! Don't drop it!" And, of course, guess what was happening most of the time? Right. Jane was consistently dropping the ball. I asked her what else she could think when she was asking for a pass. Her response, "I can catch it!" And her teammates quickly joined in, laughing, "Yes, you can catch it!" In the moment, they decided that when Jane was dropping the ball, they'd remind her that she could actually catch the ball! The answer seems so obvious and simple. Yet the change was essential. Jane started catching the ball.

Jane's game was transformed through the small change she and her teammates made. Her confidence re-emerged. She became a reliable teammate based on the one seemingly small change. Yet she was willing to honestly face her source of suffering. It seems easy as we look in, but it can be intensely difficult to be the person who has to be honest and has to make the one necessary change. And as we all know, any change is difficult. It is difficult to get ourselves to purposefully shift what we are thinking, what we are doing, or what we are pursuing. If we risk seeing ourselves—or worse yet, others seeing us—as weak or limited, it can be tremendously difficult to change. And yet, ironically, one small shift can make radical, positive shifts.

One small change can also nudge us back into living in the sweet spot. And it often just takes one additional change in effort to reap a big impact. Although because we are already tapping on our willpower each day to just keep up with our many demands, any additional demand can be taxing. We need to carefully choose what we add in consideration of our precious resource of willpower.

The question remains, what small changes in our lives can significantly contribute to our future happiness and success? Peter Senge is a leader in organizational behavior. His great contributions to the business world are integral to systems theory. A system can be conceptualized by comparing it to a baby crib mobile. Imagine a little mobile with eight little animals hanging down. When you touch one, they all are impacted and move. All parts of any system are interdependent. Systems are constantly impacting and being impacted by other systems.

Within the framework of systems theory, Senge introduces the idea of the *highest point of leverage*. The highest point of leverage is the single change that would make the biggest, most positive impact on a system. I've thought quite a bit about my highest point of leverage in my current life. I've determined that when I exercise and meditate daily, it sets my day on an entirely different course. I am steadier with the kids, my mind is clearer to write, I eat less sugar, I am more grateful for my life, and I simply enjoy my life more. There is a positive snowball effect. Exercising the physical body and tuning my mind impacts all of the systems in my personal life including my social, emotional, spiritual, mental, and professional well-being systems.

Regardless of whether you are six months away from competing in the Olympic Games or want to prepare for your first local 5K road race, making an effort to find your highest point of leverage will help you prepare. The volitional activity that you identify as your point of positive leverage may not be directly tied to actually practicing for the event. Your highest point of leverage may have to do with putting more energy into fun, recovery activities, shifting away from negative thoughts, or nurturing one relationship that is particularly meaningful and safe. It may be something you can change in a completely different part of your life. And it may be essential to making the difference in your performance when it is most important to you to do your thing well.

FINDING A SMALL CHANGE THAT MAY BE A POINT OF LEVERAGE

You may not yet know what your highest point of leverage is for your training. This book will provide many areas to consider in your training and performance life. But for now, consider what small change might make a big difference in your life. If you had to guess right now, what small change would you try to leverage? Whatever you choose, make sure it is realistically changeable. I encourage you to try implementing this plan for the next few days and see how it effects your emotions and focus.

Just the experience of purposely modifying what you think or what you do to help with training will be a great step forward. As you read on, you will be provided many essential options to help you optimize performance, which you could adopt for your highest point of leverage shift. Where you are right now, what slight shift might be of most help to you?

I've included in Figure 4.1 a quick visual of how making a small, purposeful change can affect your experience. Imagine your life now is sitting at point

Exercise 4.2. Finding a small change that may be a point of leverage

What is one change that might make a difference in my training?	Why?	Action I need to take
e.g., Spend one hour each day reading fiction	Time alone reading helps fully rest me	Go to the library or bookstore and get a few books
My small change/potential point of leverage:		

A in Figure 4.1. One small decision at this point in time, like cutting back on sugar, practicing mindfully, saying one kind thing to yourself each day about the progress you are making, or saying only positive things about teammates, can literally change the direction of your life. In one of my classes, there was a student who had been chewing tobacco for 10 years. During this conversation of small change, big impact, he decided to stop using tobacco for the week. Now, seven years later, he is tobacco free. If he had not been willing to make the key change that day seven years ago, his health might be completely different than what it is today.

You could be moving from point A toward Z (healthy eating habits and positive relationships with teammates) versus toward X (no change in direction), all initiated through one small choice. For example, you may find yourself very successful in your sport, but, at the same time, lonely and uninspired in your private life. You may always have dreamed of painting, but you never picked up a paintbrush. The small change may be to go to an art store and buy a small paint set and canvas and then schedule a two-hour block to paint. This could eventually inspire a radically different way of living. You could shift from feeling uninspired to feeling re-energized by your nightly painting periods. Consider again the singular change that you could make that might make a big impact on your system. There are many opportunities to do things a bit differently in training, while performing or during your time of rest and

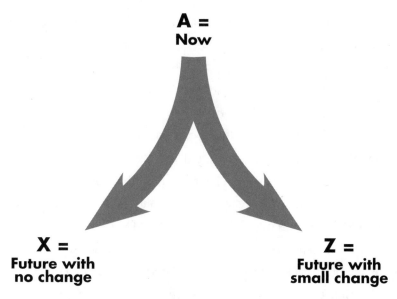

Figure 4.1: Small Change, Big Future Impact

recovery. In any of these areas you could choose to make one small change in how you think or what you do which could serve as a catalyst for a powerful, positive future change.

You may not know the answer, but I bet you have a hunch of what could make a big difference in your life. With awareness and some effort, you can figure out what would be most helpful, inspiring, or transformative for you. Or you may know what the issue is, but do not yet have the tools to make the change. Read on. The purpose of this book is to give you ideas that may resonate with you, to make a big difference for you as you prepare for big performance moments.

THREE SMALL CHANGES TOWARD YOUR NEXT PERFORMANCE

For now I'd like you to think about the next 24 hours and consider the very best way to spend your time with the goal of preparing for an upcoming perfor- mance in your life. First, consider the nature of your upcoming performance.

It may be coming up very soon, or it may be in the remote distance. Yet changes in the next 24 hours can affect that performance, whether it is close or remote.

How would you ideally spend your time? How you would choose to spend your time is clearly dependent upon your performance goals and the many other aspects of your life that are important and require your attention. Consider all of the factors in your life, like how much sleep you need, how you'd like to eat, who you would interact with, how you would interact with them, how long you would practice, the quality of your practice, and what you would do to best recover from your bouts of focused training. You may be in a phase of needing to spend the next 24 hours fully focused on recovering, emotionally or physically, or you may be lined up for many hours of rigorous training, practice, or production. Whatever it is, right now, what would you say are three small things that you could do to help you improve and prepare for your performance? What could you do over the next 24 hours that would make a difference, even if it were simply a small step forward?

Your list may seem so small that you may not think that these small changes now could make that much of a difference in the future. They may feel inconsequential. Yet these small changes could be the source of making all the difference in optimally preparing yourself for the big moments. In fact, small changes are the most important place to work to make big changes in the future.

For the remainder of the book, I will provide ideas for intervention that have helped Olympic, elite, and professional athletes over the past decade in my work as a sport psychologist. I expect that a few of the ideas will be essential to you taking the next leap in your ability to perform. It is not about making many, massive changes on top of your already demanding daily life. This book is about helping you get clear on a few small changes that could free you up to enjoy what you are doing more and to help you stay more focused on the moment to moment of what you are doing so you can do your thing as well as possible and you can get a great sense of daily satisfaction

Exercise 4.3. Three small changes toward your next performance

Action	What will you have to do to make it happen? When, where, and for how long would you ideally do it?
e.g., I'll be in bed by 10 p.m.	I'll have to make dinner sooner and turn the TV off at 9:30 p.m.
1st Action	
2nd Action	
3rd Action	

from your efforts. The ideas are intended to help you get in and remain in the sweet spot, so you can set yourself up to perform in the sweet spot.

You will know which changes will help you. If the idea seems compelling, go for it. If one feels burdensome, skip it and read on.

At the core, this book is about helping you train, prepare, live, and perform in the sweet spot. This does not mean it will always be easy or feel good. In fact, it won't. You will experience emotional swings, just like everyone else. But training and performing in the sweet spot does mean that you will be able to count on being satisfied with your efforts. It does mean that you will give yourself the best chance of being successful. It does mean that you will have a sense of peace or contentment because you are doing all that you can in your power to do your thing to the best of your ability and at the same time being open to all the good that is occurring both within and outside of your training world.

5

The Learning Approach

Getting the Most out of Your Wins *and* Your Losses

"If I don't win a gold medal this time (the athlete's third Olympic Games), then my rowing career will have been a total waste of time."
—Multiple-time U.S. team member and Olympian

The classic question from parents to their child after the child has competed is, "Did you win?" If the answer is yes, then we celebrate. And if the child says no, then most people tend to be disappointed.

But what are we celebrating or mourning? Is it just the win or loss? Of course, it is great to win and disappointing to lose. Our instinctive response to winning and losing, in the moment, will probably always be strong. We love the positive rush from a win. Is that all that there is to the story? Do we just suffer with the losses? Do we just decide that we are great for the few hours or days after a win? What else can we do but celebrate a win and mourn a loss?

I once worked with a collegiate coach who came to me because she had difficulty dealing with loss. With some sense of embarrassment, she admitted that she felt depression after her team lost a game. She said after a loss she would literally have a hard time getting out of bed the next day. She didn't know what to say to her team when her team lost, and she experienced an intense feeling of humiliation. She said that she knew that her response was unhealthy, but had no idea of how to overcome the rush of negative feelings. For this coach, winning meant feeling good and losing meant feeling bad— very bad.

A very different experience emerged in one of my research studies in which I interviewed U.S. National and Olympic team rowers. All of the study participants talked about two self-selected episodes during their elite sport training experience. They talked about an event that occurred while they were either on the U.S. team, Olympic team, or while training at a U.S. Olympic training site. The events represented times when they felt the most competitive pressure to perform. One of my study participants, Cyrus Beasley, had been the U.S. team single sculler (one-man boat) for a number of years. He was thought to be one of the best rowers in the world at this time. He is 6-feet, 7-inches tall, thick and powerful. I was very interested in interviewing him, given his great success nationally and internationally.

Just before the interview, Cyrus had been in a phase of his elite sport experience where he was wanted by the U.S. team coaches for any boat that was being prepared to race in the upcoming World Championships. He could have rowed in the eight-man boat (one oar each), the four, the pair, the men's quad (four people sculling with two oars each), or the double (two men sculling). For most athletes in the elite world of rowing, making the U.S. team is a significant mark of success. Olympic and World Championship medals are precious and unpredictable, but making the team is more predictable, controllable, and an important mark of success for most athletes. Usually, the best athletes will first ensure that they make the team and then worry about winning medals. Cyrus could have achieved this goal without a problem.

He just had to say yes to any of the boats listed above. Cyrus, surprisingly, did not make this choice.

When Cyrus decided to attempt to make the U.S. single scull (one-man boat), he had to win the series of races. The final series of races came down to himself and one other athlete. The two men were tied after the second race; each athlete had won and lost a race. The third race would determine who earned the right to race in the World Championships. Whoever lost would stay home.

Cyrus felt fully prepared; he'd never rowed so well. He was in the flow state; he was fully engaged in the race with no distractions. At the halfway mark of the race, the two boats were dead even. With 500 meters to go (3/4 of the way through the race), the other boat had pulled a foot ahead of Cyrus. He responded by pulling as hard and effectively as he could. He remembers:

> I was pulling as hard, I was asking for everything, I was pulling as hard as I possibly could. … He crossed the line I think a few seconds in front of me… I have never been so exhausted after a race as I was after that race and felt physically really ill. And I have never felt so shaky and so bad after a race… I was absolutely miserable, but I knew at the same time there were good things in there, because I knew that I had given everything I possibly could have given. That was it. That was all there was. **That was the race I was looking for.** That was it and [he] beat me. So… what can you do? I was really, really happy. It was a weird feeling. I had just lost, and I was so happy. It was wild.

Cyrus had never raced better. He crossed the finish line a few feet behind his competitor. He lost the race and lost a spot on the U.S. National team that year. Yet he had a sense of satisfaction rather than overwhelming disappointment.

Cyrus's story has sat with me for almost a decade. At the time of the interview, I found his final thoughts after losing the race almost unbelievable. At that point, I had recently retired as an Olympic athlete myself, and I could not imagine losing one of the most important races of my career and feeling happy about it. How could an athlete, at the pinnacle of his athletic career, lose such a pivotal race and immediately after his race, experience such a powerful sense of happiness? For Cyrus, happiness at that moment had nothing to do with winning or losing. His happiness was about achieving his absolute best, regardless of how he compared to someone else. He was definitely living in the sweet spot as he raced.

So what is the difference between the team coach who became very depressed after a loss and Cyrus Beasley, who felt joy after what was arguably his greatest loss? Why did one person experience devastation and one experience satisfaction? This chapter delves into this issue and aims to show how learning from our wins *and* our losses is a key to living in the sweet spot, in performance and in life.

The team coach was not prepared to learn anything positive from her team's losses; rather, she understood the loss as saying only that she was a failure and that she did not have the capacity to succeed. This plunged her into negative feelings of shame and devastation. In contrast, Cyrus learned something very positive from his big loss. He learned that he could operate at peak performance, and sustain it. It was entirely beside the point that someone else could race faster.

I suspect Cyrus valued putting forth his best effort; he valued striving toward excellence (of skill and effort). He had learned the value of trying his hardest, learning all that he could, and then taking the results as they came. I suspect this approach allowed him to become one of the top rowers in the US for many years. It also allowed him to quickly accept such a significant loss while taking pride in his effort.

There is no question that winning, being successful in your performance area, matters. The question really isn't, "Does winning matter?" Winning does matter to almost all of us. But when we want to set ourselves up for success over the long run, a different question becomes equally important (after our celebration).

When we want to set ourselves up for being as successful as possible over the long run, the critical question is, "What are you doing with the *information* provided by your own performance (whether you win or lose)?" I suspect for Cyrus that the information he took from his final race was that he rowed to the best of his ability on that day. His rhythm, balance, effort, and power application were excellent. This information was a source of joy.

A TRULY SUCCESSFUL MINDSET: A LEARNING MINDSET

What is the mindset that gives us the best chance to consistently perform our best and win as much as possible? Here is where the big mistake comes into play, a mistake that we all often make. If we highly value the outcome of winning or being successful compared to others (which most of us do), then we can fall into the bad habit of evaluating ourselves only in terms of wins and losses—when we win, we are worthy; when we lose, we are not.

Our mindset, or our attitude, toward our daily practice and training has a significant impact on how hard we try, how much we persist in the face of adversity and the emotional experience we draw from our training and practice. It turns out that our mindset toward what we are doing, toward our effort, successes, and "failures," has a powerful impact on how we evaluate our talents, skills, and abilities. Specifically, many of us draw a harsh conclusion that lack of success is evidence that we lack ability. We don't just lack success in the present event, we lack ability and our loss has demonstrated that we lack ability. With this conclusion, there is not much we can do—we lack ability and that is it.

As an elite athlete, I would often allow one win or loss to determine how I felt about myself as an athlete, whether I was talented or not, and how I felt about myself as a human being. I would generalize one performance to my talent and skill. If I won, I felt like I was good and if I lost, anything, I thought it indicated that I was less talented than my competitors. I experienced being devastated over and over. And, unfortunately, the losses or the negative events would stick with me far longer than the good ones. I carried a fear with me about how badly I would feel just after the next loss. I believed that being cut from a boat or not making a racing squad, once, meant that I was less than my competitors. And far worse, it meant that I was less worthy to be on the planet.

How can you think about your setbacks and wins in a way that will best set you up for success? Carol Dweck is the leading researcher in the area of mindset and her research gives great insight into the mindset that will best serve you in your achievement aspirations. Dweck's research indicates that there are two basic mindsets, the *fixed* mindset and the *growth* mindset. These mindsets say a lot about how a person looks at his or her abilities, talents, and intelligence.

In the *fixed* mindset, people look at their abilities as relatively stable. This means that their basic abilities will not change much; they are either good or bad at whatever they do. When we think of our abilities as fixed, then we evaluate the results of competition as direct evidence of our innate talent and skills. When we are successful, having such a fixed mindset can make us feel like we are born winners. Competition can be a public acknowledgment of our God-given talents, abilities, and (in some performance realms) our intelligence. People with a fixed mindset thrive when they are assured of success.

However, Dweck's research shows that with a fixed mindset, you tend to fear challenges. Why? Because a challenge presents the threat of revealing your lack of ability. Losing can create sheer humiliation. Losing means that we are not gifted or talented. People with a fixed mindset believe that practice and effort cannot change their (natural) talent. With the fixed mindset approach you believe that there are winners (and losers) in any particular realm. And in a fixed mindset, there predictably is a significant concern with how you might be judged.

Dweck's research shows that for people with a fixed mindset, there is often an underlying belief that if you have to try, you are not truly talented or skilled. And there is the belief that trying and failing is worse than not trying at all! Therefore, our mindset can stop us from trying, create an anxiety response to an upcoming performance, and can stop us from being willing to try our best. Our mindset can set off a series of positive (when successful) or negative (when less-than, as compared to someone else) emotional surges.

When you are on a winning streak or you are on the top of a group of performers evaluating yourself in this way (winning means that you are competent and able) has little downside in the short term. When you win and think that this reflects that you are more talented and skilled, this boosts your confidence and makes you feel good. You'll tend to perform well. Over time, however, there is a limitation to this approach because you are not learning as much as you could about why you are doing so well. You miss opportunities to purposefully strengthen and expand what is going right.

The bigger challenge lies in when you hit a slump or someone outperforms you in a setting that makes a difference to your standings. When you believe that one competition against a competitor represents some fixed talent or skill that you have, it can be devastating. In fact, such evaluation of your abilities can lead to steep downward swings in negative emotion, harsh self-judgment, and a reduction in your willingness to persist in practice and performance. I would suspect that the team coach I described earlier was working with a fixed mindset, and had become caught in such a downward cycle.

If you identify with some of the fixed mindset characteristics, don't despair—that is OK. That means you have a chance to change your mindset. With self-awareness and some effort you can shift to a mindset that can ultimately help you succeed more often. You can become aware of thinking patterns that are ultimately creators of pain and destroy our ability to perform under pressure. You can nudge yourself back into your sweet spot. With effort you can learn to take joy in your learning and effort. You can learn to be more quickly accepting of losses you cannot control. And you can learn to be more persistent in the face of great challenge.

A fixed mindset can hurt you, but it can also hurt others' performance, if you use your fixed mindset to judge them. A few years ago, I became very aware of the impact of mindset when my kids were learning to draw and write their letters. I used to tell my oldest child that she was "so smart" when she would show me her letters, and I'd always say what a good artist she was and comment on how she could draw so beautifully. (I had an over-the-top "isn't my kid great" attitude.) Everything was fine until my next child decided not to even try drawing or writing letters. He was not so "smart" or could not draw so "beautifully" compared to his sister. My comments making judgments on her abilities, based on one drawing or one line of letters, taught him to evaluate his abilities. He decided that he was no good and that there was no use trying. After a few months of changing the language (and my mindset) of my comments on my daughter's effort or progress (e.g., "Oh, that is an interesting combination of colors. You've worked really hard on that, I can tell"), my son began to try. He began to draw and write.

What about the other mindset? The *growth* mindset is the antithesis of the fixed mindset. With a growth mindset, you believe that with effort, your basic talents, abilities, and even intelligence can change and improve. The hallmark quality of the growth mindset, according to Dweck (2006), is that "the passion for stretching yourself and sticking to it, even (especially) when it is not going well, allows people to thrive during some of the most challenging times in their lives." And, clearly, this is what we need to develop in the effort of best preparing for performance. With such a mindset, you value effort and learning. There is a sense of patience as you continue to improve, grow, and learn with effort. It can still be painful to fail to meet a goal, but someone with a growth mindset is committed to learning from his disappointments and to tenaciously fighting toward improvement.

How can we change our orientation from a fixed mindset to a learning mindset? One important aspect is deciding that we value learning. Of course, most of us think that we value learning, but when really pressed, we might find that we value learning less than we might claim.

Consider this question. One of my Olympic teammates once asked me what I'd rather do: Race and *not* try my hardest and win, or race my very best and lose.

What would you choose? I remember feeling perplexed by this question.

Of course I always wanted to win. But then, I also always wanted to do my best. Why couldn't I have both options in a third scenario? The teammate who asked me was an unusually talented member of our small pool of Olympic hopefuls. She had already been on many U.S. National teams at that point. Everything seemed to come easy to her, especially her apparent ability to win whenever it mattered. I think she expected me to say that I'd rather win with a half-hearted effort. I am certain that would be her choice, because that is how she seemed to train. She always seemed to slow down or stop whenever she could. She put in minimal effort toward lifting weights. Yet on the water she was consistently one of the fastest athletes.

I clearly remember answering the question with, "I'd rather race my best and lose." I secretly wondered if there was something wrong with me choosing this answer. Why would I, an aspiring Olympian, even lean toward any preference that was connected to losing? It should have been against my nature, yet that was my authentic response. It just didn't make sense to me to prefer to put out a half-hearted try, regardless of the win. It just didn't feel right. And yet, I struggled with giving my honest answer out loud, because it sounded like I'd rather be the struggling loser versus the cool winner.

At the time, I wasn't able to verbalize with what I was grappling. I had no words for it. I'd never thought about or talked about having a training philosophy. I'd never talked about my attitudes toward training and racing. I was just caught up in the day-to-day of trying to move up the elite-rowing ladder to make the U.S. National and Olympic teams. I wasn't able at that time to work out the implications of my teammate's question. If I could have, I would have asked myself some of these questions:

- If you only put yourself in situations in which you won easily, would you be developing your skills as much as you could be?

- How satisfying is it to give a half-hearted try and end up successful?

- What might your ability to perform in the next two or three years be if you always tried your best and were willing to take the hits of losing?

The question that my teammate posed to me was about values: Was it more important for me to feel fulfilled by doing my best, or was it more important to demonstrate success in comparison to others? But is this really what we have to choose between? Is there another option?

I think we can have both. Clearly, winning and being successful is important and is a dominant value in our society. However, the win in-the-moment desire can cloud our thinking and make us unable to see and feel the positive emotional shot that can come from doing our best and learning from it. The key, as this chapter argues, is the learning.

HOW CAN WE LEARN FROM OUR WINS AND OUR LOSSES?

Once we have decided that we really value learning, and that we want to promote a growth mindset, we have to work with what we learn from our wins and our losses. What do you do with the information that led you to a particular loss or setback, or to a win? What could you learn from the experience that can make you better next time? What new information do you have that you could leverage in your practices so that you could come back stronger? Some information that may be relevant to your performance realm includes how well you focused, what you focused on, how your performance felt, how you implemented your strategic plan, how you emotionally responded to the upcoming event, how you were able to tolerate negative emotions, and how you were able to shift out of a negative emotional spin. Whether you win or lose an event, being aware of such data could be critical to how well you are able to perform the next time you are competing.

I worked with Jenny, a young 15-year-old swimmer who was a highly competitive, nationally ranked swimmer. Jenny's best event was the 100-meter butterfly. She came to work with me because she was having a difficult time with her emotions during the time period just before she began to compete. Though she was the fastest in this event compared to her club teammates, she would begin to cry intensely right before her races. The experience of racing this particular event was miserable for her. She was terrified of not hitting her "time" at the end of each race. When I began to talk with her about what was happening during the process of racing from the moment after the gun went off to just before she touched the wall on the last lap, she literally had nothing to say. She had spent almost no time thinking about her thought process or her physical experience while she was racing. She raced mindlessly. She could recall only thoughts of intense fear when she thought that she might be falling behind while racing.

Jenny could learn little from racing until she could begin to become more mindful of what she was doing. Through our work together, she began to purposefully pay attention to what she was physically feeling, on what her mind was focusing on, and—when out of the water—on good past performances (through some visualization work). Jenny became more aware of the process—or actual experience—of racing. She realized that she had many negative thoughts going through her mind like, "What if I can't finish?" "What if I don't make my time?" and "What if I can't pass her?" The most significant thought that she noticed was, "Here it comes." That was the red flag. It was the consistent first signal that she would soon start to have breathing problems. With this awareness, she could begin to make changes to what she was paying attention to while competing. She had to shift her attention from only caring about winning to what she was feeling and thinking while racing.

Jenny was able to shift her attention to how she'd like to be swimming. She was able to focus on how she could swim most effectively. She thought about power and efficiency. She also focused on her strengths. We created cue words and phrases that would allow her to swim to the best of her ability by paying attention to the actual in-the-moment process of swimming. Jenny was also able to notice when specific physical sensations were off, so she could make corrections.

Jenny made a radical shift from worrying about the end result of her races to paying attention to what she was doing while she was racing. Over time, we developed strategies that helped her race more effectively and helped her directly face her fear of not being able to breathe. Jenny stopped crying before she raced and cut down her time in the 100-meter butterfly. In fact, in one national level series that included nine races, she got her personal best time in every event after about two months of purposefully paying attention to what was actually happening in her mind and body while racing (racing mindfully).

Jenny's experience represents a radical shift in her mindset. Though winning and being successful remained very important to Jenny, her focus while racing was primarily on factors over which she had control. She was paying attention to factors that both would help her perform better and ones that she could actually change or strengthen with focused attention. She began to learn to evaluate the quality of her racing and the improvements she was making. She learned from her experience and came to believe that growth is possible. And with these changes in thinking she nudged herself back into the sweet spot while both training and competing.

WHAT ARE YOU LEARNING?

What do you do with the very specific information of what you are focused on, what you are thinking, and what you are feeling as you prepare and actually are engaged in practice and performance? Consider the examples in Exercise 5.1. Consider how differently your experience can be with the two different mindsets after a win and after a loss.

When there is a fixed mindset approach, there is little attention on what could be strengthened or improved. There is almost an exclusive attention on negative feelings from sub-par performance or celebration from a win. The more information you are able to glean about how you'd ideally like to be training, practicing, and performing, the better you will ultimately perform. In Exercise 5.2, take a moment to consider what you learned today or recently in training. Notice how you felt when you had the awareness of what you could learn and consider the positive impact on future performance if you begin to put into practice the necessary changes. The emotions may be negative. Sometimes with insights in the moment, the new awareness can be emotionally painful. But there is also a possibility to improve your ability to perform.

Exercise 5.1. What are you evaluating after training or performance?

Event	Evaluation	Emotion	Contribution to future performances
Lost race	*Fixed:* "I'm just not as good."	Frustration, embarrassment	None
	Growth: "I pushed too hard in the 1st lap."	Feel badly, have hope	Information to change race strategy
Won race	*Fixed:* "I'm better than everyone else."	Happiness, joy	None
	Growth: "My focus on my rhythm helped me through the last lap."	Happiness, joy, interest	Information to maintain the particular focus for the next race.

The in-the-moment awareness can be a powerful source of positive emotion as well. When we are able to focus on our own effort and our own progress, we suddenly have much more good to enjoy.

Consider the moments in training or performance that were particularly challenging or particularly excellent. What could you learn from a recent training bout? If you only evaluated the moment as a chance to improve, what would you specifically consider? What kind of emotions may emerge with such an evaluative approach? How might actually putting this new idea into action impact your future performance? With these questions in mind, either think through or jot down your answers in Exercise 5.2.

Our focus is so heavily weighted on outcomes that we have forgotten about the value of both doing our best and learning from our training to set ourselves up, ultimately, to perform our best. Nurturing a growth mindset can be the key to manifesting our performance goals. The focus on learning, versus chronic self- and other-judgment, is the shortcut toward success. If, instead, we decide to make a performance outcome determine what our talents and skills are for the future, we set ourselves up for failure (unless we can always dominate in all settings—and in this instance, one's mindset doesn't matter).

MINDFULNESS IN PRACTICE AND PERFORMANCE

Just beginning to pay attention to what is happening during performance is a great step in being more mindful of what actually is occurring in your body, how you are applying your skills, and what is occurring in your mind. All of these experiences can be signals to what could positively change. The other option is to tune out, go through the motions, and hope for a win at the end of a competition. Paying attention to what is happening as you compete is essential in learning what needs to happen to take the next step in improving performance.

In Exercise 5.3, consider what is happening in your body and mind as

Exercise 5.2. Growth approach to training and performance

Event	Evaluation/ What I learned today	Emotion	Contribution to future performances
Practice/ Performance	"I need to remember that I still get to do my things and keep pushing even when I get passed."	Determination	Potential new mental habit
Specific aspect of your training			
1.			
2.			
3.			

you go through a segment of performance. You can consider a slice of performance in which you are least comfortable and could use some progress. You may not be able to fully describe the segment of performance now, but I encourage you to start thinking about it so you can make some positive progress with what you learn when you think about your performance.

There is so much to pay attention to in training. Taking a moment to notice your physical cues and what is happening in your mind may provide all the information you need to make positive improvements in your ability to perform. But time is lost when we spend it comparing ourselves to others, feeling disappointment from a loss, worrying about whether or not we will win the game or play the best musical segment, or worrying about being negatively or positively evaluated by someone. As we allow our minds to wander or tune out, we miss opportunities to truly enjoy what we are doing and to accelerate our abilities to perform our best. We can always learn from what is occurring if we open ourselves to this.

Exercise 5.3. Mindful performance

Performancing	Examples	Your Experience
Event:	5-K running race	
In-the-moment of the event	The halfway point of the race	
Physical sensations	Burn in my thighs and throat	
What I hear	Rhythm of my feet striking, others breathing	
What I think	"What if she passes me?"	
My emotions	Fear	
What I can learn	Change to more empowering thoughts; change how I perceive the physical sensations	

CREATING THE HABIT OF LEARNING

When many of my students first read the ideas related to the *fixed* and *growth* mindsets, they become internally reflective and somber. They shift, all at once, deep into thought regarding their own well-developed fixed mindsets. They report concerns such as thinking how they are worried about how they are judged and how they compare to their classmates. Unfortunately, many of us have been trained to love the win and be very hard on ourselves when we lose. We've been trained to put on our 2% blinders of what is wrong and have little practice in holding all of our abilities, accomplishments, and desire for improvement and success. We miss out on the 98% of what is right, regardless of how we stack up against someone else in a discrete moment of time. We expect ourselves to always know, understand, be competent, and ultimately be successful. We have our high standards, but haven't thought much about how to become so competent, knowledgeable, and successful. We want the outcome, but haven't considered how to get there. And even if we've considered the healthy way to get there, it is really hard to consistently live this way. It is possible to live and compete in the sweet spot—but we must train ourselves to create habits of thinking and evaluating that serve us better.

We have not created the habit of authentically thinking about what we can learn without cruelly judging ourselves (back to the 2% blinders). This habit of mind, our habituated response, can be changed. To create a different response we must put into practice a different approach.

As the saying goes, "Insanity is doing the same thing and expecting a different outcome." We can strengthen or weaken our habits of mind through practice. A habit is developed through practice and dissolved by lack of practice. To develop the habit of learning for performing requires us to pay attention to what is happening in training and performance that could be improved (without judging yourself as bad!). After the awareness has arisen, we must then purposefully practice making the changes that are related to what we are learning. This learning could be as specific as slightly changing a breathing pattern during a particular movement in performance. Another example could be to notice when a move or execution of a move feels particularly good physically, or just *on*. Noticing when the good happens and making an effort to replicate the feeling or focus are examples of strengthening the habit of learning. It can be either paying more attention to what you can learn or putting into practice what you are learning.

Another aspect of developing the habit of learning includes purposefully noticing any whispers of positive emotions that arise as a result of engaging in this purposeful learning process. It is important to notice the good energy that arises from practicing and making subtle positive changes in your skills or abilities. We have been inoculated to pay attention to the good that comes from winning and the bad that comes from losing. We must strengthen our ability to notice the daily good that we can generate through paying attention and doing the best that we can in the moment.

This, of course, sounds so simplistic. The idea is clear. The challenge is manifesting the change. The challenge lies in the moments when we have learned habitually to ignore the data to make us better (and to boost our enjoyment of the process) and in the moments when we are harsh with ourselves. In both these areas, we can make shifts to develop and strengthen our habit of learning.

Paying attention to the small moments that acknowledge our strengths and abilities, the fleeting moments of positive emotional surges when things go right, are essential to develop the habit of learning. The next, perhaps more difficult, task is to notice where we could improve technically, cognitively, and emotionally in our performance realm. Noticing how to improve technically or strategically is a normal part of training for all of us. We learn to pay attention to how we could create a better rhythm, throw more accurately, or slightly change the angle of our body in a particular moment. However, our negative emotional surges, such as embarrassment, are a great sign for a need to shift in what we are valuing—learning (growth mindset) or being the best (fixed mindset).

We often get the negative rushes after a performance or practice segment

Exercise 5.4. Developing the habit of learning

Event	What I've done well	How it feels when *it* is going right and well
In practice:	1.	1.
	2.	2.
In performance:	1.	1.
	2.	2.

when we immediately move to judging ourselves harshly. Reducing the strength of the habit of chronically judging ourselves harshly comes from noticing, with kindness and attention, what we are doing. Harshly judging ourselves in trait-like terms such as being worthless, hopeless, or permanently less-than does us no good. But we have to become aware of these occurrences in order to make positive changes toward strengthening the habit of learning.

We have to become aware of the truth of the harshness of the judgment. We need to notice how it creates negative emotion, makes us feel less-than (when we are beaten or make mistakes), and reduces our resolve to push through difficult moments. When we purposefully pay attention to judging ourselves harshly, and not buying into the truth of the judgment, we are taking a first, significant step toward dissolving this habit. Even if we don't rationally believe it, the judging mind can create painful, negative reactions within us. After noticing the harsh judgment, it is then time to quickly shift to thinking about either what you have done well or what you can learn from the same performance or training bout. It is important to spend as little time as possible in the judging mind, in the polarized thinking of talented/untalented or good/bad.

We all have times when we are fixed in our mindsets about our own or others' skills and abilities. We all hold both. We all, probably, can't fully shake the self-judgment, the profound disappointment of coming up short against others. However, with practice we can reduce the strength of the habit of self-judgment. We can train ourselves to consider what we are learning and what we could learn with as much attention as we can muster toward learning.

It is hard to make a global change in one's own mindset. However, you can make progress if you focus only on one area of practice, be it in how you are giving feedback to your children, how you are evaluating your performance during practice, or how you are assessing yourself after a date. If you focus only on one area and make a commitment to yourself to notice three things that you could learn each day in that area, you will be making positive progress toward strengthening your habit of learning. Strengthening this habit is unquestionably necessary to help prepare yourself to perform your best in whatever you are working toward.

6

The Positive Perspective

Building on Gratitude and Optimism

"I get joy out of playing in front of others. Though it is such exposure, I really want to share it with other people. It gives me a lot of joy doing it."

—Vanessa, of Vanessa Trien and the Jumping Monkeys

Our overarching philosophical attitude toward what is happening in our lives, that is, our perspective, may be our greatest asset when the pressure is on. So the question is, how do we develop a mental perspective that frees us up to focus on exactly what we are doing for our big moments? There are ways to cultivate a constructive perspective that allows us to focus effectively on what is occurring and where our energies are most effectively used, moment-to-moment, when it matters most. That is the focus of this chapter.

What kind of positive, constructive perspective would work when you are one of 500 musicians trying out for a premier orchestra? Being selected will mean a six-figure salary and playing consistently with other world-class musicians. Not making it will mean having to wait another few years for such an opportunity. What kind of constructive perspective would be called for when you are going in for a final round of try-out that will determine whether or not you will earn a starting spot in your team's line-up? What type of perspective is needed when your team is trailing by one point in basketball and you are on the free throw line in the last second (if you miss the first shot, your team loses)? What kind of perspective is needed when you go in for a job interview and you very much want to land the job? The job could mean doubling your income, doing more of what you love to do, or working much closer to home. In that job interview, the pressure is on.

Whether trying out for an elite orchestra, an elite sport team, or giving the job presentation of your life, chances are that we do not succeed or fail based on our abilities. Usually in such instances, our skills and abilities are essentially equal to our competitors and colleagues. All performers have slightly varying levels of strength, quickness, skill, or natural ability. However, the best competitive events bring together those who are essentially matched in ability. The question is, what will elicit your ability to consistently be able to shrug off the distractions and be fully present for whatever task lies in front of you—playing your instrument, catching or hitting a ball, or running as fast as your body will move?

Our overall mental attitude gives us our edge. There are various ways of conceptualizing the type of attitude that will best serve us. On race day, we do need to call on our ability to be mentally tough, to be able to focus on what will best serve us moment to moment. (I refer to this as motivational flexibility, which I address in Chapter 14.)

Oddly enough, our ability to focus in the high pressure moment is something that we must develop over months and years. We can build an overarching attitude during the many months and years of preparation for our biggest events, an attitude that sets us up to be tough when the time comes. Our ability to maintain a positive and hopeful outlook in our day-to-day training for our future performances proves to be crucial in helping us to be tough and focused on the task at hand, when we most need to be. And the impact of a positive perspective is not limited to just the high stress moments. When we have a positive perspective, we can use less willpower in just getting present. We want to train. We want to get better. We are able to tap into the love of what drew us in from the start. So not only does the cultivation of this positive perspective help us in the high performance moments, it makes our months of practice more effective as well.

What defines this positive perspective and approach to daily training? Though we could conceptualize it in many ways, maintaining a positive perspective is essentially driven by our willingness to focus on the good in our current lives and the expected good in the future. And in our performance lives, this means focusing on what is good and right with our current training situation and expecting that we will be able to perform to the best of our abilities when it counts.

Focusing on the good in your current situation could encompass a large number of activities. It could include purposefully making you aware of the fact that you are well prepared, that you have an opportunity to see how well you can perform, and that you've worked hard and earned the right to be right where you are. Other examples of focusing on the good in your current life experience could include bringing awareness to the fact that you can breathe, that you can move, and that you are loved. Being present and grateful to all that is good in your life in the moment can elicit a sense of focused presence.

How can we focus on the good in our future life? It hasn't happened yet, so how can we focus on it? Many people harbor a negative attitude toward the future, fearing that it will turn out for the worst. Focusing on the good in the future involves an imaginative optimism. For example, you could be hopeful that your performance will go well; you can imagine the good that will come with success. You could look forward to becoming even healthier and stronger. You could look forward to further enjoying the love that is always available to you each day you are alive. You could look forward to becoming more skilled and more strategically adept. Focusing on the good in your future will lead to progressively more confidence in your ability to perform.

The irony for many performers is that they do just the opposite. They often think about what will happen if they perform poorly, get out-performed, do worse compared to a competitor, or get cut. They often think about a mistake that they just made or a mistake that they could make. They spend time worrying about the type of negative feedback they will receive or chronically comparing themselves to someone in their domain that is slightly more talented, receives more playing time, or receives more attention. In our world of competition and performance, it is easy to get lulled into believing that your human worth is limited to how well you perform on any given day. And this harkens back to the fixed mindset, the perspective that can put us in danger of being nudged back into our 2% blinders.

We've all heard the phrase, "You are only as good as your last performance." This phrase may represent how we are selected or the opportunities that we may be offered in our sport or performance domain on a particular day. And with this, we can easily lose perspective on our present and future good. We can get tricked into believing that who you are as a person is defined by your ability to perform. We can get tricked into thinking that a poor performance on one day must "mean" something bad about our ability, now or in the future. All of us can get trapped in such negative habits of assessing. Your attitude toward your present and future can easily become corrupted by worry, comparisons, and dread.

I learned this the hard way (and this is why I became a sport psychologist). In the fall of 1983, just a few weeks into my freshman year of college, the captain of the rowing team invited me to try out for the team. After my first row, my college coach-to-be said, "You could make the Olympic team." I was delighted. Could I really have some natural talent? Could there really be someone who saw my potential and could help me to develop it?

So began the dream. I loved the long morning practices, the weight-lifting sessions, and mostly having a place to belong. I joined developmental rowing clubs in the summer and made my first U.S. team in 1989. I was filled with appreciation for the training and all that I was learning. I was filled with hope and could easily imagine what I might be able to achieve in the future. My perspective was positive and empowering.

As I achieved higher levels of success, such as winning national championship races and making U.S. teams, my desire to be the best and my concurrent fear of ultimately not doing so created a fear of failure. I slowly became obsessed with this thought: "What if I'm not successful when it counts?" I developed a fixed and fearful mindset as I moved up the ranks of elite rowing.

Though I continued to make U.S. National teams, my fears of ultimately failing grew as the 1992 Olympics approached. For me, making the Olympic team would represent the ultimate achievement in life. My heart, mind, and soul were drenched in fear. I had no idea of how to hold onto the positive perspective with which I began. I had no idea how to shed the fear. Though, of course, it is possible to develop, reclaim, or strengthen one's positive perspective, it is easy to become victimized by one's fears.

Fast forward nine years. One early summer day in 1992, I was overwhelmed by fear. The upcoming series of races over a one-hour period would determine whether or not I'd realize my dream of becoming an Olympian. I was vying for the last spot in the eight-woman boat on the 1992 U.S. Olympic rowing team. I had already made two U.S. National rowing teams, won an international gold medal, and had won a dozen national titles. Yet, my sense of self-worth was on the line and my confidence was deeply shaken from years of nurturing my terror of failing. My day-to-day training was filled with negative emotions and hopelessness, and my expectations for my most important series of races were grim.

I cried in fear for almost two straight days before the final race for my spot on the team. I was afraid of not being able to perform when it counted, of looking bad in the eyes of my teammates, and perhaps most importantly, of losing a sense of belonging. I had lost the ability to tune into what my body knew to do to create a powerful, positive racing rhythm. My fear and angst were totally in the driver's seat as the set of races neared. My mind was filled with devastation over the possible loss to be had.

While racing, my physical body was blocked from being able to perform the way it had been trained. My breathing became constricted and my muscles fought against themselves. I rowed ineffectively and lost my final round of racing, shattering my hopes of racing in the Olympics. (I did end up being selected as an alternate for the team.)

In retrospect, I can see what I could not see then. I had lost perspective. I had lost my appreciation of the positive in my daily training and I had lost my ability to remain optimistic about the results of my efforts in performance. I had no perspective. I had no faith in how hard I had trained. I had no trust in being present and just doing my thing. I had been made sightless by my 2% blinders. I could only consider what was wrong and what could go wrong. I was far from living in the sweet spot.

POSITIVE PERSPECTIVES TOWARD TRAINING AND PERFORMANCE

Our mental attitude, our habitual way of thinking about training and performance, has a huge impact on our ability to perform when it counts. What habits are best to develop in our quest to optimize performance when it counts? What does it really take on race day to be able to feel relatively at ease and totally focused on the task at hand? We need to be able to nurture a perspective that strengthens both our experience of positive emotions and positive expectations. Of course, we cannot always be upbeat, positive, and hopeful about what we are doing and what we hope to achieve. However, we do need to develop perspectives that allow us to mostly enjoy what we are doing and to maintain hope about our future performances, be they many months or just moments away.

What habits of mind and character help strengthen the positive perspective? There may be many answers to this question. I, however, have experienced and have professionally observed that when paired together, *optimism* and *gratitude* help us to create a mental approach and perspective that can get us to train harder, longer, and to have more courage when faced with important competitions. What I mean by courage is that we can feel internal or external fear and still focus on the task at hand and perform to the best of our abilities.

How do optimism and gratitude work? Gratitude helps generate positive emotions and perspective about one's *present* situation and optimism generates positive emotions and perspective about one's *future*. When we are able to consistently put to use, as much as possible, these character strengths, we can develop a positive perspective in which we free ourselves up from unnecessary distractions and allow our energy to be focused. With this positive perspective, we can best develop our skills and abilities in the moment to set ourselves up for the future performance.

GRATITUDE

Gratitude, at its core, is about being grateful for the good that is currently in our lives. The good can be anything that you value, whether it sounds significant or trivial, and to which you bring your awareness. The good can be enjoying a moment of rest between sprints during practice. The good could be enjoying the quality of air that you are breathing in. The good could be the moment that your teacher or coach notices the progress that you've made in your technique or strategy. Anything that you experience as added value to your life in any big or small way can be considered part of your good. Gratitude is sometimes conceptualized as the positive momentary emotion that is evoked by perceiving that you have received some sort of gift or benefit in your life. Robert A. Emmons and Charles M. Shelton, in the *Handbook of Positive Psychology,* refer to gratitude as "… a felt sense of wonder, thankfulness, and appreciation for life." Gratitude, then, can be conceptualized as noticing any good in your life that you have received and, from this awareness, generating positive emotions.

Does noticing the good really matter? Aren't we better suited to just focus on what we are doing, learning to better execute and to get stronger and more fit? Do elite athletes really purposefully nurture such an attitude? Some top-level athletes purposefully look to the good to keep up their spirits and motivation. They have learned that with some brief moments of appreciation and positive emotion that they are better able to face challenging bouts of training.

Tripping Lilly is a young acoustic folk pop band. The four musicians work diligently in their efforts to follow their dream, while still making a living. They give music lessons and travel up and down the East Coast performing. This past summer, they were performing about once a week, giving lessons, and recording a new CD. At one point, they had recorded the music for their new CD and lost it on a hard drive. They had to re-record their entire CD. After staying awake for two straight days and nights, one of the band members, Alex, told me how he was feeling. He smiled and said, "I feel so lucky to be doing this. I love music. I love doing it all the time. The new CD sounds great!" He could have complained about being exhausted, his lack of money, or the pressure to perform. His mind immediately shifted to gratitude when I asked him how things were going. Imagine if we all were able to shift to gratitude for all the opportunities that we have, all the good around us, and our chance to still do our thing.

OPTIMISM

Optimism is the second habit of mind that can contribute to developing positive perspective. Optimism is about experiencing a mood or attitude associated with positive expectations about some aspect of one's future. Remaining optimistic about how you could perform or how you hope to perform is important. We must have the requisite skills and abilities in a particular domain, but beyond that, our attitude and expectations about how we will perform have significant implications for how we will be able to focus and what we will tune into while competing and performing. When we are focused on expecting things to go well, we give ourselves a better chance at allowing our own minds, our psychology, to help things go well.

In addition to valuing the good in our current lives, we also need to maintain a positive expectation about our ability to perform in the upcoming competition or performance. Martin Seligman is the leader in helping the professional world of psychology understand optimism. His work on optimism is based on *attribution theory*. He became fascinated with how people explained their successes and failures. For example, if someone lost a big game, what would their explanation be for the reason that they had lost? Or if someone got a personal best racing time, to what would they attribute their success?

What Seligman found out has a lot to do with our optimistic (and pessimistic) styles of explaining the successes and failures that occur in our lives. He found that those who have developed an optimistic outlook tend to explain bad events in a way that empowers them. They see the difficulty as temporary and unique to the given moment in time. They tend to believe that with effort and using their abilities, they can overcome the challenge. Charles S. Carver, Michael F. Scheier, and Suzanne C. Segerstrom's research indicates that when we have an optimistic attitude, we keep trying (and when we have a pessimistic attitude, we tend to give up).

I conducted two studies with a total of 38 elite rowers. Many had been on multiple U.S. and Olympic teams and all of them were training at a U.S. Team Training Center. I interviewed them all individually to get a better sense of how they coped with competitive pressure. All of them selected to discuss times in which they were either in the last round of selection for the U.S. team or were competing at the Olympics or World Championships. Retaining hope or optimism was essential to those who were able to maintain themselves under intense competitive pressure. Specifically, more than half of them reported that in such competitive situations when they didn't cope well with the pressure, they had mentally given up. They had lost hope that they could perform well. While in the middle of the race to make the Olympic team or win a World Championship or Olympic medal, they gave up.

For one rower, who I'll call John, his position in the selection process for the Olympic team was dependent upon his performance on the indoor rowing machine. When John reported his worst coping scenario, he remembered, "My focus went from this kind of mission to, 'Oh shit, I am not accomplishing it, and I am not feeling well and the coaches are going to be disappointed.' So I was done before I was done. I was like, 'I am done. I can't. What am I doing?'"

In stark contrast to that, John recalled being able to call up a more determined, hopeful approach in his next opportunity to demonstrate his ability to his coaches on the same type of indoor rowing machine. A few months later, when the pressure was on again, John was given a particular time that he had to meet based on a 6,000-meter ergometer test (the athletes are going as hard as they can for about 20 minutes) as one of the tests to make the U.S. team. He recalled, "I was expecting that I was going to do it, that I had to do it." So this athlete–in this instance–exuded a determined optimism.

John goes on to emphasize how he had also been committed to not thinking about all that could get in the way of him accomplishing his goal. He said, "But it is crazy to think that over 6,000 meters you are two seconds over what you have to break. That comes down to one or two strokes or being a little less rested. If I thought about all the things that could have gone wrong just to make up those two seconds. It kind of blows my mind." This positive perspective made all the difference in this athlete's ability to perform when it counted.

Developing a positive perspective in our performance domain

Having a positive perspective in a performance domain would require maintaining an awareness of the current and future good that comes with training and performing. How do we nurture such a positive perspective? Is it really possible? Aren't we just the way we are? If we are ridden with fear, isn't that just our personality? If we exude confidence and only expect the best for ourselves, aren't we just born that way? Research does suggest that some people are born with a more positive attitude than others. But the most crucial research is about what we can do about our inborn tendencies. Current research increasingly finds that our habits of mind can be strengthened. In the positive psychology research world, there is great interest in the character strengths and habits of value and action that can get stronger with practice. So yes, with practice, we can strengthen our positive attitude toward our present performance lives and our expectations about our ability to perform in the future.

Martin Seligman is one of the leaders in understanding how to enhance one's optimism. In his book *Learned Optimism* he suggests that there are two basic ways to boost one's character strength of optimism. One way to strengthen one's optimism is through *modeling*. This means searching out and learning from someone else who is already optimistic. It would mean watching and understanding how they respond to difficult, neutral, and good experiences in their lives. The second way to learn to be more optimistic is through *cognitive therapy,* which is essentially becoming aware of your thinking and learning to think in more empowered, constructive ways—typically with the help of a therapist. We, too, can generate more optimistic ways of viewing our futures. First, we can become aware of how we'd like to be as we watch others who are more optimistic and positive than we are. Then we can learn to be aware of how we think and make conscious shifts to more constructive ways of thinking, This shift is far from easy, but it is possible.

In the performance domain, there are some specific ways, as well, to build your positive perspective. Some of us may need to experience a wake-up call about how devastating a negative, fear-based perspective can be. But we can also learn from how other top performers have taught themselves how to focus into determined optimism. We can learn how to set up our situation so we, too, can savor and enjoy our current circumstances, even when those circumstances are filled with intense competitive pressure.

Strategy 1: Focus on the good
To begin to strengthen our positive perspective and our gratitude, it can be helpful to think about the good in our lives. Thinking specifically about the good in our day-to-day training and lives can be a great boost to our ability to train well and to generate the positive emotions that help push us to try harder and learn more. One of the great thinkers in the area of optimal human functioning was Abraham Maslow, who discussed what it took for people to fully realize their potential, to become the best of what could be. He coined the term *self-actualizers* to refer to those who reached their potential. He emphasized how self-actualizers were chronically grateful for their daily lives. He stated that self-actualizers had the capacity to "appreciate, again and again,

freshly and naively, the basic good of life with awe, pleasure, wonder, and even ecstasy, however stale these experiences may have become to others." This sense of gratitude about their daily lives helps maintain a source of positive emotion and perspective, and leads away from irritations and distractions that can thwart one's ability to make the best use of one's daily training.

Consider who and what you are grateful for in your life and in your training. Consider the good that you could appreciate. Take a moment to consider these in Exercise 6.1. It doesn't matter how good or simple your points of gratitude sound to others. What matters is that they resonate and are true for you. As a reminder, it can be helpful to write onto an index card the best few examples of good in your life for which you are thankful. You can put it somewhere where you will see it on a daily basis. It will be a reminder to continue building and strengthening your gratitude for the good in your daily training. This will, in turn, help strengthen a positive perspective about your training and possibilities for future performance.

I suggest that you consider both who and what you are grateful for. Is there anyone who is there for you no matter what? Do you appreciate some segment of how you are coached, or how you access your critical information to improve? Are there things about your training that you like? Even if seemingly

Exercise 6.1. Strengthening gratitude:
The good in your day-to-day training

Who I am grateful for	What I am grateful for
e.g., My best friend and teammate, who's there for me no matter what.	e.g., The fresh air when I am running. The ability to breathe, move, love.
1.	1.
2.	2.
3.	3.

unimportant, it can be very helpful to bring awareness to all the good that surrounds you and especially the good that you can glean from your training arena.

Developing and strengthening your gratitude is a great step in building a positive perspective. It is important, as well, to nurture hope and optimism about how you could perform if you were able to fully express your skills and abilities when it counted. It can be very difficult for some performers to truly have hope for the manifestation of their best performance.

In one group workshop, I worked with a group of 60 swimmers who were preparing for their national competitions. I asked the group who had spent time thinking about how well they might be able to swim for the upcoming competition. Only one athlete of the 60 raised his hand. Unfortunately, the idea of maintaining optimism and hope for best performances can be eroded by worry. Worry comes from our desire to have control; we want 100% assurance that we will be able to perform well. We all know that is an impossibility, but it doesn't stop us from worrying. And worry saps our positive perspective.

After this workshop, one young swimmer, Becca, came to talk with me. She asked me, "What if my best isn't good enough?" Becca was literally losing sleep each night because she worried about how badly she might feel, even after swimming to the best of her abilities, in a competition coming up in two weeks. I asked her, "What else can you give?" To develop an optimistic perspective, we must be able to imagine and hope for ourselves to do the very best that we can in the given competition. However, with this comes being able to accept that being prepared, being present, and putting yourself fully into your performance is enough. We can ask no more from ourselves. We cannot guarantee success. If we cannot accept this, then we will continue to be ridden with fear and will continue to be pessimistic. Of course, there is no hope when our goal is to do better than we can realistically physically produce.

Strategy 2: Wave your magic wand
It remains very helpful to have the intention to manifest performances just the way that you would like them to unfold. Envisioning possible future successes

can be a way to put your fears aside and imagine the best possible future outcomes. One of the ideas that has always fascinated me was the idea of considering how the future would unfold if it went exactly as you would like it to go. As a small child, I used to love to play the game, "If you had three wishes, what would you wish for?" I used to love to imagine how amazing things would be if I had the power to actually manifest radical change in the future.

I often ask my clients, "If you could wave your magic wand, what would you like to happen?" I ask this question to performers when they are thinking about preparing for an upcoming performance, an audition, a team try-out, or a national championship—or when trying to cope with a difficult coach or teacher. It is an important question to consider. This wave-your-magic-wand question allows you to put doubt and fear aside for a few minutes and to consider what you truly value. This approach allows your optimism and hope to expand.

In your performance area of choice, try waving your magic wand just for a moment. What do you wish would change, improve, or manifest? What would you love to happen? Would you like to hit a particular race time? Make a specific team? Lead in scoring? Give an impactful speech? Express your music fully when performing in front of an audience?

It is important to both be able to imagine performing to the best of your ability and to be willing to accept the possibility that you may not be able to manifest such a performance. Optimism is about hope, about possibility. Of course, there are no guarantees. Those who maintain a positive perspective realize that they cannot guarantee that they will hit their desired mark of success. But they keep their attention on what they hope to manifest. They must draw on their courage to maintain hope. Even when it appears that they won't be successful, they keep trying and persisting. They continuously give themselves a good shot at success.

Strategy 3: Purposefully create an atmosphere that you enjoy
If you are in a situation in which you are not able to enjoy or take pleasure in any aspect of what you are doing, it may be time to make some subtle or

significant shift for a short period of time to infuse the possibility of feeling grateful for the good that is present. One athlete from my study with the elite rowers, Jenny, recalls a time just prior to selection for the national team. She purposefully created a quiet, (relatively) luxurious space for herself just prior to the series of final selection races for the team. Jenny recalled,

> "So this time it was a real challenge for me. I was definitely really excited. I was in my zone immediately. As soon as he [the coach] said we were going to be in singles [each athlete would race in their own boat], I just isolated myself from everybody else and I knew that I had to be really selfish in how I treated myself and my time, my rigging, the weather, and practice time. I was on my own. I had a car then and a little money in my pocket, so I was able to take care of all of the variables... We just spent whatever money we had. We got a nicer hotel with one of my roommates. She ended up being [on] the Olympic [team] as well. We just put ourselves away from the rest of the team. We had a car, [were] close to the course, and we had lived there, too, [so it was] a little bit of home advantage. We knew what we were doing. And I remember we spent a lot of money on this nice hotel; it was like a bed and breakfast. So we wanted to be really comfortable. It sounds kind of strange, but to be relaxed and comfortable, in a comfortable atmosphere, was important. I remember doing my rigging really early. So I set myself up for a positive atmosphere."

You may not be able to change where you are living, but you can ask yourself, "What could I do to make my day-to-day life more enjoyable?" It may be as simple as deciding to buy high-quality fruit and vegetables. It may be to spend 30 minutes a day reading the types of magazines or books that you usually don't give yourself time to read. Perhaps it is making a decision to run next to certain teammates and not others. Only you know what will contribute to your daily sense of enjoyment. Particularly when in a pressure-filled environment (which all of us are probably facing most days), it is important to imbibe that which is pleasant and soothing to us. This can help us be more resilient

Exercise 6.2. Increasing daily enjoyment
(good in your day-to-day training)

What can be changed or added?	What do I need to do to make it happen?
e.g., Schedule 30 minutes a day to read what I like	Put the reading time in my planner (just like I do for my training/practice time)
1.	1.
2.	2.
3.	3.

to challenge when it comes. What is one thing that you could change today?

At first you may have wondered what the topics of gratitude and optimism are doing in a book about preparing for performance. Though these topics are generally missing from similar books, they are essential to create the habits of mind that help us in times of great pressure, such as performance pressure. The more that we can maintain a positive perspective, the more we will enjoy our day-to-day training, the more focused we will be on learning and stretching our physical abilities, and the more open we will be to feedback. And, perhaps most importantly, as we strengthen this ability to maintain a positive perspective, progressively, we set ourselves up to better handle the intense moments of competition pressure. With a positive perspective, we hope for the best in our performance, we tune into what is going well, and we are able to persist in the face of difficulty. We are able to believe in our abilities and talents. We are able to hold onto the possibility of how well it can go and are wise enough to know that it won't always go our way—and that we will be OK either way. Practicing a positive perspective in our daily training is essential so that when the pressure is on, we are able to truly optimize performance with the best of our body, mind, and soul.

PART II
PREPARING FOR PERFORMANCE OR COMPETITION

7

Flow and Engagement

**Nurturing Enjoyment and Engagement
in Training and Performance**

> *"Sometimes I add tricks during
> boring drills or I practice skills during
> down-times of practice. Now I
> know how to make it fun."*
> —NHL player

In 1991, I was part of the U.S. women's rowing team and we were racing in Lucerne, Switzerland. This is the international race where all crews go prior to competing in the World Championships. We were in the women's final eight (rowing) race against a number of countries including Germany. We lined up for the race and we all felt a powerful sense of anticipation. We had a new coach from Germany and the US had not beaten the the former East Germans in international competition for more than 10 years. As soon as the flag went down and we started, the boat felt perfect and the rowing almost effortless. I knew that I was racing at 40 strokes per minute at the start of the race and settling into 36 strokes per minute (which is a full-out sprint), but there was no pain and our boat was flying.

We pulled in front of the Germans, and all the other boats, at about the first 500-meter mark (which is about 1/4 of the way down the race course). The race felt too easy. I kept performing quick body scans to make sure that I was pulling as hard as I could. I kept pushing harder, yet there was no pain. My effort felt totally engaged with the boat; I felt perfectly in sync with my teammates. We just kept pulling away from the pack of boats and easily won the gold medal.

As I was racing, I had no concern about winning or losing. Of course I wanted to win, as I always did, but I wasn't thinking about it. During the race, I was mesmerized by the ease of the race and I was savoring it. Usually, the physical experience of racing is intensely painful. I used to dread the pain, especially through the last 1/3 of the race when I wished the pain would just end.

Mihaly Csikszentmihalyi (Chick-sent-me-HI) is the leading researcher in understanding optimal performance experiences that are fully engaging and enjoyable. His research perfectly explains the racing experience that I had. He would deem my experience as *flow*. Similar phrases to describe flow are "in the zone" or "in the groove." He has learned to understand the shared characteristics and potential antecedent factors to this magical, altered state. He presents his ideas and explains flow in his seminal book, *Flow: the Psychology of Optimal Experience* (1991, 2008).

When we are in flow, we are in a state of concentration or complete absorption on the task at hand. Being in flow requires that you truly enjoy the activity itself—you are intrinsically motivated toward the activity. Intrinsic motivation means that you want to do the activity regardless of what others value or want. You want to do the activity because it is an inherently enjoyable activity for you. When in flow, you are totally absorbed in the activity and you are stretching yourself to make the best use of your skills. When I was racing, this is just what I experienced. I loved being in the race and would have continued racing as long as possible just to remain in that state of mind. Clearly, on some level, I did want to win, yet this was not the focus while racing.

As you can imagine, the idea of flow has caught on in the performance psychology world. Athletes and all other performers love to be in this state (and we all love it in any context). We hope for it, yearn for it, and love it when flow manifests when we are performing. Often when performers experience flow while performing or competing, they think of achieving this state as a highly unusual event, something that cannot be purposefully recaptured. The flow state can feel as fleeting as the sense of being washed over with joy. It can feel like something wonderful but too elusive to plan for, too elusive to try for.

Nevertheless, there actually are ways of getting closer to or achieving flow every day. With self-awareness and purposefully directing what you think about and what you do, there is engaged joy to be had every day. We don't have to wait for our equivalent to getting selected for the Boston Symphony Orchestra or for our tryouts for an elite team. But first let's consider in more detail what comprises the flow state itself in performing.

Csikszentmihalyi paired up with Susan Jackson and, together, they wrote *Flow in Sports*. This book provides a detailed explanation of the flow experience while performing. They outline nine characteristics of flow, which emerged from many research studies on flow states. Table 7.1 includes the nine characteristics of flow with a brief explanation of each.

The idea of being in the flow state is highly compelling for all of us, especially when performing. It is a lovely part of living in the sweet spot when performing. When in flow, we authentically enjoy what we are doing. In that moment, having the opportunity to be in your performance arena of choice and being engaged in running, competing, or performing feels like a gift. Concurrent with this sense of joy and enjoyment, you also are stretching the limits of your abilities and doing so with full confidence. You feel no fear and you are willing to fully put yourself on the line. You have no negative thoughts. You are totally present in the moment. You are absolutely performing to the best of your current abilities.

Table 7.1. Characteristics of Flow in Performance

Flow Characteristics	Description
1. Balance of challenge and skill	The challenge of the activity must meet your skills. If the challenge is too great, you will feel anxiety and if too small, you will feel bored.
2. Merging of action and awareness	When in flow, we are totally absorbed in what we are doing. We almost feel unified with our instrument or equipment while performing. While in this state, we are performing to the best of our ability, to the limits of our capacity. And at once our fully engaged experience feels effortless.
3. Clear goals	Our goals help us to know just what we want to do behaviorally in the moment. We are confident in knowing where best to direct our energy and attention.
4. Unambiguous feedback	Paired with our goals and action, we need to be tuned in to the information we are getting back from our performance. The feedback is essential so that we know if we are, for example, hitting the sweet spot on the baseball bat. Clear feedback lets us know we are performing the way we want to and can.
5. Concentration on the task	One's irrelevant thoughts are absent. The idea of focusing on performance can be so easy, yet the challenge of keeping our minds off of irrelevant thoughts is ever-present. There are many distractions to contend with: worries about recent mistakes or the final score, about whether we will be able to keep up, whether we can tolerate the pain, curiosity about who is in the stands. These undermine flow.
6. A sense of self-control	There is a strong belief in yourself and belief that you will have access to whatever resources you need to have in the moment. You believe that you can handle whatever challenges or opportunities arise.

Flow Characteristics	Description
7. Loss of self-consciousness	All negative thoughts about yourself are absent. You have a confidence or sureness about what you will do moment to moment.
8. Transformation of time	One's sense of time becomes changed during the flow state. This can be experienced as a speeding up or a slowing down of how you normally experience time.
9. Autotelic experience	Csikszentmihalyi refers to this as an "intrinsically rewarding" experience. You do the activity for the enjoyment of the activity, regardless of the rewards, money, or attention that you may receive. You may greatly enjoy the rewards at the end of the performance. However, while performing, you would choose to do the activity exclusively for the sake of the experience itself.

Source: Adapted from Jackson and Csikszentmihalyi, 1999

When have you been in flow? Think back to a time that you most enjoyed yourself and felt totally engaged in practice or performance. It doesn't have to be a perfect performance moment, just one in which you were totally engaged with what you were doing with no conscious focus on the past or future. Think back to a time, recent or far back, in your performance area in which you felt like you were in the flow state. What were you doing? How did your body feel? What kind of emotions were you having? Where was your attention? What was the challenge? What skills were you drawing on to meet the challenge? What were the goals that you had to meet in the moment to be successful? What information were you receiving that indicated that you were meeting your goals moment to moment? What was it like to feel totally at ease while stretching your ability to perform to previously unattained levels? What was it like to be fully enjoying what you were doing while feeling an absence of negative thinking and worrying?

Exercise 7.1. You in flow

You in flow	Description
Your flow experience: When and where?	
What skills (strengths) were you drawing on?	
Your emotions?	
Your thoughts and focus?	
Your physical experiences?	

Not only will this memory provide a shot of positive emotion, recalling this moment may also contribute to future performance in a few other ways.

Remembering a time when you performed as you'd ideally like to perform can provide a model of how you'd like to perform in the future. Instead of thinking of a flow state as an elusive, impossible state to replicate, it can be helpful to notice specifically what was happening in terms of focus, thoughts, and physical sensations both before and during flow. When you do so, you then can begin to work toward recreating such an experience or at least aspects of the experience on a daily basis. Recalling these positive performance moments can also serve as a source of hope or intention for future performances. If you conjure up and hold this flow state experience, you are going to make yourself more likely to have a similar experience in the future. We tend to manifest what we think about and what we focus on. Of course, it takes more than just imagining being in an optimal state. But thinking about how you'd like things to manifest paired with focused, determined effort will set you up for creating flow experiences more often.

GETTING INTO THE FLOW STATE FOR GAME DAY

Can we really prepare ourselves to get into the flow state for important performances? Can we really get ourselves closer to this state through high-pressure performance? Yes, we can. Susan Jackson delivered evidence when she conducted two studies with elite athletes to explore what may be precursors to experiencing the flow state in competition. Of course, she couldn't get at unconscious factors or perhaps even at some habits of behavior or mind of which the athletes themselves were not even aware. But through in-depth interviews, she was able to discover some shared experiences that occurred prior to and during high stakes competition. In her first study, she interviewed U.S. National champion figure skaters. In her second study, she interviewed athletes from a variety of sports who placed in the top 10 in worldwide competitions. She found shared experiences of these athletes as they reflected on an event in which they had one of their best performances (when under high pressure to perform). What follows are some of the main themes that emerged:

1. Positive mental attitude: The athletes in Jackson's studies had a positive attitude toward their competition. They felt hopeful and optimistic about their abilities to perform. They were confident about their skills and strengths. Having a positive attitude is a habit of mind that can be nurtured, and it is a habit that needs to be strengthened over time. It may seem easier for someone who is on their way to becoming a national champion—in anything—to have a positive mental attitude. But it is possible to nurture a positive mental attitude regardless of whether you are dominating or you are the long-shot underdog.

When we focus on what we would like to achieve, appreciate the effort that we are investing, and can accept the outcome (win or lose) we can immediately begin generating a positive mental attitude toward competing. From her second study, Jackson also found that within their positive mental attitudes, these athletes reported a clear motivation to perform. The athletes were not afraid of performance; they actually wanted a chance to demonstrate their abilities and to engage in the highly competitive atmosphere.

2. Positive pre-competitive and competitive affect: In Jackson's studies, she also found that the athletes primarily experienced positive affect, meaning positive emotions and feelings, prior to and during competition. Our emotions are not always cooperative, particularly just prior to a significant competitive event. Many athletes struggle with just the opposite. Many athletes feel a sense of dread and anxiety prior to competing (this will be covered more fully in Chapter 12). There is such a desire to win that it can be difficult to stay focused on the event itself versus worrying about what might happen at the end of the performance or competition.

It is possible to move toward a more positive emotional state before we begin performance. When we keep in mind all the good that is associated with competing or performing we can begin to create or nurture a more positive emotional (affective) approach. Maintaining a focus on the good, such as an opportunity to push the limits of your skills to see what you can accomplish or to be engaged in activity that you love, can help nurture positive competitive emotions (affect before and during performance). Jackson's findings on this are in harmony with the principles discussed in Chapters 3 and 6.

3. Achieving optimal arousal level before performing: In Jackson's second study, the athletes reported that achieving the correct level of physical and mental excitement was an important aspect of getting into the flow state while performing. It is critical to know what type of energy level works best for you in your performance realm. Historically, coaches are known for giving a big pep-talk before a game. This can actually push some athletes into anxiety mode. Yet for others, it allows them to hit their effective peak of energy.

I like to think of arousal, or excitement to compete, on a scale from 1 to 10, where 1 represents feeling totally at ease and calm and 10 represents feeling intensely hyped up. If you reflect on your best performances, what is the arousal level that best sets you up for competition or performance? Generally, in a room full of performers, about one-third feel best at 3 or below on the scale; one-third feel best between 4 and 6, and one-third of the group feels best between 7 and 10.

There is no universally correct answer to this question. Depending on your personality, your experience level, and your performance realm, you may perform best anywhere in the entire range. What matters is being aware of what works best for you. I know as an athlete and performer that I easily arrived at a highly energized state, and the more I could bring down my intensity and feel calm, the better I would perform. I knew that I could always count on being explosive and intense. This natural mode would only serve me if my arousal levels were on the lower end.

What works best for you? This may be a highest point of leverage for you to work on. In the following chapters, you will learn skills to help you to increase or reduce intensity levels before competing.

4. *Maintaining appropriate focus:* In Jackson's first study, one of the main categories for preparation was having an appropriate focus. What is the appropriate focus? It is fully individualistic and really depends on what works best for you. In an earlier chapter I mentioned an athlete who was considered one of the up-and-coming single scullers (single boat rowers) in the country. I asked him about how he prepared for racing. He talked a lot about chatting with friends, making jokes, and maybe stretching if he had time. Privately, I thought that his avoidance approach to preparing for racing was a great setup for failure. I was wrong. This athlete went on to be one of the best single scullers in the world. For him the appropriate focus was to distract himself before he raced. He was well prepared, technically and physically, to race. He could depend on his well-trained habits of mind and physical output when it counted. For him to dwell on racing before he went off the line was not an appropriate focus for him (though this type of focus does work well for many of us).

There is no universally correct way to focus. However, there is an appropriate focus for us all as we prepare to perform. The key is to honestly reflect on what works best for each of us so we know where to focus our attention prior to competing.

5. *Physical readiness:* The last main idea from Jackson's first study on flow is the importance of physical readiness. It seems so simple, yet it is profoundly important. The idea of one's body being ready for performance is essential. As human beings, we rely on our bodies for our lives, our movements, and our existence. It can be easy to forget the importance of preparing your body.

I once worked with a lightweight rower who was trying to make the U.S. national team. Sasha came to me because she was experiencing high levels of anxiety. The challenge of anxiety was not a new subject for me as a sport psychologist. Many athletes that I have worked with over the past decade have been challenged with anxiety as it related to preparing to make a team, compete, or perform. However, Sasha's challenge was more global than I'd ever seen before. She reported that even when she would try to lie down at night to relax and watch a movie that she would have such intensely anxious feelings, especially with her heart racing, that she could no longer turn to movies as a source of comfort and relaxation. I began to ask her about her eating. I asked her to tell me about what she ate and drank in a normal day.

It turned out that Sasha was drinking the equivalent of 10 to 12 cups of coffee per day. This high level of caffeine intake paired with her limited food intake (lightweight female rowers race internationally at about 126 pounds) was triggering a physical anxiety response. I worked with Sasha to reduce her caffeine intake to two cups of coffees per day. Her anxiety issue was solved. Though this is an extreme story about the importance of being physically ready, it is revealing. It can be easy to believe that your body is stable in its ability to perform. But we know that what we eat, what we drink, how much we sleep, and how well we stretch affects our physical readiness. Also, how we deal with the stress of relationships, how we deal with fears and other negative emotions, and even how we deal with our financial lives can affect our bodies and our physical readiness. To be truly ready for performance physically, you must consider how to take care of yourself, holistically. This holistic approach to taking care of yourself will actually help you achieve your flow state more frequently and more readily. It is a good start to think about being in flow state when competing or performing; however, there are many opportunities to experience flow outside just the few opportunities of top performance.

Using Exercise 7.2, I encourage you to think about some of the primary precursors to getting into the flow state for competition. It can be helpful to consider which of these factors you could work on that might get you closer to flow more frequently when competing.

CAN WE ALWAYS GET INTO THE FLOW STATE?

The truth is that no matter what we do, we cannot ensure that we can achieve flow state in one or the few most important performances of our lives. Getting into the flow state when it really counts is elusive. One of the most respected

Exercise 7.2. Helping you get into flow state

Flow: What can help get you there	What you experience/ What you need to do to nurture this aspect of flow
Positive mental attitude	What thought (e.g., I love what I'm doing) best supports your positive mental attitude before you perform?
Positive pre-competitive and competitive affect	What emotions work best for you right before your perform?
Optimal arousal level	What intensity level in your body best prepares you to perform on a scale from one to ten (1=sleeping to 10= jumping out of your skin)? What can help you get there in preparation for key moments?
Maintaining appropriate focus	What are your few go-to points of focus that help you get ready to perform?
Physical readiness	What represents you being physically ready? What do you need to do to get there? Sleep more? Drink more water? Stretch more?

sport psychologists in the United States, Ken Ravizza, noted once that even professional baseball players are only performing in the zone about 15% of the time. And in Susan Jackson's studies, about half of the athletes thought that they could manifest flow purposefully and half didn't think that they could, ever. And note that these were some of the best athletes in the world in each of their respective sports.

It is difficult to feel physically ready, have a positive mental attitude, be well-prepared for competition, and have appropriate focus for every competition. We all face challenges when we are not fully prepared or when we are distracted. The professional players are also competing with other distractions such as negative thoughts, concerns about a missed play, hopes for being bumped up in salary or to make a better team (not to mention their own personal lives and difficulties). As we rise in our abilities in performance and excellence, we face progressively more distractions. Even if we are excellent in what we do, our expectations for ourselves and expectations from others can make getting into a fully absorbed, engaged state progressively more difficult.

FLOW AND TOP PERFORMANCE ARE NOT SYNONYMOUS

Where does that leave us? One of the challenges in the performance psychology realm is that we often assume that flow and top performance are one and the same. They are not. When we think back on being in flow state, we often think about one of our best performances. Flow and top performance do tend to coincide much of the time. When we are performing at our best, we do tend to be fully engaged in what we are doing, experience almost no distractions, and enjoy what we are doing. It may be more difficult to get into flow state when under the pressure of performance. Yet we can experience flow even when we are not performing at our personal best. We can actually be in flow when we are tired, or not executing perfect technique. Flow is a broader concept than top performance. Flow is about being engaged in what you are doing. It doesn't mean you are necessarily better than everyone else doing the same thing.

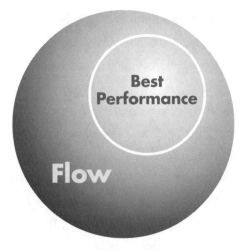

Figure 7.1: Best Performance: Only one aspect of Flow

The more we can practice getting there, or getting closer to the flow state in everyday training and life, the better chance we will have to get there when we are trying to put it all together for key performances.

GETTING CLOSER TO OR EXPERIENCING FLOW, EVERY DAY

Getting closer to flow in daily practice is possible. It is useful to consider the antecedent factors (precursors to flow). These factors, having a positive attitude, being fully prepared physically, having a well-developed plan, and having the appropriate focus, are the things to work on developing on a daily basis. These factors point to aspects of training that we could be developing every day. However, we don't have to wait for the moment to get these factors in line in order to experience flow. We also don't need them to be perfect each day in order to be in flow, to be enjoying in and fully engaged with our activity.

It may be more important to consider how to get closer to and experience flow state in daily living and in training than how to manifest the flow state when under great pressure to perform. As the saying goes, "You perform the way that you practice." It is unwise to wait until race day to see if the magical state will manifest itself. And we cannot wait until we are fully prepared to experience flow. Flow—or getting closer to flow state—is available to us daily, every moment we are engaged in activities that we, at our cores, enjoy doing.

I worked as a performance psychologist with Betsy, an aspiring musician. She had a difficult time performing under pressure. I asked her to talk about what it was like when she was practicing alone. I asked her, "How much of your attention is on creating your music when practicing?" She estimated that 50% of her attention was on her creating her music when practicing alone. It turned out that the balance of her attention would be on her worries about mistakes, about not expressing the music the way that she would like to, concerns about how she was being or would be evaluated by others, and anxiety about practicing certain phrases of the music that were the most challenging. I asked her the same question about playing with her teacher and then performing for an audience. She said when she was practicing alone, 50% of her attention was on the music; when she was with a teacher, 30% of her attention was on her music; and when she was performing, 10% was on her music. The balance of her energy was a summation of fear and thinking about the past and future. I found this information fascinating. She paid so little attention to doing her thing. Only when she had her attention on creating her music did she have a chance of hitting or coming close to a positive flow state.

We worked on increasing Betsy's focus on and attention to her music for all three scenarios, practicing alone, with her teacher, and for an audience. As you can see, she was quite distracted by her fear of mistakes and of others' judgments of her ability to play. I found that the best way to help Betsy was through daily practice in preparation for an audience of any size. I wasn't trying to get her to 100% focus and enjoyment every day. Rather, she had a goal of moving from a 50% to 70% focus on her music while practicing. Our everyday practice is rich with opportunities to pay attention to connecting to the good, the fun, and the opportunity to learn, moment to moment.

To experience flow or to get closer to flow more often, we need to choose to focus on activities or particular aspects of activities that we authentically enjoy. This is, ultimately, the answer to best preparing for performance. For Betsy, her answer was focusing on the emotions she was trying to create through her music and being available to connect and communicate with her audience. In an interview for one of my research studies, a participant made a comment that has stuck with me ever since. Essentially, I was asking him about how he coped with competitive pressure. He said that he did not experience pressure to perform. He explained, "It doesn't matter if I am racing alone in the rain on Sunday morning or racing at the Olympic finals. I race the same."

We perform the way that we practice. I have found through my work with performers that the more we fully engage in what we are doing—day to day—the more likely we are to optimize performance when it counts. This idea seems obvious and rational when you are asked and encouraged to think about the following:

- What do you love about practice where you are challenged? Focus on doing that as well as you can.

- What did you originally love about your craft or your sport?

- What was most fun and challenging about practice today?

- When were you most engaged in your training today?

When you notice your mind wandering to worries, use this as a reminder to get back to the aspect of practicing that is so challenging that it absorbs all of your attention.

The fascinating aspect of flow is that it signals that we are concurrently performing to the best of our abilities and enjoying what we are doing. It seems to make sense that we would all pursue being engaged in activities that we authentically enjoy and do them in a way that works for us on a daily basis. Or it seems to make sense that we'd make an effort to enjoy the aspects of training that are possible to enjoy while we are doing them. There is no question that some aspects of training simply cannot be inherently enjoyable in the moment. This can be particularly true of athletes or performers in a team setting. Sometimes you truly feel exhausted, you know you are unable to get any more out of practice, yet you must continue because your teacher, coach, or director demands it of the group. At such times, it can be very difficult to truly get into the flow state. However, there are many opportunities in training when it is easier to be present with an effective mental attitude and purposeful focus on the good.

Marco is a national level fencer. He has a fantastic ability to image how he'd like to perform when facing one of the best fencers in the world. However, the everyday training appeared too mundane to keep his attention. This caused some problems for Marco. He had difficulty finding sparring partners who were able to challenge him enough to give him a good training session. Marco was frustrated with his lack of local competition. He felt like he was wasting his time in practice and was not preparing himself as best he could for upcoming international bouts. Marco was just going through the motions in his training bouts. He didn't have to try to win, so he did not and often found himself distracted and bored.

We decided to focus on the fact that you achieve flow only when the challenge at hand stretches your skills; otherwise, you can predictably find yourself experiencing boredom. Marco had to consciously try to come up with particular moves that would challenge him. He would try these moves while sparring to regain energy and continue learning in practice. The moves that he chose were difficult for him. He would risk losing points against a less skilled fencer, but would benefit from both improving his skills and again injecting energy and challenge into his training. Marco found himself more excited about going to practice and he again made progress on his fencing skills in preparation for the big moments. He also found himself more energized and excited about just showing up for training.

The study of flow in sport and performance has been almost exclusively focused on times of *best* performance. As you can see from Jackson and Csikszentmihalyi's research on flow in sport, the findings are based on some of the world's best athletes' best-ever performances. It can take years to develop such habits of calm, focus, and enjoyment when faced with a performance that may determine your standings internationally or professionally compared to your peers.

However, it's important to remember that flow can be experienced frequently; we don't have to wait for those few times of highest performance stress. There are many more opportunities to achieve flow state. In some disciplines, it can be months if not years to prepare long enough and develop the requisite skills to become outstanding and to have an opportunity like the one I described when we were racing the Germans. A very narrow understanding of flow as only being associated with such events can be very uninspiring and limiting.

We don't have to wait to be the best in the world to create the habit of being fully engaged in what we love. Csikszentmihalyi's initial study of flow was not about flow experienced during best-performance and peak performance. The concept of flow was born out of the study of normal people living their lives. Csikszentmihalyi was interested in when the flow state naturally occurred throughout a normal day of living. Csikszentmihalyi gave beepers to thousands of people. The beepers sounded at unpredictable times throughout the day. The task of the study participants was to record what they were experiencing in the moments that the alarm rang throughout the day.

It turns out that people experience flow a lot in their daily lives. We often feel flow while doing activities that we enjoy and that are engaging or challenging to us, like gardening, reading, and even conversing with friends. It makes sense that we become engaged in activities that are inherently compelling to us. For example, I have found making bread by hand to be a highly enjoyable experience. I love the feeling of the ingredients uniting. When I knead the bread, it feels like the bread is literally coming to life. Clearly, making bread is not a high performance endeavor. Yet this process can create a highly enjoyable present state of focus for me. The key is to find this love and presence in daily training and practice.

A cornerstone of the concept of flow is that people inherently enjoy the activity with which they are involved. And their abilities are stretched so they must focus all of their attention on the task at hand to be successful in their moment-to-moment efforts. What are the aspects of training or performing that you love, that you enjoy that require this type of full-focused effort? For the purposes of getting ready for the big moments, it is critical to hone in on nurturing positive emotion and engagement in your daily training and practice. Creating more enjoyment and the potential of feeling fully engaged with what you are doing sometimes comes easily. There are magical times when everything seems to click and there are times when you just feel really well, both physically and in terms of your confidence. There are times when no matter what the challenge, you can rise to it and maintain an upbeat positive attitude about it. Yet, we live in a reality where there are many more times when we feel off, frustrated, anxious, angry, and irritated. We may not like some of the people that we are competing with or against, we may not like the way we are being coached and taught, or we may not like the heavy responsibility of living up to the expectations of others. Whatever our goals may be, there are both compelling and repelling elements to the aspiration process.

My main introduction to sport psychology came about when Terry Orlick, a world-renowned Canadian sport psychologist, was hired to work with our America's Cup women's team. (In 1995, I was part of a professional sailing team that competed on 16-person boats. We competed only against men.) During the middle phase of that year of racing, Terry was brought in to help us with our mental approach to racing. I asked to meet with him one day because I was feeling intensely frustrated with a few teammates. I didn't think that they were working hard enough or taking the opportunity seriously enough. I would look at a few of my teammates and feel surges of anger and frustration.

Terry encouraged me to pay attention to what I liked and who I liked. He encouraged me to literally turn my body when on the boat more toward those that I enjoyed being around. (About 18 of us spent nearly eight hours every day on a 20 x 10 foot surface on each boat that went out to train. We were literally dripping sweat on one another or sitting shoulder-to-shoulder most of that time.) This intervention sounds simple, yet it had a profound effect on my attitude and my ability to race. I started really enjoying the many other teammates who I respected and liked. The intervention allowed me to focus my energy on learning to race more effectively rather than being caught up in the anger toward teammates. With this shift I had more of my attention on doing my thing versus being consumed by distractions. This shift supported a better, more enjoyable performance on my part.

Using Exercise 7.3, take a few minutes to consider the aspects of your training or in your daily life that you authentically enjoy. Again, it doesn't matter if what you enjoy sounds impressive to anyone else. What matters is to tap into what could be enjoyable in your training. Even moving from *dreadfully boring* to things being *all right* or *pretty good* would be a great success.

Consider paying attention to what you enjoy while training or practicing. Regardless of the importance of the outcome of the activity, what is compelling to you? Regardless of others' evaluation of you, what is compelling to you? It can be difficult, sometimes, to allow yourself to become aware of what truly resonates with you. I recall when I was in college in the 1980s that I loved lifting weights. This was a time when women were not fully encouraged athletically. Somehow, I very much liked lifting in a free-weight area where only the male athletes trained. I recall feeling quite embarrassed about going into that area to lift weights, yet I still did it because I truly enjoyed the physical experience. I had to tolerate my embarrassment to go toward what resonated with me. I am certain that lifting four or five days a week helped me make the Olympic team. Honoring the aspects of training that you love, versus what you think you should or should not love, does not have to be so extreme. However, taking time to consider what resonates with you will give you the keys to increasing your ability to get closer to flow state and learning to optimize performance. The focus on what you enjoy can also give you a better shot at living in the sweet spot. It is not enough to train hard, we must also be able to recognize when our training is going right. We need to learn how to recognize what is compelling to us as we push ourselves to achieve. Without noticing the good or positive, it is impossible to be in the sweet spot.

In Exercise 7.3, give yourself a few moments to consider how you could begin more purposefully being present to and engaged with activities in your life that are inherently compelling to you. I like to think of it as going toward

Exercise 7.3. Going toward the light

Your performance realm	Things that I love or enjoy
Practice	e.g., Stretching, keeping a training journal, watching video, lifting weights, running, visualizing best performances 1. 2. 3. Even when I am exhausted or feel frustrated, I still love: 4. 5.
Performance	e.g., The energy of the crowd, the reality that you are so prepared, the chance to see how well you can do 1. 2. 3. Even when I am exhausted or feel frustrated, I still love: 4. 5.

the light—going toward the good. The more we move in that direction, the better it gets. It doesn't mean that training won't be physically painful. It doesn't meant that we won't have moments or periods of doubt. But it does mean that we will more frequently be able to get ourselves into a fully focused, engaged mental space. Consider aspects of both practice and performance that you love or enjoy. Also consider aspects that you love even when up against great pressure, like being exhausted or in a position of losing.

Sometimes it takes shifting your attention or what you are actually doing in your training or practice to make the effort as fulfilling as possible. For one of the items on your list above, consider how you could purposefully pay attention to this factor while in the middle of your next training session. Consider writing the word down on a piece of paper that you could see to remind yourself of what to notice. If you are a runner, you could select a certain point in your training run to shift your attention toward your source of enjoyment. If you are a classical musician, you could make a note on your music sheet of what to think about in the middle of a practice session or in a concert. If you are a public speaker, you could plan for certain points of your speech to cue into the sources of what is most engaging for you.

All of this takes practice. If purposefully engaging in flow on a daily basis could be a highest point of leverage for you, you will need to come up with a simple, clear way to get your mind to refocus toward the light. The next five chapters will provide specific skills to help you make the psychologically based performance changes that most resonate with you.

8

Facing Negative Emotions

Recognizing, Accepting, and Shifting Negative Emotions

> *"I can't sleep. My U.S. National races are only two weeks away and I can't think about anything else. I feel so much fear."*
>
> —Top-ranked high school swimmer

> *"I hate going to the rehearsal hall with my teacher. I feel so embarrassed when I make mistakes. I feel like I'm letting her down."*
>
> —Graduate school musician with professional aspirations

Negative emotions such as fear, angst, anger, disappointment, and frustration are a natural part of striving and learning. Let's face it, training and performing can be an emotional roller coaster. Whether we lose an important place on a team, lose a match, are heading into a big event, or are preparing for a speech, we can't always feel internally steady and at ease. Sometimes, we are able to endure the negative and pretend that we are fine. But everyone in the performance world has to deal with negative emotions.

Most of the chapters in this book deal with ways to increase and sustain positive emotion. In this chapter, we will look at how to work productively with the negative emotions that are inevitable in our lives. In fact, I will argue that negative emotions can be a gift, a clear and readable sign to us to make changes that need to be made. If we can learn to recognize, accept, and shift our negative emotions, they can actually help us flourish.

THE TWO WAYS THAT NEGATIVE EMOTIONS CAN HELP US
Signals of immediate problems

The first way that negative emotions can help us is by warning us of something that may harm us. As every human being knows, sometimes our negative emotions are flooding in to protect us. We are in danger, and our brain systems are telling us that we need to take action. On a very practical level, negative emotions can help keep us safe and goad us into action. Sometimes, our perception that something is a threat to our well-being from the outside world is fully accurate. In these cases, our negative emotions serve us by energizing us to focus in and address problems, threats, and concerns that need our attention.

For example, our negative feelings may be telling us that we may need to get out of an abusive training situation or get out of a bad relationship. They may be telling us that we need to ease up on our training regime to avoid injury, or we may need to begin to train more consistently. If an elite runner begins to feel chronically irritable and easily frustrated, these emotions may be a signal that he needs to back off of training for a few days. He may have been putting too much strain on his physical system and the negative emotions are a sign to give himself some recovery time. We've all had days when we are scheduled for a hard day of training and our bodies are breaking down. We feel an emotional pull to go, but our bodies are screaming to stay in bed. If we override our negative emotions and force ourselves forward, we become sick or injured.

Admittedly, for high achieving performers, it is not always easy to read these signals. By taking part in the *performance culture* of sport, music, or other types of work, many of us have learned that we must conform—we must fit in with what our coaches, leaders, or mentors envision for us. We must do what teammates are doing. This conformity we've learned to abide by is a major challenge when it comes to dealing with negative emotions signaling a real danger.

Dan O'Brien, a gold medalist in the decathlon, had the insight to correctly read his own signals and he was willing to honor those signals. Decathaletes are pushed to their physical limit and must adhere to their body's warning signals. They must notice potential breakdowns before they push themselves too far physically, which can result in injury or burnout. Dan was able to listen to his signals, even when it meant upsetting his coach when he didn't follow through with a pre-planned workout. It is a mark of his overall ability that Dan was able to listen to himself, and his experience gives us insight into the importance of adopting a mindset of listening to oneself, which is contrary to the suck-it-up mentality in the traditional sport culture.

Non-urgent signals about the need for change

The second way that negative emotions can help us is often more difficult to see and requires some thoughtful action on our part. Sometimes we are clearly not in immediate danger, and yet we feel intense negative emotion. Most people simply try to ignore such feelings. I have found that if we pay attention and respond to such feelings, it can help us reach our goal of living and performing in our sweet spot.

I worked with May, a 14-year-old swimmer from the Midwest, a few years ago over the telephone. She was dealing with a seemingly insurmountable challenge. She was unable to breathe when training and racing. Often, in the middle of a race, she would stop to cling to the side of the pool to regain her breath. She was taken to many medical specialists to determine whether or not the challenge was a physical one. It turned out that it was not. She had nowhere to turn, so her mother considered the possibility of it being a psychological problem.

It turned out that May was afraid. She was very afraid. She thought a lot about what would happen if she could not continue breathing when competing. May's fear was particularly triggered when neck-and-neck with a competitor and beginning to physically tire—a situation that affects all of us. At these moments, her mind would become filled with intense images of drowning, of her lungs stopping functioning, and of an inability to breath. Concurrently with these feelings, May felt embarrassed, full of fear, and anxious. These factors together would lead to constricted breathing and to May feeling as if she was physically drowning.

May was not aware of any negative thoughts about swimming or of any fears of not being able to perform her best. She thought that her fears were all about her difficulty breathing and the danger of drowning. She would simply be totally overwhelmed by the inability to breath. It wasn't until we took some time to talk through what she was actually feeling and thinking before her races and before her breathing problems showed up that she was able to notice the initial signs of panic and anxiety in her mind. May discovered that she actually did have an emotional and fearful response to competitive swimming itself. This new awareness of her emotional response to racing was pivotal to her ability to learn to face and accept the fear such that it would not manifest as restricted breathing, muscle bracing, and, ultimately disastrous race results.

Often, when feeling negative emotions, we are thinking about our training and performances in ways that don't serve us. In this negative emotional state, if our minds are not redirected, they will be filled with fearful thoughts, or we will have powerful urges to escape and leave the situation. Obviously, it doesn't help us to dwell on the negative throughout a three-hour practice session. And when we feel terrified just before performance, the best option is not to run away. We must carry on. We must go practice or perform. So what should we do about these negative emotions?

When we feel strong negative emotions and we know we are safe, it is time to use the negative emotion as a marker of needed change. In these moments, we have a great opportunity to shift how we are thinking. When we consider what needs to change in our thinking, with careful consideration, we can regain balance in our training or performances. The negative emotion could be the result of how we are responding to a teammate, teacher, or coaching relationship that needs attention. We may need to respond to losing differently. Though often repugnant or aversive, our negative emotional responses are important in helping us pay attention to what needs tending. With a goal of maintaining a sense of well-being and ultimately optimizing performance, our negative emotions serve as key guides to just what needs to be addressed.

HOW CAN WE WORK WITH NEGATIVE EMOTION?

You may wonder, "What choices do we really have? Don't we just feel the way that we feel?" Yes, but then the question is, what do we do with those feelings? Can we influence the extent to which we have negative feelings? Yes, we can. Can we use those negative emotions to help us flourish? The answer is yes.

In fact, current research indicates that we actually need some negative emotion to thrive. This negative emotion, however, must be in balance. Current research in positive psychology has shown that in order for us to thrive, we generally need to maintain a certain ratio of positive to negative emotions. This magical ratio of positive emotions to negative emotions is between three-to-one (3:1) and five-to-one (5:1). These ratios are based on research by Barbara Fredrickson, a world-renowned researcher of positive emotions, John Gottman, a well-respected researcher on why marriages last, and Marcial Losada, a well-known researcher on team success. Their findings about these ratios of positive to negative emotion suggest that if you have more than one episode of negative emotions for every three episodes of positive emotions, you may put your ability to thrive at risk.

But how do we achieve this ratio of positive to negative emotion? Most of the chapters in this book are about increasing the frequency and quality of our positive emotions. This chapter concerns what we can do with the negative ones. There are three consecutive steps we can take to work productively with negative emotions.

1. **Recognizing potential problems and acting if necessary:** First, we must try to recognize and understand what the negative emotion is telling us. What is the negative emotion like? Is it telling us we are in immediate danger or in a harmful situation? Is there some clear action we can take right away that will help us? Sometimes, we need to use the wisdom learned from the negative emotion to make a change in our actions. Negative emotions can also help provide the energy necessary to help us leave a dangerous situation or relationship.

2. **Shifting the negative emotional state:** If Step 1 does not seem to apply to the negative emotion, we have to ask whether our negative emotions are coming from the way we are thinking about our situation. It may be possible to shift our feelings from negative to positive by working with our appraisal and understanding of our situation.

3. **Accepting the negative emotional state:** Sometimes, we are stuck with the negative emotion. It may be impossible in some cases to get ourselves, in the moment, to shift out of a negative emotional state. We must learn to accept the presence of the negative emotion to minimize the impact of the anxiety.

Before we explore these steps more thoroughly, it might be helpful to think about how we can recognize the contents of our negative emotions. This has to take place before we move on to taking action.

AWARENESS OF OUR NEGATIVE EMOTIONS

Emotions are our engines to action. Our emotions can powerfully direct our intensity, passion, and commitment. Our emotions can also derail us. In our success-driven world, the importance of emotion can be undervalued. We are expected to be rational beings. Yet we all have intense feelings and there is no question that our feelings are the drivers of what we do, how hard we try, and when we give up. The power of emotion is clearly demonstrated when we perform. When we feel confident and inspired, watch out! If we feel less than, terrified, or unable, the results are often disastrous.

To have some influence over the powerful impact of our emotions, we need to first be aware of how we are emotionally responding. Having an awareness of what we feel is particularly important as we approach practice, training, or competition because, oftentimes, how we feel when going into an event can strongly influence our ability to focus and optimize training or performance. The key to coping most effectively with negative emotions is to be aware of when they are happening and what they are about.

This seems like an obvious thing to do. We should expect that we all can easily be aware of our emotions, right? Well, it turns out that this is not the case. Sometimes, we don't notice a small fear or sense of discomfort until it becomes monstrous, and then it can become very hard to handle.

Consider times in training or performance when negative emotions that you think might hurt your performance manifest themselves. In Exercise 8.1, take a moment to think about or jot down any negative thoughts or fears that you might have that could help generate negative feelings in practice or performance. Next, consider what thoughts you may have that could trigger this cascade of negativity. Through building your awareness, you then create the possibility of acting, shifting out of such states, or otherwise minimizing their impact on your performance.

Once you become aware of when the negative emotions show up and what they are, you can begin to make a plan for responding.

Step 1: Recognizing real problems—and acting

The first thing to consider when you are experiencing a strong negative emotional state is what you could do to change the situation. It is helpful to ask yourself what you could do or what you may need to say to relieve yourself of the negativity. Negative emotions can be a sign that some sort of action is necessary. It may be that you are injured and need to take a break. You may feel repulsed by having to go to practice (again) and need to discover a way to make practice more compelling. You may feel like you are not training in

Exercise 8.1. Building awareness of negative emotions
(practice/ performance)

The event/challenge	Your negative feeling:	Thoughts that might trigger the negative emotions:
Your experiences of negative emotions	e.g., Fear e.g., Boredom	"I must be successful or I'm worthless." "I am so tired and sick of this."
You in practice		
You in performance		

the right place or with the right coach/teacher and that you have an urge to change things up. You may feel uninspired and it may be time to make a plan, for example, to transition to another training group. Or it may be that you need to train differently.

When we feel negative emotions and we are not physically or emotionally safe, the obvious answer is to take the necessary steps to get to safety, as soon as possible. Some situations call for quick, clear action. If you are injured, and you know you are hurting yourself, it is time to stop training. Sometimes, however, this is easier said than done.

I recently worked with Mitch, a runner who had sustained a foot injury. He was told that if he kept running, he would permanently damage his foot. He felt angry and frustrated by the situation. We discussed in detail the pros and cons of continuing to train. Though he knew that he risked incurring permanent injury on his foot, he continued to run. He did damage his foot and when he reflected back on the situation, he wished that he had taken the necessary time off to heal. Though in the short term he would have had to miss some performance opportunities, in the long run, listening to his body would have served his training much better.

There are other types of changes that need to be made that are signaled by negative emotions. We can be on the wrong team, in the wrong program, or in a setting that somehow is just not conducive to success. A few years ago, I worked with John, a top-ranked tennis player who was very uncomfortable with his coach and team. He had a strong sense that he needed to move south to a nationally ranked team where he would receive the type of attention and competition that would allow him to thrive. He fought the angst and discomfort that he felt.

We explored his thinking around continuing to play where he was and to reinterpret how he was making sense of the situation. We worked on helping him learn to accept the negative emotions. None of this worked. It became apparent that this young athlete did need to leave his current situation. He transferred within a few months and competed for one of the top collegiate tennis teams in the country, happily. His negative emotions motivated him to make a change that was necessary for him to make. And, thankfully, he listened to himself.

When we are emotionally uncomfortable, the right answer is not always to leave the situation. Yet, we must be able to entertain the possibility of quitting, leaving, or changing where we train and with whom. With John, we talked quite a bit about both what he was hoping to find in the training opportunity elsewhere and what he would lose if he left his school, scholarship, and current training situation. To consider a significant change, we've got to think through the pros and cons of both leaving or staying. It is important to consider both the emotional information (like "I can't stand it here anymore") and the logical consideration of the impact of whatever the choices will be on our lives in the immediate future, a few months later, and then a few years down the road.

Negative emotions can also be a signal to work harder or to back off of training. It is quite typical when preparing for performance to push too hard for too long. At some point, performers will feel uninspired and feel a sense of not caring, exhaustion, or a loss of interest. These signs are invaluable. When we are able to pay attention to such signs, we can learn to take the necessary breaks before we physically break down and are forced to take precious months away from training.

In contrast, sometimes negative emotions can signal a problem of not working hard enough or not achieving sufficient focus. Sometimes feeling unfulfilled and frustrated can be a function of simply needing to work harder and to be more focused. Such emotions can put us back into focused action that is necessary to ultimately optimize performance.

I recently worked with Luke, a college basketball player who was frustrated by the fact that he was not in the starting lineup. In our sport psychology sessions, he would talk about feeling flat and frustrated in practice. He felt he was just going through the motions, stating, "It doesn't matter if I try, he (coach) will just start the senior in front of me." But it did matter to Luke. He was irritated all through practice. He knew that he had more to give and wasn't feeling satisfied with his daily effort and training. His sense of frustration was a great negative emotion to acknowledge. It was a signal that he was not starting and that he was not challenging himself enough in practice. Through our conversation he also started to realize that the effort that he was putting forth would keep him on the bench much longer than he could tolerate. After we created a plan for him to be more purposeful and present in his training, his negative emotions dissipated. The negative emotions were critical to experience and pay attention to, because they were a signal that he needed to shift into a more purposeful, focused mindset while practicing.

Consider any current negative feelings that you may be experiencing in your training. Think about whether some specific action, in terms of what you need to do or say, is necessary to help you take the necessary step toward your success. Consider both the pros and the cons of the possible change.

Sometimes, just becoming aware of how you are feeling can help you become aware of the action that needs to be taken. Other times, thinking

Exercise 8.2. Pros and cons of changing the situation

The negative feeling	The situation	Possible action response	Pros of change/ action	Cons of change/ action
e.g., Irritation	Practicing three hours per day	Option 1: Skip Practice	I'd feel relieved.	I'd get behind.
		Option 2: Practice with a friend	I'd be more energized.	I might feel embarrassed.
Your feelings: 1. 2.				

through the options of what change you could consider making and the pros and cons of such a change can help you determine the best course of action (or no action). The key is that if you are experiencing strong negative emotions and you can relieve them by doing or saying something that will ultimately contribute to your performance and well-being, it is invaluable to think about what that change might be. The next step is building up your courage to do or say what you must for your own well-being.

Step 2: Shifting a negative emotion
Most of the time, coping with negative emotions in the performance realm means handling emotions that are intensely strong but generally do not help with performance. Often, there are no magical words or actions that will relieve us of such emotions. There is no clear danger or threat: we are safe, and yet we feel strong negative emotions. The negative emotions are often generated from our expectations or judgments of how we should perform. These expectations can morph into feeling too much pressure, embarrassment at not competing at a particular spot, fear of not living up to your own

or others' expectations, or simply the fear of not being well enough prepared for an upcoming performance.

In order to understand how we can shift these feelings, we first have to understand more about emotions in general. Recent research has been very helpful in shining a light on this domain.

How emotions are created. Understanding how our emotions are created is an important first step in regaining influence over how our emotions affect our training and performance. Our emotions are the direct result of how we are making sense of all the cues and information of what is happening around us. Our emotions are composed of both our explanations of what is going on around us and how our bodies respond. How we make sense of our world, ourselves, and the specific demands within it are unquestionably the driving force behind our emotions.

Figure 8.1 is a simplified version of how emotions are understood. The key to this figure is the Assessment. How we evaluate or make sense of a situation makes all the difference in terms of how we emotionally react to what is going on. Imagine that you have a speech to give. If you assess it as, "I'm worthless if they don't love me," then you may experience great fear. If you assess the same situation as, "I love having a chance to share all these fantastic ideas with all these people," you may experience joy or excitement when going into the same situation.

If we are willing to see ourselves differently, our world differently, or our challenges differently, we can transform our emotional reaction or state. Our psychological interpretation of the environment, what the situation means to us, has the biggest impact on determining how we will feel about the situa-

Figure 8.1: How emotions are understood

tion. Richard Lazarus is a leader in understanding the importance of emotion. He emphasizes that how we make sense of the demands of our environment depends on our goal regarding the challenge or demand. The importance of the goal relative to other goals in our lives determines how important the outcome of the goal is to us—and how much distress would result from failing to meet the goal. A retired marathoner going out to run a marathon for charity may feel much differently about achieving that goal than would be the case if he were running a marathon early in his career, trying to earn a qualifying time for the Boston Marathon. As our goals shift, our emotional responses to the same goal will also shift radically. When the goal is at the top of our list, we predictably will generate much more emotion (negative or positive) when pursuing the goal and when we do or do not achieve our goals in the end.

Examining and shifting our appraisal: a key to change. The key point is that we have a choice, and it lies in how we appraise the challenge. One of the most promising ideas that I have gleaned from Lazarus's theory of emotion is based on the simple phrase, "Change the meaning, change the emotion." What he means by this is that if we think about any challenge differently, we can respond differently.

According to Lazarus, our "beliefs about self and the world" affect how we interpret the demands around us. Our emotional response will also be tempered by how we judge ourselves. If we see ourselves as able and competent, we are more likely to respond to a demand more positively. It really doesn't matter if we are highly skilled and competent. Competence isn't the key. Believing in our ability is the key.

Also, how we see the world impacts our emotional responses. Do we see the world as a safe, warm place, full of possibilities? Do we see the world as nurturing us, guiding us in the direction that best suits our abilities and skills? Or do we see the world as harsh, unkind, and judgmental? We have a choice in how we see the world. Whatever we pull for seems to gain our attention and grow. We can transform our emotional responses if we encourage ourselves to look for the good, the kind, and the benevolent that surrounds us at all times.

Our ability to rely on our "personal resources," according to Lazarus, is also key in terms of how we react emotionally. I have a 6-year-old son, and with that comes many opportunities for me to observe strong emotional reactions in both his and my own responses. In particularly challenging moments, my son will say and/or act in a way that is consistent with his go-to statement, "I want what I want when I want it." Clearly, he can't always get what he wants. When he is pushed, he will quickly become overwrought with intense, negative emotions like anger, frustration, or indignation.

Historically, I'd match his surge of emotions; I'd begin to feel what he was feeling. I'd have to force myself to try to kindly guide or instruct myself how to act when racked with negative emotion. I thought for a while that I was just going to have to endure the negative feelings. I didn't know that I had other resources, my own personal resources, on which I could rely. I learned that it is possible to move to an authentic centered, peaceful, and self-controlled space. I can be the emotional leader in my own life and, subsequently, for my son as well. This probably should have been a realization that I had when I was 10 or 15 years old, but better late than never.

We all have extraordinary, perhaps limitless, personal resources. But we must first acknowledge them and sense them, before we can lean upon them. Part of learning how to effectively cope with our emotions includes figuring out how to rely upon ourselves. Otherwise, we can become victims of great angst and fear as we interpret the myriad challenges around us as things that we can't handle. It is essential that we are aware of the 98% of our skills and abilities that are already in place. We must take off our 2% blinders in focusing on what is wrong and be willing to acknowledge what is, already, good about our world and ourselves. This shift helps us learn how to more effectively respond to the ongoing challenges that we face.

The earlier example of the young swimmer, May, represents a shift in how a performer can change the meaning of an experience and how this can help shift the emotional response. With the stress that May was experiencing, she felt like she was drowning when racing or training hard. With May's new awareness that the drowning sensation was created by her own fear, we were able to develop a plan for her to use when the mild feelings of fear and anxiety surfaced. (We had to get at them before they got too strong.) May went from not being able to finish races to actually going faster in her best events within about six weeks. She made this change because of her newfound awareness of her fears and the basic sport psychology strategies to cope with them (she used imagery and memorized tailored key phrases to say to herself when the fear began to surface during a race). Her progress started with her becoming aware of her negative feelings. She had no way of addressing the issue until she was able to face the emotional challenge head on.

May experienced a great fear of not being able to breathe. Her fear was a function of her believing that when she was racing and getting tired, that her body could not handle the challenge. When her fear surfaced, her muscles tightened and her lungs constricted. May had to consider her belief that she couldn't handle it. She had to decide that she could fight the feeling as opposed to feeling beaten by it as soon as it showed up. She changed how she responded to the fears. May was able to shift from feeling intense fear to feeling determined while racing and doing hard sets in the pool. It took tremendous effort on her part to refocus her mind on her swimming (instead of thinking about not being able to breathe). She also had to be able to face her negative emotion head on. As part of her intervention plan, she literally said in her mind, "I can beat this monster." This phrase helped her shift to a purposeful determination instead of being pulled out by the riptide of fear. She needed to learn to shift how she was thinking to be able to transform her emotional response.

Can we really shift from one emotion to another? When caught in the throes of anger, jealousy, frustration, or indignation, is it possible to shift to an equally authentic, more effective emotion? The answer is yes. And, yes, it is difficult to get ourselves to shift to a constructive, authentic mindset in such instances. Living in the sweet spot can be tough at times. And purposefully changing how we assess a situation when we are deep into a negative, destructive emotional reaction may be the hardest part of staying in our sweet spot. It is not a matter of just faking it and trying to experience something that we don't authentically feel. The answer to shifting out of a destructive, disempowering emotion lies within our ability to think about the challenge differently.

May had to shift from thinking, "Oh no, here it comes. I'm not going to be able to breathe. Oh, I have to stop or I'll drown!" She shifted to, "OK, here it comes. I can beat this. I can beat this monster. Stretch. Pull through the water. Cut through. I can do this." Shifting to more empowering thoughts that May truly believed was key. We had to work hard to figure out where she could shift her mind to a thought that she would believe was as authentic as the fear. If we don't shift to a thought that we believe, the strategy won't work. For example, if she tried to think, "I can always beat this," it wouldn't work because she was still unsure of her ability to always overcome the fear.

In the performance world, emotional shifts are more likely to happen when you plan for them in advance. It is difficult to shift when your entire system is inundated with anger, dread, or fear. We can't always predict when the unhelpful negative emotions are going to hit, but we all have some moments when we can predict that they will. Consider a time in practice or performance when you are most challenged by negative emotions. Consider the event, your typical appraisal, your typical emotional reaction, and how you could more effectively appraise the challenge. By considering these things, you could also consider how thinking about the challenge would make you react emotionally differently, as well. I've given some practical examples that I've seen many times in my practice as a sport psychologist. The key is to, first, be aware of the unhelpful emotion and, then, come up with a new appraisal (new interpretation or assessment) in which you authentically believe.

Practicing making emotional shifts is very challenging, but very rewarding. With awareness and practice, it is possible. To prepare, it is important to first select an event that you know will typically trigger a negative emotion at a particular instance. You then can work through the chart in Exercise 8.3

Exercise 8.3. Thinking differently about the same challenge

The event	Your typical appraisal:	Typical emotional response	New appraisal	New (possible) emotion
Practice	Boredom	"I am so tired and sick of this."	"I'm going to work on a specific skill today."	Engaged
			"I'm thankful for the chance to train."	Upbeat
			"This is making me better."	Determined
Your experience				
Important performance	Fear	"I must be successful or I'm worthless."	"I've trained hard."	Determined
			"I've done all that I can do."	At ease
			"I'll just perform, each moment, the best that I can."	Slightly more relaxed

to help yourself tailor a new appraisal so you'll have a plan for how to help yourself shift out of the negative emotional state. To be authentic, this shifting appraisal takes time and practice in order to work.

It's important to select a shift in thinking (a pre-planned thought or phrase) that you will believe, that you will know is true even when you are wrestling with fear, anger, indignation, or disgust. Take a look at the *New appraisal* column in Exercise 8.3. Whatever you come up with to attempt in practice or competition, the thought must be one that resonates with you. The only way to make such an emotional shift is to be able to authentically and honestly shift how you are making sense of the challenge or difficulty.

With our young swimmer, May, the only way she would be able to shift her emotional response was to come up with a way of thinking about the particularly challenging moments in racing when she felt like she was drowning. She had to shift her interpretation of the physical symptoms. She had to shift to a thought that was more empowering, one that she would believe in the moments of great stress.

Step 3: Accepting the negative emotional state

When you recognize a negative emotion and have worked through Steps 1 and 2, to no avail, you may have to consider Step 3. There are times when we have visceral, negative reactions to someone or something in our world. Sometimes our signals are just too strong for what the situation really warrants. We may be at some risk such as losing a game, making a mistake, or not performing to our potential. Yet the intense fear and desire to flee is too strong for the situation and can actually be a significant source of distraction, ultimately hurting our performance. But sometimes, it is not possible to shift the emotion, as described in Step 2.

Sometimes, no matter what we think or how we try to reevaluate the situation, the too-strong-for-the-situation negativity surges within us. As an elite and professional athlete, I've had the experience many times of facing intense fear and having no idea what to do with it. I'd try to think about the challenge differently, but just couldn't make a shift away from it. I felt helpless and the victim of negativity countless times. I always wanted to win so badly and then consistently had the fear of, "What if I don't win?" surging through every cell of my body.

When we cannot shift out of the negative emotional state, we must learn to tolerate it. When we are not in danger and our emotional system is overreacting, learning to accept, tolerate, and carry on are highly important skills.

During such times, we must learn to minimize the impact of such negative emotions so we can focus on what will ultimately help us perform to the best of our abilities.

We are best served if we are mindful of the emotions and remain productive. By being mindful, I mean we need to be able to fully feel the uncomfortable emotions while at the same time holding our feelings with kindness. Sometimes it is difficult to imagine providing this support for yourself. But I am certain that you have had an experience when you provided such kind, loving support to a best friend or teammate. When someone you love is sad or hurt, you don't treat them with disdain. You pay attention to them and help them any way that you can. Sometimes this might just mean sitting with someone and demonstrating that you care about them.

In 1992 I was an alternate for the U.S. Olympic team. It was a difficult few months. I made the team but was only going to race if someone suffered an illness or injury. I had significant negative emotions to deal with every day. I tried my best to stay upbeat, but internally it was ugly. I'll never forget the kindness of my teammate Trace (Rude) Smith. One day she asked me to go get ice cream and asked me to tell her how I was really doing. She could not do anything for me in that moment, but she was willing to sit with me and help me deal with my significant disappointment. At that moment her willingness to be honest and supportive to me meant the world. Her presence was simply kind, loving, and accepting.

Think about the next time you feel badly—hurt, anxious, or angry—and there is nothing to do to solve it. Imagine a time when you just can't shake the intense negativity. To minimize the impact of such negativity, sometimes the best that we can do is to notice that it is happening and to accept it. The task is to accept the powerful negative emotion with kindness and interest. This idea is not a new one. Being able to accept with kindness one's negative emotions is discussed by leaders in the field of mindfulness, including giants in the field such as Jon Kabat-Zinn and Thich Nhat Hanh.

I worked with a professional musician of 30 years. He spoke of the intense fear he still felt before going on stage. He tried many things to rid himself of this emotion, but to no avail. He has had to learn to accept that the intense fear will show up before he goes on stage. He accepted this experience just as he does the need to warm up. Both are part of his pre-performance experience. He no longer labels the experience with things like, "This means I'm going to bomb" or "I hate this and want to quit." He has learned to treat the negative feelings like a passing storm cloud. They arise in particular moments and then, just as quickly, disappear. It doesn't mean he is comfortable with the feelings. But he learned not to give them power. He learned not to fan the flame of negativity. This reflects his ability to be mindful of the negative emotion without strengthening the negative experience or allowing it to determine the quality of his musical performance.

This musician's experience is not unique to high-level performers. Prior to significant performance events, it is typical for elite athletes to feel rushes of anxiety. A common physical state prior to competition includes sweaty palms, an elevated heart rate, an increased breathing rate, or tightened muscles. Researchers have concluded that top-level performers still have these sensations. The difference lies in how they interpret the physical signs.

Over time, the top performers have learned to interpret these physical signs as indications of readiness to compete rather than signs of weakness or fear. Sheldon Hanton and Graham Jones conducted a study of top U.S. swimmers in which they found that these swimmers were all overwhelmed by negative emotions when they were young athletes. Over time, they learned to both accept and work with these emotions. Some athletes even reported being concerned when the rush of anxiety did not show up before a race. They had learned that this energy was a vital part of getting ready to perform. In our terms, they have been able to use Step 2 described earlier in this chapter to deal with these negative emotions. But this is not always possible.

There are many common instances when we must tolerate the rush of anxiety or self-doubt. For example, if you must do a presentation in front of others, confront someone who has hurt you, or cut an athlete from a team, it is probable that you will feel a rush of unwanted and uncomfortable emotions. We can reappraise all we like and it is still, at times, impossible to rid ourselves of the negative emotional rush. What do we do? To most productively move forward, we must be aware of the emotions and then focus our energy on that which will help us succeed in the moment.

Accepting one's negative emotions and then having to continue with the task at hand is like facing one's monster. It seems like running away in the moment would make for great relief. Yes, for the short term—for a few moments—it would be great. But to learn to optimize performance, we often must choose to remain in situations (when we are really safe) that, in the moment, still elicit feelings of terror, incompetence, or frustration. The practice of accepting the negative emotions and embracing them and yourself with compassion and love is a skill that is essential to be able to optimize performance.

Exercise 8.4. Cues for accepting negative emotions

Negative emotions to be accepted	Specific situation	Thought that can help with acceptance	Physical cue to help with acceptance	Image to help with acceptance
Anger	Coach yelling at me in the game	"She yells at everyone."	Take a deep breath	Visualizing myself at ease and comfortable
Fear	An audition for a top orchestra	"Everyone is nervous. I can use the energy to express the emotion of the piece."	Breathe out all fear for a split second	Visualize myself playing a difficult passage at my best
Your 1st emotion: Your 2nd emotion:				

In Exercise 8.4, I encourage you to think about the few predictable in-stances when you will experience negative emotions in your performance realm that do not signal authentic danger. Think about times it is unlikely that you could shake the surge of negativity. Consider in these instances how your energy would be best focused. After considering the example, try coming up with a time when you would be willing to accept and sit with negative emotions with the goal of ultimately learning to perform better. After you've considered the situation, consider coming up with a thought or phrase, a physical cue or an image, that would help remind you of how you could be more mindful and accepting the next time you are called to endure such a surge of negative emotions.

Though unwelcome by all of us, negative emotions demand our attention. We can grow wiser about how we train and perform when we notice the negative emotions. Whether we need to make some necessary changes, learn to shift the emotion to a more effective emotion, or simply tolerate the emo-tion and focus on the task at hand, becoming more aware of our emotions and our options about how to respond to them will ultimately help us be success-ful. Though often not comfortable, learning to face and cope effectively with our negative emotions is an essential component of living and performing in the sweet spot. This particularly holds true as we prepare ourselves for the big moments.

9

Coaches, Family, Teammates, and Friends

Letting in the Good and Letting Go of the Negative

*"My coach screams at me for every
little thing that I do wrong.
I find it so humiliating."*

—Full scholarship
collegiate softball player

It has long been recognized that we need to have positive relationships to thrive. From Greek philosopher Aristotle's discussion of friendship in the Nicomachean Ethics to current research in happiness, it seems that we need others to experience happiness and thriving. According to Chris Peterson, a leader in the positive psychology movement, having positive, meaningful friendships is one of the strongest correlates of happiness. The research indicates that people who tend to have close, positive friendships and relationships also tend to report being happier (and the opposite holds true as well).

You may respond, "What I care about is performing, not what others think and feel. Why is it important to have good relationships with others in my performance life? Doesn't it really matter more how skilled we are and how hard we try?" While the answers to these questions depend upon our own circumstances, for most of us, the people around us do have a significant impact on our performance and our general well-being. This impact can be positive or it can be negative. This is why our relationships matter as we aim to maximize our time in the sweet spot.

First, the significant others in our performance lives can help us in many ways. We often may need to rely upon these others to thrive in our performance realms. Consider someone who is part of a team, an orchestra, or a performing group. That person must depend upon others' abilities to perform in order to his or her own success. And even for individual performers, our social world can significantly contribute to our ability to perform when it counts. It is particularly important to look for the good from the important others in our life. The good might be key information, emotional support, or guidance.

Second, we need to make sure that the significant others in our performance lives do not undermine our attempts to achieve our best, either intentionally or unintentionally. In our performance realms, we are frequently exposed to opportunities to receive good from others, but just as frequently we are faced with the challenges of being hurt, embarrassed, or disappointed by them. Sometimes these negative experiences come from the actions of others, but sometimes they stem from our own negativity being projected onto those around us. Both can have a deleterious effect on our performance lives.

This chapter is about these two sides of our relationships with coaches, teammates, teachers, mentors, colleagues, friends, and family—in short, the important humans in our lives. How can we let in the good and filter out the unhelpful or harmful from these important people? In this chapter we'll cover a variety of issues that examine this question. The chapter is organized into three sections, each of which shines a light on one particular kind of relationship: coaches, parents, and teammates/friends.

GETTING THE MOST OUT OF YOUR COACH!

In my work as a sport psychologist, the player-coach relationship is a prominent point of discussion. One of the biggest challenges for the performers is learning to cope with a harsh coach or teacher. Athletes often see the player-coach relationship as one way only—from the coach to the player. And, typically, they do not see themselves as having any power.

At first, as a young practicing sport psychologist, I thought that each athlete I sat with had a difficult or harsh coach. But I soon learned that regardless of what their coach is really like, most athletes have a difficult time negotiating the emotional strain that results from being chronically pushed to the edge physically and, then, consistently (or relentlessly) being reminded of what needs to be improved. Our coaches and teachers tend to focus on the 2% that needs improving. Most don't have the time, energy, or priority to focus on the 98%, to remind us of what is going well.

Yet if we really want to optimize our performance, it is imperative to learn how to take in the information that the coach or teacher provides and to minimize the impact of the seemingly harsh delivery. One spring, I worked with Sarah, a young collegiate rower, who had a particularly harsh coach. Sarah talked quite a bit about feeling emotionally crushed by the coach. Her feelings oscillated between anger, frustration, and embarrassment. She felt that her coach was only negative with her. She felt that the meanness was personal. Sarah had a particularly strong visceral reaction when her coach would yell at her. Sarah said that as soon as her coach said her name, she would start to feel a strong negative emotional reaction.

Sarah had several options. She could choose to remain in emotional hell, choose to leave the team, or choose to learn to deal with the way that her coach coached her. First, we explored whether or not Sarah was ready to leave her team. She was not; though, of course, she wanted to be free of the night-sweats and nightmares inspired by the thoughts of her coach.

The next step was to figure out a way to help Sarah feel at once emotionally safe from her coach's harshness and remain open to the good information that the coach was giving her about how to improve technically. There is not one right way of learning to bring in the good and block out the hurt. With some creativity and effort, it can usually be done, but it can take some experimentation to figure out how to do this for ourselves.

In Sarah's case, we next talked about the coach's intention. I asked her what she thought the coach was trying to do when she was coaching Sarah. I asked, "Is she trying to make you miserable? Is she trying to humiliate you? Does she try to help you improve?"

After considering her coach's intention, it became clear to Sarah that the coach was indeed trying to help her get better. She noted her insight when she said, "I know that coach is trying to help me, though how she does it is awful!"

Once she was able to separate the delivery style from the coach's intention, Sarah was able to better tolerate the way in which her coach consistently yelled at her and was able to look past the yelling to hear the good information about improving performance. Sarah was able to consistently note that the coach was intending to help her, and with this awareness, Sarah was more able to take in the useful information and detach it from the harsh delivery style.

Sarah was particularly sensitive and felt hurt by her coach's style. I looked to humor and lightness to help take away the sting that came from Sarah being "screamed at." In one of our sport psychology sessions, I asked her to tell me what kind of animal the coach reminded her of when she was yelling at her. She laughed and said the coach reminded her of a howling wolf. Though the information that the coach gave her was quite helpful, the challenge remained to cope with how the coach communicated that information. Together, we created a plan for how Sarah would deal with her coach's style.

When Sarah heard the coach say her name, she planned to envision a howling wolf (which made her laugh inside and put her at ease) and then she would purposefully filter for good ideas. She would purposefully not allow the meanness or harshness of style to get to her. She would remind herself that, though the style was awful, "Coach is trying to help me."

This is a situation in which Sarah had to honor how she felt so she could come up with a strategy to cope with the situation differently. If she tried to talk herself into feeling positive about the coaching style and the feelings were not based on authentic interpretation, the intervention never would have worked. If Sarah had tried to tell herself "it doesn't matter" or "I just have to deal with it" she would not have succeeded in creating the positive outcome she sought.

Sarah had to honor how she felt so she could find a way to make her situation work better for her. With her new strategy of acknowledging the harsh style (the wolf image) and her acknowledgment of her coach's positive intention, Sarah's negative emotional reactions to her coach subsided over time. And almost immediately, she was able to go to practice and put to use the good coaching information she was receiving from her coach.

There is no question that coaches and teachers are human beings and that they all have their weaknesses. We are all sensitive to those people who have significant power over our lives. We are very aware of what they are not, and what we think that they should be. Almost all coaches have many good ideas that will help us get better. The more we can be open to their ideas, their coaching style, and how they relay information, the more we can benefit.

In order to benefit, we must be able to learn to take in the good and screen out the hurtful ideas or styles of delivery. Sometimes, it can be helpful to think logically through what is happening when we are dealing with a harsh coach or teacher. I have found it helpful to have my clients acknowledge the situation, how they feel about it, the intention of their coach/teacher, and then to develop a strategy to deal with the difficult aspects of the relationship. In Exercise 9.1, you can develop your own tailored strategy to cope with a particularly challenging aspect of someone who is coaching, teaching, or leading you.

First, consider the situation and how you usually respond to them. If it is difficult, consider a way to think about the situation that will elicit compassion for them (this will help take away some of the negative power they hold over you). Next, consider the intention of the coach, teacher, or leader. What are

Exercise 9.1. Your coach/teacher's intention:
Getting the most from their feedback

Situation	My emotional response	Compassion for them	Intention of my coach	Strategy to get the most out of the situation
e.g., Coach yells at me when giving me feedback	"I feel hurt and close down. I think coach doesn't believe in me."	"They are doing the best that they can."	"Coach is trying to help me get better."	Think, "Take in the good information."
1. Your challenge:				
2. Your challenge:				

they trying to accomplish? Now, most importantly, what could you do or what could you think about that would help you get more out of the situation in terms of it contributing to your performance? It can be helpful to think about or even write down your potential responses.

YOUR PARENTS' EXPECTATIONS VS. YOUR CORE MOTIVATIONS

We all think about what the significant others in our life hope for and expect for us in our performance world. The expectations of parents or family can have a very positive impact or a negative one. It is up to us to be aware of these issues and work with them in a proactive way.

Jack was a collegiate men's hockey player. He was so obviously talented that he was drafted by the NHL even before attending college. He was kept on a retainer, with the expectation that he would be fast-tracked to the professional level once he graduated from college. Jack was quite successful throughout his collegiate career, but found himself sitting on the bench his junior year of college. Having been a very successful athlete since the age of four, sitting on the bench was a very unfamiliar and embarrassing experience for Jack. The hardest part of the situation was that Jack's brother already played in the NHL and his father fully expected that Jack would follow in his brother's footsteps.

Jack's dad lived about a five-hour drive away from campus, but would loyally show up for every one of Jack's games. After each game, Jack became more intensely frustrated and embarrassed. In our sessions, Jack would note that his father was darkly silent after each game. Jack felt that his father was so profoundly embarrassed of Jack's being left on the bench, with no ice time, that his father couldn't speak.

This scenario went on for about two months. Jack was short-tempered, had stopped talking with friends, and was on the brink of being left by his long-time girlfriend. The hardest part of sitting on the bench for Jack was the game-by-game disappointment of his father. I encouraged Jack to talk directly with his father, to find out what his dad was really thinking. With great trepidation Jack talked with his father.

With great emotion, his father told him that it broke his heart to see Jack so upset and that he didn't say anything after the game because he didn't want to further upset Jack. He told Jack that it didn't matter to him if he continued playing after college; he just wanted Jack to be happy. Though Jack didn't play in a game until the end of the season, his attitude radically changed. Once he knew that his father was with him, regardless of his performance on the ice, he was able to tolerate not being played. He then was freed up to begin focusing on actually improving his skills on the ice to regain playing time (which he did). In this instance, the challenge was Jack's speculation as to what his father might think of him riding the bench.

Notice that again, we are coming back to understanding the intentions of others. Just as Sarah had to consciously consider her coach's intentions, Jack had to realize that he did *not* know what his father was thinking. When he finally got the courage to ask, he found that he had been misreading his father. Instead of disappointment and thwarted expectations, his father held only hopes for his son's happiness.

Sometimes, of course, parents or other relatives are not simply content hoping for our happiness. Sometimes they have intrusive or inappropriate expectations for us. What do we do then?

An extreme example of this was Nicole, a young swimmer with whom I worked, who was demonstrating a significant anxiety response to racing. She was doing a lot of crying at night, before practice and after. Her grades were slipping at school and her times were beginning to slow down in the water. Nicole's mother contacted me to work with her daughter. She was very concerned about her daughter's significant signs of anxiety and simply didn't understand why Nicole was feeling so much pressure. Nicole's mother said that she was not pushing Nicole and that she "just want[ed] Nicole to be happy!"

Within a few minutes of our first sport psychology session, the reasons for Nicole's high anxiety became readily apparent. As I often do toward the beginning of my work with performers, I asked Nicole to talk about what was happening in her mind before and during competition. Because her mother reported that Nicole was very anxious before meets, I asked her to tell me a specific instance when she felt the most competitive pressure. Nicole told me about a time recently when she was trying to make the cuts for the next national championship races. She said that her mother had volunteered to help keep track of the times that the swimmers raced. Her mother would stand next to the pool, keep track with a stopwatch, and record the times that all the swimmers got, including Nicole.

Nicole's mother had told her just before she raced, "Don't worry about your time. I've got the stop watch and I'll make sure to stop it before the cut-off time. No matter what time you race, you'll make the cut." Nicole's mother was overtly cheating to make sure that her daughter had "success" in the water. She thought by stopping the stopwatch early, and telling Nicole about her plan, that Nicole would be relieved of the pressure she was feeling. Her actions had the opposite impact. Though this is an extreme example, others in our lives can become over-involved in our desire for success.

Some of those close to us have so much invested in our success that they themselves totally lose perspective. How can we keep connected to our positive feelings and give the effort required when a close family member is acting like Nicole's mother? In addition to creating confusion and upset in our minds, others' over-involvement can lead to a heightened sense of an I-must-be-successful-or-I'm-worthless attitude.

Stories like this indicate why it is imperative that we become clear on what is truly important to ourselves, regardless of how others evaluate our success or progress. When we are able to fully reclaim the value of pursuing our goals for our own reasons, regardless of what others think, we can greatly reduce the pressure we feel from the expectations of others.

In my work with Nicole, just as with Sarah and with Jack, we first worked on the question her mother's intention. What was her mother thinking? Why had she done this? It took some time for Nicole to see that her mother truly had good intentions. Her mother was willing to cheat the system because she so much wanted Nicole to have success. Her mother was trying to reduce the pressure that Nicole felt to make the next cut for performance. Clearly, however, there are ethical issues that need to be addressed here—yet the core of the motivation of Nicole's mother was the love that she felt for her daughter. In realizing that her mother had developed a misguided plan because of her desire to lower Nicole's anxiety, Nicole was able to put this behind her.

This was not enough, however. Any time a parent is too strongly focused on their child's success, there is another important step to take. The performer has to get back in touch with his or her own motivations. I helped Nicole focus on the reasons that she swam and wanted to do well. I worked with her to separate her core values from the desires and expectations of her mother.

We must all keep our attention on why being part of our performance realm is important to us, regardless of what others think (or what we may guess that they are thinking) to prepare ourselves to perform our best. Nicole had to move away from thinking about a mother who wanted her to perform so badly that the mother cheated. Jack had to move away from thinking about a father who he thought was so disappointed in him. To optimize their performance they had to get back in touch with the reasons that participation in the performance realm had aligned with their own interests and souls in the first place. We all must do this. The more we value what we want as opposed to what others want, the more we are freed to do our thing when the pressure is on.

If it is relevant to you, consider a person who you may feel pressured by to perform well. Note the situation and consider what is important to them. Now, most importantly, consider what you value, your intentions, and your purpose for training and competing. What is a phrase or word that can remind you of why training in this domain matters to you? Take a moment to write it down or to make a mental note of your thoughts.

Consider developing a phrase or word that would help you accept their values and focus more on putting more value on why it is important to you.

Exercise 9.2. Clarifying your reasons for competing/performing

Situation	Their values	What I want/value	Mental reminder/ cue word of my value	Acceptance of "their" values (cue word)
e.g., Try out for a leading symphony orchestra	Husband and teacher want me to make the orchestra because…	To play the clarinet to the best of my ability. To enjoy creating music	"Create and live"	"They just want the best for me."
Your situation:				

FRIENDS AND TEAMMATES

Your go-to person – When I was on my first U.S. national rowing team I was wildly delighted. I felt like I had been given a gift and that every day was energizing. As the days and months went on, however, I began to feel more and more pressure to continue making the U.S. team and to make the next Olympic team. As my ability to be present to my love for rowing dwindled and my fear escalated, I had no idea of what to do with these emotions. I was not wise in terms of with whom I shared my fears. I was keenly aware of what I was feeling, but was not thoughtful as to with whom I could and could not share my intense feelings of fear. I wasn't aware of who could really help me and who might just help strengthen my fears and negative feelings.

Sometimes, when feeling particularly fearful or anxious, I would talk with a teammate who would quickly dismiss me and scoff at my feelings. This just made me feel worse and mentally weaker. I did not always understand how to move toward relationships that were safe, nurturing, and kind. Yet, when we are pushing ourselves to the edge, trying to reach a peak of performance, we all deeply need such social support.

It is important to be able to choose our confidants wisely, particularly in the competitive world where we are expected to be strong and powerful in all ways. It is essential to have at least one person with whom you can share your moments of fear, weakness, and failures. It is also essential to have some-one with whom you can safely share your long-terms performance goals and intentions. Ideally, this is a person who loves you and cares about you, regard-less of how well you have performed lately. It is important that this person is supportive of your performance vision and goals. Such support can come in unexpected forms. You may have a dear friend who gives you a sense of being loved and cared for. There may be someone who is not a best friend but who nevertheless makes you feel safe and supported.

It is important to know who that go-to person is before you get pulled into a negative emotional vortex. Dr. Steve Durant, a well-respected Boston-based psychologist who works with troubled boys, introduced me to the idea of a *go-to person.* We all just need one. Take a moment to think of a person who you can truly trust. Who is someone that can listen to you wholly without judgment? Who might be someone in your life that respects you, regardless of what you accomplish or don't? Just bringing to your awareness who is actually there for you can be a wonderful contribution to your sense of connection and well-being.

Your go-to person can be a critical resource in tough times. For example, if you begin noticing that you feel burned out and uncaring toward practice, you may want to be cautious with whom you share this information. Telling all of your teammates may be unwise. Telling no one is unwise. Telling a trusted mature player who could understand and help you make good choices to get out of the negative spiral may be the best choice. Or, if you have decided that you want to become a nationally competitive elite athlete, you may again want to consider with whom you share this information.

As social beings, we can be quite reactive to the opinions and judgments of others. We can become easily hurt by important others. We also can be buoyed, inspired, or experience joy through our connections with others. We need to know when we can tolerate others' harshness and judgment and when it works best to keep our more personal issues private. We need to know with whom we can celebrate our successes with an open heart and love.

We are emotional beings and our emotions have a significant impact on how hard we push, where we commit our energy, and how long we are willing to try. We must be able to check in and see how well we are able to focus, how we are feeling emotionally, and how energized our bodies feel in practice and performance. We also must be able to check in to see how our social relationships are working both within a team setting and within our normal social lives. We must know how we feel around others and respond to them, in order to make good, healthy choices about with whom we spend time and what we share with them.

Clarify what you have to give to others – Being a source of support to others can contribute to a team's or group's performance. It is important to consider what is being asked of you and to also ask yourself what you have to give. I worked with Betsy, the team captain for a women's collegiate softball team. Betsy struck me as a steady, confident, and upbeat person. Her challenge was not her own attitude or performance. Her main challenge was the chronic demand of her teammates to support them. She had a winter training camp coming up and Betsy was concerned about the high demand that she would be under to support her teammates.

She felt like being around her teammates drained her energy, and she wanted to figure out a strategy to deal with this challenge. Most of her teammates would come to her for support. Though she liked this role, it could become too much in a training camp environment. We came up with a strategy, which turned out to be very helpful to her. She said that when a teammate needed her, she would be there to support her no matter what. However, she thought that often they just *wanted* her attention. Though in such instances it was helpful to them to talk with her, they really didn't need her.

Her strategy was simple. If they needed her, she would talk with them. If they wanted her attention, she would only give her attention to them if she wanted to do so (if she didn't feel like it, she wouldn't). Betsy had a good sense of the difference between being needed or wanted. She used her judgment. Essentially she would talk with a teammate initially, no matter what. But if it appeared to be a re-hash of the same complaints with low emotional charge, she would give herself the option to leave the conversation. In fact she had pre-planned strategies to leave the conversations that were draining to her in which she could give no good. With this strategy, Betsy was able to help her teammates get the most out of training camp while also protecting her own energy.

Negative feelings about teammates: How empathy can help – When we are fully engaged in our performance lives, we can tend to become focused on our own goals, progress, and day-to-day struggles. When teammates or those with whom we work are frustrating us, it is really easy to identify a character flaw in the other—and so starts a negative social spiral. We become so self-focused that we can forget that everyone else has a history and reasons that lead them to act in particular ways.

It can be quite difficult in the performance realm to be tolerant of others when they are not trying as hard or giving as much you think that they should. Coping with an under-performing or under-committed colleague or teammate can become a great source of irritation and distraction from your need to focus on continuing to learn and be competitive in your own performance realm. Essentially, it can be very difficult to cope with others who have attitudes and values that clash with your own.

When I was on an America's Cup sailing team in 1995, I found myself in an extremely frustrating situation. During that year on the team, for the first eight months, we spent about 14 hours every day preparing for our series of races. We would show up at 6:30 a.m. sharp to do 30 minutes of push-ups, sit-ups, and stretching. We would then spend from 7:00 to 8:15 a.m. lifting weights and/or doing intense fitness exercises. After a quick breakfast, we were out loading the boats and then sailing until the sun went down. And then, usually late into the evening, we were cleaning, scrubbing, and fixing things for the boat.

I had a teammate who had become good friends with the coaching staff and was allowed many absences from our morning strength and fitness training sessions. Rumors abounded of her absences. I never knew where she was, but I did know that she skipped practices that would have made her more fit and stronger. We shared a position of *grinding* on the boat, which is an intensely physically demanding job. I was highly irritated that she wasn't training as hard as I was, yet I had to rely on her when we went out to race.

For those who don't know much about America's Cup sailing (which I knew nothing of before I joined the team), the grinders provide the physical power for the boat. We turn handles that look much like bicycle pedals which are made for our hands. The faster we spin the handles, at higher gears, the more power we generate. As we spin the handles we generate power on gear-connected drums (winches). The power from those winches is used to pull sails or people (to fix things at the top) up the 100-foot mast or to pull sails from side to side on the boat.

As grinders, our sole role on the team was to provide physical strength to handle the heaviest physical demands of the boat. To have a teammate who was consistently skipping morning training was infuriating. The logic was simple to me: She would not be as strong as she could be because of the lack of training, which simply left more hard work to the rest of us.

I found myself feeling angry whenever I was with her, which was all day long. I often shared the same winch handles with her. I was filled with judgment and frustration. How could she be so lazy? How could she take such advantage of the situation?

I, luckily, had the chance to work with Terry Orlick, our team's sport psychologist. He was incredibly helpful. He asked me a few questions that significantly changed my attitude. He asked things like, "Is it possible that she is doing the best she can with the situation?" Note that we began physical training at 6:30 a.m. and often did not get home from the compound until 8, 9, or 10 p.m. (and sometimes later). Terry also asked me, "What is happening to your performance when you pay attention to what she is doing?" These two questions were quite profound to my thinking. I realized in my conversation with Terry that my teammate may have been doing all that she could to survive. I also realized that my negative attention on where she came up short (my opinion only, of course) was hurting my own performance.

If I had begun with considering my teammate's perspective, I may have avoided much anger and frustration. I spent precious little time thinking about how she might think and feel about being on the team. I thought nothing of what she might value. I did not consider how difficult it might have been for her to be on the team. I never considered what her habits or values were before she joined the group. I also never knew where she was or what she was doing. I made up a great frustration in my head without, first, considering where she was coming from. The idea of empathy, understanding or feeling what another feels, was lacking in my self-focused approach to training. And what a lonely, distracting approach to training I employed!

Whether our frustrations or judgments are about a teammate's abilities, training habits, attitude, or values, it can be helpful to ask ourselves some basic questions to begin considering building a sense of perspective and empathy. With this approach, we can minimize the negative impact of others who have a different style, approach, or values than that or those of our own. Here are a few key questions to ask yourself:

- Is it possible that they are doing the best that they can with what they know?

- How is my attention on their "faults" impacting my own performance?

- How might my performance improve if I focus on what they are contributing or on the good of others around me?

- What is good about them, just as they are?

- How are they already contributing, even in the smallest way?

- How might they be feeling in this situation?

- Who around me is a positive contributor? An inspiration? Who would I like to become more like? Who can I spend more time with?

Though these questions will not automatically manifest a change in the situation or in your relationship with the difficult other, they can help you quickly take the focus off of what is wrong with the other that you cannot control. And more importantly, get your attention onto what is right.

As you shift your attention to what is already good about them and to what they already contribute in a positive way, the negativity will begin to abate and you will be able to bring your focus back to your own training. When you concurrently focus on the good of others around you, when you consider who does inspire you and make an effort to focus attention on them or spend more time with them, your negativity will continue to dissipate and your positive emotions will strengthen. The goal is to do whatever can help you with your performance. As you strengthen the positive relationships in your performance world and minimize the impact of the negative ones, you will be able to pay more attention to training and performance. You will also be less stressed and more at ease.

NURTURING POSITIVE RELATIONSHIPS

One of the essential components of happiness is nurturing positive, life-enhancing relationships. We need to allow ourselves to be drawn to people who will bring out the best in us, who will support us when we need it, and who will also be open to our love and support. There are times that a colleague, teammate, or relative can be toxic. They may thrive off of anger, meanness, or power. We need to be able to recognize these situations and keep ourselves safe. We don't necessarily have to end the relationships and, many times in fact, we cannot.

We must figure out a way to disallow the negativity, meanness, or jealousy from impacting our souls and our lives. We have to know when it is sage to rely upon others and in what ways it is no longer productive, safe, or nurturing to our souls. We must also be aware of those around us who are committed to helping us thrive. We need to remain open to those who will help us with our sport (performance realm) information, emotions, and even finances. The help can come in unexpected places and it is important that we keep our antennas up for such help and benevolence. We must know who we can turn to, to help both buoy us when we are down and to celebrate when things go well.

We must, at the core, be honest with ourselves in terms of who authentically supports and believes in us. It may or may not be our teacher or coach. It may or may not be our best friend. It may or may not be a teammate. It is important to be fully aware of who we feel good with, who we feel safe with, and who we do not feel safe with. We can train and perform with almost anyone.

We need to keep our attention on what is good in others and be willing to take in that good. We also need to be able to reach out and help our teammates, family, and friends when we have the resources to do so. We need to trust ourselves to say "yes" when it works, and "no" when it doesn't in our interactions with others.

10

Imagery and Scripting for Performance

Creating Your Intentions for Performance

"I raced in my head before I raced. After a while, I just believed that I could beat these people out of sheer mental thought."
—Olympic rower (preparing for team selection)

Sport psychologists have found that for athletes facing a high-stakes performance, it is useful to use mental imagery to help shape the outcome. The performer creates a mental picture or image and rehearses it consistently, and this supports their efforts to achieve a certain performance outcome. Long before I had read any of the research on imagery, I discovered its usefulness in a high-stress situation.

My unexpected introduction to using imagery occurred in Los Angeles at a try-out for the American Gladiator television show. One of my dear friends, Siren, was one of the core female American Gladiator personalities. She and her manager strongly encouraged me to come and try out as a contender.

They thought I'd make the show and that it would be fun to be together during the week of filming in L.A.

I stood in a line with hundreds of people to have my shot at being in the show. I was vying against about 500 other women for one of about a dozen spots on the show. I had just finished a year on the America's Cup sailing team and I had never been more fit or strong. I had been a grinder—one of the people that generated the power to pull sails and people up a 100-foot mast and provided the power to pull the sails back and forth on tacks and jibes. After grinding for a year, I was in tremendous physical condition and thought that I would have a good chance to become a contender on the American Gladiator show.

I began the series of physical tasks without a hitch. I did my pull-ups (you had to do at least seven). And then it got hard. I next barely made the cut-off time for the 40-meter dash. The next task was the rope climb. Actually, I had never tried it before, but as a sailor, I thought that I should be able to climb the rope. I had to climb about 15 feet of rope in under 10 seconds. I started, struggled, and made it to the top. I came down and was told, *"Nice try, you just missed the cut-off time. You should come back and try next year … Next!"*

I hesitated, wondering what to do, and I decided to get right back in line. I was determined to figure out a way to get through the rope climb. As I scanned my mind for ways to make it up that rope, I began asking others around me the best way to climb. I was told to use both my arms and my feet. You reach as high as you can with your hands and hold tight. You next grip the rope with your feet with your knees bent. You can then push your legs straight up. With this process you rely on your legs more than your arms. I quickly got the idea, but the next step was getting my mind and body coordinated to do the motion.

I had never tried imagery before, but thought that this was a good time to at least try it. I was still in the moving line of auditioners, so I closed my eyes as much as I could. Almost all of my attention was on the image I was trying to create. At first my body felt incredibly heavy in my imagination. So I shifted to seeing myself as a cartoon character. With this image shift, my body was super light and could do anything. I still had a hard time in my mind's eye co-ordinating the movement of my body, even in my mental cartoon land where my body felt weightless. Finally, in my imagination, I was able to visualize the motion of climbing up the rope quickly.

My turn finally came around again. This time, I repeated the pull-ups and the timed run with success. And then, I was onto the rope climb. It felt light and easy. I climbed swiftly. When I came down the rope, the timer said, *"Hey, great. That was the fastest time of the day so far!"*

So how did the tryouts go this time around? I was not selected. Stand-ing almost 6-feet tall and having significant muscle density from my years of rowing and sailing, the producers said I would not look right on camera with their gladiators. I would tower over them. My good friend Siren was only 5-feet, 7-inches. So I didn't get the Gladiator gig, but I did learn first-hand the tremendous power of imagery. After this experience, I became a believer in the power of visualization, and I've used it successfully with many clients over the past 15 years.

Imagery is a powerful and under-used skill. Imagery, also referred to as *visualization* or *mental rehearsal,* is a way to use your imagination to mentally practice in advance what you'd like to create or manifest. It really is amazing how powerful just a few moments, daily, of imagining how you'd like to feel can be. Visualizing how you'd like your performance to end up, and how you'd like to feel in the process of training and performance, can actually help you get there. Imagery is a practical way to help support you in your quest to create whatever you intend to manifest.

A great example is how two-time Olympic and three-time World Cham-pion medalist rower (I'll refer to him as Zack) used imagery in his daily train-ing. In the instance below he talks about how he used imagery to improve his overall rowing technique, which is essential to moving the boat fast. As you would guess, the more efficiently you row, the faster you go. Zach used environmental cues to remind himself to practice his imagery. He recalls, "I tried to study different rowing techniques or just a body angle that I liked and similar to what the coach wanted me to get to. I would get a picture of that next to my bed or somewhere where I could see it, like at work. I could close my eyes and think about my body in that position."

Zach's example is about much more than a momentary daydream imagining himself performing well. (Though momentary daydreams of yourself performing well are great! If these are happening, allow them to keep flowing.) He was methodically and purposefully practicing mentally how he would like to perform in the future. By having an external prompt to get himself to practice it, he was able to integrate his imagery practice throughout his day. He was purposefully filling his mind with how he would ideally like to row in terms of the ideal, repetitive motion. Zach was purposefully helping himself through imagery practice to manifest his ability to row technically well.

Another Olympian from one of my studies (I'll refer to her as Grace) recalls how she used imagery to help her make the Olympic team. Grace envisioned herself beating her opponents the week leading up to the selection for the Olympic team. She notes that trying to do your best is not enough. First, you need to see (visualize, imagine, mentally rehearse) doing your best. Grace recalls,

> I really wanted to make that Olympic team. I did a lot of visualization that week, for the most part seeing myself winning. And I took care of myself really well physically, too, in terms of nutrition and a lot of food. I definitely remember seeing myself doing everything perfect. Not just going out there and just trying to do things perfect[ly]. I tried to race in my head before I raced. After a while, I just believed that I could beat these people out of sheer mental thought.

In this segment above, Grace points out that going out and trying to do your best isn't enough. For her, she had to see it, first, in her imagination, through visualization. Once she saw herself competing the way that she ideally wanted to—and doing so repeatedly—she believed that what she saw was possible. Her belief in what she created in her visualization became a powerful source of confidence.

Using imagery can, practically speaking, mean putting forth very little additional effort with huge potential impact. (Of course, working hard is a baseline requirement to optimizing performance and performing in the sweet spot.) You can use imagery for changes in the implementation of any future movement, skill, strategy, thought process, or even emotional response. There is plenty of evidence from the research that imagery is an effective mental skill including a comprehensive review of imagery research done by Deborah L. Feltz and Daniel M. Landers and strongly supported in Tony Morris, Michael Spittle, and Anthony P. Watt's book *Imagery in Sport.*

The question is, "What is most helpful for you to imagine as you prepare for performance?" The purpose of this chapter is to help you to plan to use imagery for key aspects of preparing for performance. What will best serve you in your effort to take radically positive steps in your ability to perform? It's particularly important to build awareness of how you are already using imagery (to your benefit or possibly not) and keying on new places to use imagery in support of your goals.

I have come to three basic conclusions about imagery in terms of helping people get ready to perform. Most seasoned performers

- have already developed excellent imagery skills (even if they don't use them on purpose),

- sometimes unconsciously use imagery in negative ways, and

- have aspects of preparing for performance that could greatly benefit from productive imagery use.

Often, seasoned performers use imagery for some aspects of performance, but still miss out on key opportunities to further improve their ability to perform. They may use imagery to practice skills for the next logical step in their preparation (e.g., a basketball player may use imagery to execute a new way to follow through on her free throw shot). They may also use imagery to practice performing the way that they expect to be able to perform. Given their training and habituated response to performance, they imagine their performance going optimally, given the constraints of what they believe is possible for their next performance. Surprisingly, seasoned performers and novices as well may sometimes use imagery in a negative way: involuntarily, negative imagery in the form in nightmares—or *daymares* will arise. These can include images of how they fear their next big competition or performance will go.

The sections of this chapter will help you to become aware of

- when you are using imagery in ways that are hurting your performance so that you can put an end to this,

- when you are using imagery to your benefit, and

- other aspects of your training and performance that could benefit from imagery use.

And once the awareness is developed, you can then create imagery scripts to help you create the change that you would like.

BUILDING AWARENESS OF THE NEGATIVE USES OF IMAGERY

A first place to start is to consider how you may already be using imagery in daydreams or waking nightmares that may, in fact, hurt your performance. I have spoken with many athletes over the past 15 years who have unknowingly strengthened negative performance patterns by allowing their imaginations to run amok by picturing negative outcomes as they were preparing for high-pressure competition. They didn't know to stop these waking nightmares and to purposefully shift their minds to a more constructive focus.

I worked with Joe, a collegiate ice hockey player, who was committed to playing professional hockey after college. Joe was a highly talented hard worker who had been playing hockey since the age of four and came from a hockey family. Joe seemed to have it all, except for one major problem—Joe hated try-outs. Joe was so talented that this fear never got in his way of being able to make top teams up to this point in his career. However, as Joe was facing graduation shortly, try-outs for professional teams kicked his old fear patterns into high gear.

And his waking nightmares returned. His mind was filled with images of coaches yelling at him and criticizing his ability to play hockey. He would see old high school and league coaches criticizing him. He also imagined the coaches for whom he would be trying out being critical of the weaker parts of his game (which were actually quite strong). He visualized them criticizing him, too. He imagined being cut. He imagined feeling humiliated. Joe was using his incredible ability to visualize to actually strengthen his fears. As he talked about this, Joe became progressively more anxious and physically tense.

I asked Joe to talk about a time when a coach was highly supportive of him. Joe had to go back to the age of about 10 years old. He recalled a coach who was tough, but always believed in him. He recalled a specific time when the coach praised him for his talent and potential. The coach praised him about a specific difficult move that he had made. As he spoke, Joe's entire body relaxed. It appeared that he shifted into a confident, at-ease state. Joe had developed the ability to bring up very clear, detailed images that powerfully impacted his emotional system. He had used his imagery skills up to this point only to his detriment.

From this point forward in the intervention, we began to put to use these well-honed skills. Together, Joe and I developed a script for what would most benefit him in preparation for the try-outs. He imagined how he wanted to skate, what he wanted to focus on, and how he wanted to feel physically. For Joe, the plan was to become aware of when his waking nightmares started, and then to purposefully shift his attention to bringing up images of him skating at a try-out just the way that he would ideally like to do.

When do you have negative images flood through your imagination? You may not have these *daymares* (and if you've never had them, you are quite lucky). You may never have seen such specific images as Joe. However, some people do experience the emotional-physical aspect of daymares without the visual images. You may have felt dread in anticipation of performance, with vague feelings of physical discomfort and anxiety.

It can be very helpful to become aware of your daymares or related feelings. You can use them as a reminder to get refocused on thoughts and images that will actually help you with your performance. You can use these imagery skills to your advantage. To put your imagery skills to use takes awareness of what is happening and a plan to replace these unhelpful images with more empowering or supportive images.

Later in the chapter, I will give you the best of what I have given to other high level performers to help you develop a script or two that will serve your performance needs. You can begin thinking about moments when you have random images of performing that would, in fact, hurt your performance. I remember that while I was preparing for the Olympic team I would have fantastic and crazy dreams. I would dream that I was racing in a boat that was made of material like an air mattress (instead of the sturdy, light resin of an actual racing boat). I would race and my boat would pop. In some images, the course I raced on would become extremely narrow and windy or would literally dry up.

At the time, I laughed at these visions, though secretly I felt great fear. If I had been prompted to think about it, I, too, could have used this great imagery skill to my advantage. I could have used these images as a prompt to purposefully bring up confident, focused, empowered images of racing successfully. If you have negative, unwelcome images, don't worry! It means you have good imaging abilities and that you can learn to harness these powerful skills and use them to your advantage.

PREPARING FOR PREDICTABLE CHALLENGING MOMENTS USING IMAGERY

A great example of learning how to use imagery to shift from a fear state to one of powerful presence is represented by Dawn Moore, who used imagery when performing in her own band, Random, and as a backup vocalist for tours with major artists in Tokyo. In an interview I conducted with her, she was able to talk clearly about her frequent experience of having significant fear just before performing and how she consciously and purposefully used imagery to combat that fear and strengthen her confidence. She used imagery to get herself into a state of mind that would allow her to do her thing, night after night. This is what she had to say:

> Sometimes, I would go through the songs in my head and imagine the performance going well and remembering all the lyrics. I focused on the story I was trying to tell to the audience. And then I would try to take on a personality that was bigger than myself to get through it. She was fierce. She had perfect pitch. She was strong and beautiful and powerful and in control of the performance, the stage, the audience. They would melt when she appeared. I would try to feel that I was that person. I had so many insecurities that I didn't want to come out on stage.

Dawn used her imagery to overcome her normal, human insecurities before going on stage. She needed to put her fears and worries aside and draw on the best of what she had in order to consistently be able to do her thing well.

It is invaluable to plan for the times that are predictably challenging. Everyone has a moment in performance that is, predictably, their hardest. In performance, we must bail ourselves out. It would be heaven to be able to turn to someone outside ourselves to help us get through, but there are times in performance when no one can be there to help us. We all have a great power inside of us that we can rely upon when things get tough. We all have a unique bundle of strengths on which we can draw. It is really important to notice what these are and how to use them so that we don't have to hit the wall. That's where the planning comes in.

Consider the mile runner. She may be doing fine until she is going into her third (of four) laps on the track. At some point in the race she may hit a strong urge to stop or to stop pushing so hard. Her mind may be telling her that she can't make her time, can't go on, and her body just can't respond to what is being asked of it. She may have powerful feelings that she wants to quit, doesn't care, or just wants to walk it in. At this point, her mother on the sidelines cannot pull the runner into a psychologically strong state of mind. Her coach cannot do it for her. Their words could be helpful, but the runner must be able to draw on her own internal strengths to keep going, to keep pushing. The trick for all of us is to have a plan before such predictably hard moments arise.

Consider for a moment a few of your most predictable hard points in performance. For a musician, it may be hitting a wrong note. For a marathoner, it may be having someone pass you in a race. It may be when the lactic acid builds up and you are in physical pain. It may be after you get knocked down or miss a basket. It may be when you lose a tennis game. With only a moment of consideration, most of us know when we feel weak or irritated in training or practice.

What are your tough spots? Take a moment to note the situation in Exercise 10.1 below. Describe briefly what it is like. Next, if you could put reality to the side, how would you like to respond to that same situation? If you could wave your magic wand, how would you like it to be? As you begin getting a sense of how you would like to respond, you can begin to think about creating an imagery script that would support this change in response to the same situation.

Exercise 10.1. Predictably hard moments—A new place to use imagery

Situations	What's it like?	Wave a magic wand: How would you like it to be?
e.g., Being passed in a race.	I want to give up.	I become determined.
1.		
2.		
3.		

BUILDING AWARENESS: WHERE ELSE CAN I USE IMAGERY?

Being aware of your most challenging moments is a great place to consider where you could put imagery to work (more later on how to create scripts to help you do this). Yet, I am guessing that there are other key places in your performance that you would not even consider using imagery, but where it could be very helpful. These are the spots that you consider as just the way you play or just a weakness that you have. You may accept being limited in particular aspects of your performance realm that you may not yet have considered working on to improve. You may have decided you're just not good at *that*. Well, you might be able to be good at *that*—if you work on it.

The challenge and key to using imagery effectively and powerfully is to go beyond how you already use imagery or the more obvious places that you could use it. It is important to take stock of what you are doing so you can see your new opportunities to use this skill. For a moment, review in your mind how you use imagery. You may not use it at all or you may have already developed some specific areas of focus for your imagery practice. Pause to consider if and when you use it.

Now, the next question is, "How else could you use imagery to your advantage?" You may ask, "Wouldn't it be obvious where I need to use imagery?" Not necessarily. We become so used to how we do things, it can take some work to see your own life or your own training through a fresh perspective in order to see alternative ways to use this skill. For example, I recently worked with Brad, a nationally recognized golfer. When teeing off, he has an excellent long game. Yet he lacks consistency in his putting and short shots from the fairway to the hole.

I asked if he could imagine preparing for a teeing off on a difficult course. Without hesitation he nodded yes. He had imagined himself successfully having the ball land, just where he wants it to go. In an instant, he could imagine all that went into taking this shot. When I asked him to describe it, he said, "I can just feel where the ball will go before I take the shot." I asked him to tell me what went into feeling the ball go just where he wanted it to go. I asked if he had thought about it. Brad hesitated before responding.

He said, "I never really think about it [how he took his successful long shots], I just do it." But with some reflection, he realized that he actually does take into consideration the specifics that will impact his shot. He has just learned to do this automatically. He takes into consideration the shape of the terrain, the distance to the hole, the wind direction and speed, and the temperature. After considering all of this, he reflects, "I notice where I do want to put the ball. I choose the shot that gives me the best chance of getting the ball to do what I want it to do."

With a little prompting, Brad is very clear on what it takes for him to hit a good shot off of the tee. He has been using his imagery skills every day as he feels where he wants the ball to go for his long game. With this clarity, I figured that Brad would be able to make the leap directly to his short game. I figured that he would be able to see the connection between what he already does incredibly well and transfer this to his short shots and putts as he approached the green.

No go. I was totally wrong. Here is how the conversation went. I said, "OK, great! Now how does this work for your short game?" Dead silence. Brad had never considered using these incredibly well-honed skills for his short game. He had never thought about how to transfer this skill, though he was known for his tee-shots and had extraordinary confidence in his imagery skills for that aspect of his game. With this insight, a radical and positive shift in Brad's game became possible.

He gained new knowledge of how to use imagery to help improve his short game. He already had carefully honed imagery skills. Yet he had never put it all together. From this point, we developed an imagery script so he could practice his short game and plan how to think to give himself the best chance to put the ball where he wanted it to go.

In your quest to prepare for performance, I am guessing that you already have some solid imagery skills. The question is, "Where can imagery best serve to help you prepare for the big moments?" As we prepare to create an imagery script for you, it will be helpful for you to start with either an example of how you already use imagery or call up aspects of your performance that represent your strengths in motion (like Brad's long game). It could be some aspect of how you practice or how you perform. If you already use imagery, jot down the different aspects of your image—thoughts (internal or external), emotions, and physical experience. If this is new to you, consider a time that you felt most confident, recall a time (or a few times) that represents your strength in motion. Take a moment to imagine it in your mind's eye. What words describe the focus? Describe where your attention is focused and how you body feels. How do you feel emotionally? Take a few minutes to fill out the chart in Exercise 10.2.

Scripting for Success—for YOU

After you've considered a place that you already use imagery or the strongest part of your performance, consider a place that you would like to work on. Where else might you put scripting to use in your game or practice? It could be a part of your performance that is most frustrating to you. It could be a place that you've never thought you could change (like the golfer's short game). Or it could simply be practicing strengthening what you already do well.

Exercise 10.2. You at your best

Specific situation	External thoughts and focus	Internal thoughts and focus	Physical feeling	Emotion(s)
e.g., Teeing off	I consider the win and shape of the course.	Point of swing & follow through	Perfect plant of leg	At ease; confident

One way to start is to consider what you might like to talk with a performance psychologist about. You can also take a look at the previous exercises to get ideas. Once you've come up with a part of training or performance to work on, I ask that you imagine how it would look and feel if you were able to perform just as you would ideally like to perform. Don't think about how you usually perform. Consider how you would look, feel and think at your best.

If you can, in your imagination, try just for a moment to see yourself performing with the change. Imagine performing ideally: What would you be thinking, feeling and how would you be responding? Take a few minutes and come up with words that could help elicit this image. Reconsider your strengths or previous imagery practice. What ideas can you take from those to also use on the aspect of performance that you'd like to improve or strengthen?

I have been using a modified form of imagery scripts with hundreds of athletes over the past 15 years that I call scripting. In addition to considering all of the senses (what you see, smell, feel, taste, and your physical movement), I have found that adding what you would like to emotionally feel is essential to creating effective scripts. I learned this the hard way as a young sport psychologist.

I worked with a lacrosse goalie, Chris, who would become angrier with every shot on goal made against her. As her anger increased, she would hit the goal posts, the ground and eventually her own body with her stick. Chris came to me so I could help her with this angry response. Her legs were literally covered with bruises. In my youthful confidence, I decided that imagery practice would be the best intervention for her. After our first session, I sent her off to visualize herself every night. I asked her to make a few saves and then miss a block. When she went to retrieve the ball she was to tell herself what she could improve on next time, pass the ball back, and start fresh. She was to repeat this 10 times in her mind every night.

The poor goalie dutifully showed by up a week later, exhausted. I asked how she was doing. She said she couldn't sleep! The imagery practice made her so mad and agitated that she had a hard time sleeping all week.

I had missed something vital (which most interventions in imagery practice miss as well). To be effective, you must incorporate how you emotionally want to feel, not how you usually feel (unless that is just how you *want* to feel!). So how did I help our goalie modify her angry response to being scored against? I asked her in our next session when she feels most relaxed. She said, "In the shower." So we incorporated the shower into her imagery sessions.

I had her repeat the same imagery practice with one significant change. After she got scored against, I had her immediately go to the shower (in her imagination only). Once she was calmed down, she took the ball out of the back of the goal, noticed how she could block the ball better next time, and passed the ball out to play again with a fresh start. After this added dimension to the imagery practice (and lots of hard mental practice on her part to change her habituated harsh self-evaluation and to focus on simply how to improve), this young goalie was eventually able to control her temper on the field. By learning to move away from self-judgment to accepting mistakes and learning from them, her negative emotional reactions were reduced. The shower was essential in her imagery practice because she learned how to be at ease in the face of mistakes on the field. She learned to nudge herself back into training in the sweet spot. And most importantly, she stopped bruising herself with her lacrosse stick.

Scripting includes all of the senses and emotions. But how do you create your own script? I have found it most helpful to have the performers start with a few best past performances to be able to have access to emotions, thoughts, and points of focus that will help them create in their minds, their ideal performances, and thereby their script. I ask you to take a few moments to consider on which part of your performance that you would like to focus. This is where you are the only one who knows what is most compelling to you. I've successfully had performers create scripts for *before* competition, for *during* competition, and for coaches about how they wanted to *be* in practice and during game day. For the script, I encourage you to pick an aspect of performance that is most compelling for you to focus on. Where could you use the most help or inspiration? But to get going it can be helpful to think how you'd like to be both before you perform (a few hours before) and how you'd like to perform during performance.

In whatever aspect of performance you choose for the script, consider the following in Exercise 10.3. What would you like to be thinking about? What would you like to be feeling? How would you like your body to be feeling? In this reflection, you want to make sure that you also consider the emotions that you were feeling. You can jot down some of your ideas below—using short phrases is most helpful. Feel free to write down whatever comes to mind. A few phrases or ideas, per category, is best. Once you have done this for the *Before performance* segment, go ahead and fill in the *During performance* section as well. Doing this exercise is essential in helping to create your script.

Exercise 10.3. Scripts for before and during performance

Specifics	Before performance	During performance
	WHAT EVENT?	WHAT EVENT?
Emotions	(e.g., I am calm/excited)	(e.g., I am confident)
Thoughts	(e.g., I've earned this)	(e.g., I want to be here, powerful, steady)
Physical	(e.g., I am ready. I've trained hard for this)	(e.g., Powerful, energized)
Movement	(e.g., I feel steady on my feet)	(e.g., My body is cutting through the water.)

Now that you have in mind some points of focus that will remind you of performing just the way that you would like to, we are getting ready to have you write your script. There are a few things to keep in mind before you create a script that you read many times over:

- **Stay constructive.** One of the essential facets of scripting is that you capture the points of focus that are constructive and positive. If you generally feel so nervous that you are going to throw up, you don't want to include this in your script. You'd want to include a positive interpretation of the anxiety. You could use something like, "I am energized and ready. I'll use this energy well to help me perform." Make sure that the word *not* is absent from your script. Instead of writing "I am not anxious" state the positive: "I am calm."

- **Use "I" statements** in your script and use present tense verbs. Having verbal cues like this in your script helps you imagine that the experience is currently happening in your imagination. Practically, I have found it most powerful to have performers start their sentences or phrases with, "I am… " or "I feel…" and then fill in the blank with points of mental, physical, emotional, or movement phrases that represent you at your very best as it relates to your performance. (I'll provide a sample script below to give you a clear example of this.)

- **You must believe it is possible.** Scripts are only helpful if what you write down is within the realm of possibility for you to manifest. So, for example, if you write down, "I love how this feels" before performing and you know that for now you would not be able to feel a surge of love for pre-performance emotions. You may instead focus on something that is definitely true for you, such as, "I have worked hard for this," or "I am prepared." You must believe in the ideas you write down. They must be thoughts that you believe even when you are alone, feeling nervous before you compete or what you would believe when you are performing.

- **Use emotions you want to have.** We can become so conditioned to feeling a particular way before or during competition—or heading off to the practice room—that we may not even consider that we could actually feel different and better emotions (like joy, love, interest and excitement). A key to effective scripting is creating an experience of what you would *like* to experience, and not what you expect to experience. Your emotions are drivers of your experience. Creating a focus that you can fully buy into—that is emotionally constructive—is key.

Ultimately, it will be most helpful to choose an area of performance that you would like to enhance. It works best to choose a specific segment of performance. Some of the time periods that have been very successful targets for scripting include before practice, during practice, before a race, or during a performance. I have included a few simple scripts as examples. It seems to work best using an 8 ½ x 11 sheet of paper and filling it up. I encourage you to repeat phrases that resonate most with you.

I have taught many athletes to do this over the years. In one instance, a 17-year-old swimmer came up to me one year after I had worked with him. He showed me a very tattered, old sheet of paper. He reported that he had used his script throughout his entire swim season and that it had helped him prepare mentally. Here is a start to a script for a swimmer, runner, or rower before the race:

> *I want to race. I look forward to feeling the rhythm. I want to be here. I feel strong. My body is ready. I am energized and focused. I have trained hard and I am ready. I've earned this. I want to go. I want to see how fast we can go. This matters to me. This time is for me. I'm quietly energized. I love this. This is for me.*

Scripting can be used for any segment of performance. I've used this technique with athletic coaches. Michelle, a volleyball coach, used her script for her talk to her team in between games during a volleyball match. Michelle wanted to have the confidence to refocus her team and get them ready for the next game. Here is the script that she used that she reports helped her:

Exercise 10.4. Your script

Time period/moment Remember to use physical, technical, and emotional cues.
1.
2.

I will give my energy to them. I help the team refocus their attention when it needs to be done. I am empowered. I have the attention of the team. I have my time. They listen to me. They pay attention to me. My words are meaningful to them. What I say has meaning for them. The right words are coming at the right time. I am confident in being a coach.

With awareness and a plan, you can better use your energy to focus on how you would ideally like to perform and feel. Creating an imagery script has two powerfully positive outcomes. First, it can help stop you from focusing on how you don't want your performance to go. (I encourage you to read it daily or when you are feeling particularly lethargic or apprehensive.) Second, a carefully planned imagery script can also help you begin believing that you can perform the way you would ideally like to perform. Making a shift in performance can also include a shift in one's belief of what is possible—you could perform with confidence, focus, and even joy. Wayne Deyer (an internationally recognized motivational speaker) wrote a book whose title says it all: *You'll See It When You Believe It.* A great practical way to begin believing in how you'd like to perform, ideally, is to see yourself successfully doing it, just the way that you'd like it to happen.

11

Mental-Emotional Goals for Performance

**Creating Clear, Specific
"Highest Point of Leverage" Commitments**

*"When I feel down about not starting,
I think … 'It's still hockey.'"*
—Collegiate Division I hockey player

In this chapter, we will go beyond the normal ways in which we often think of goal setting. Most of us know quite a bit about goal setting. We've learned how to decide on a long-term goal to achieve. Some long-term goals could be "I want to be a starter"; "I want to be the first violinist"; "I want to run a marathon"; or "I want to make the next U.S. team." And most of us know that we also need some weekly or daily goals to help us achieve our long-term goal. Some short-terms goals could be to lose one pound this week, get eight hours of sleep each night, or to practice three hours each day for the next six (and then take a day of rest). These types of action goals are often positive and powerful. Having such goals helps us know where to direct our energy and attention to ultimately achieve what is important to us.

We also often think that having such goals and doing our daily training is enough. We think that if we follow our schedules of physical and technical training, we give ourselves the best shot of achieving our goals. Most collegiate and elite athletes have their fitness, strength, and technique training laid out months in advance. Many musicians have practice times set and scheduled sessions with a teacher. Will these goals get us living and performing in the sweet spot? Will such goals, alone, give us our best chance at ultimately being successful?

I vividly remember one of my national team coaches bringing all the candidates for the 1992 Olympic team into a room to talk about our goals. We were each asked to state our goals out loud. As you would expect, every one of us said, "I want to make the Olympic team and win a gold medal." Of course, this is what we all dreamed for, and this is what we were expected to say. We were all following the national team training program. We were doing the runs, lifting the weights, and rowing up to three times a day. We spent endless hours perfecting our technique.

Yet, I recall distinctly walking out of the room feeling slightly sickened inside. I knew I did everything that the coaches asked of me, but still wondered if there was more I could do. I wondered what could give me an edge. I wasn't very confident that what I was doing would get me to an Olympic gold medal (and it didn't).

The point of telling this story is that I know something now that I didn't know then. The grueling training I was doing with my action goals were not enough. How could anyone in such a position get to the sweet spot? I could have turned the goal-setting skills that I was honing for the *physical* and could have focused them on the *psychological*. In this chapter I will first provide an overview of the time-honored goal-setting strategies of sport psychology. And, second, I will turn these invaluable strategies specifically toward helping you set psychological goals that may make the small change that could make all of the difference.

A QUICK REVIEW OF GOAL SETTING: START WITH THE END

Before you decide what you are going to commit to changing—psychologi-cally—let's consider the time-honored core elements of goal setting. I will focus this segment on ways to tailor your psychological goals. That way, when you consider making a change, you'll have just considered some of the most important aspects of how to effectively set yourself up for success from your tailored, short-term psychological (mental, emotional, or attentional) goals.

There are many ways to conceptualize the essentials of goal setting, but the one that I like most is the one that uses the acronym SMARTY. The SMART part is typically used in the sport psychology world. (It is unclear to whom the acronym should be credited. Some suggest that it originated with Zig Zigler, a motivational speaker in the 1950s.) More recently, there has been an em-phasis on the importance that the person setting the goals, to make sure that the goal is aligned with the individual's personal interests and values. This is where the *Y* comes in.

And this makes great sense. To be most effective, goals need to be impor-tant to the person trying to manifest them. Some add an *S* for *self-determined* goals. And others, like my student Kristen Chipman, who first suggested it to me, add a *Y*, because the goal must be chosen by you, which I'll address later in more detail (this SMARTY acronym is also found in the business world). And when it comes to setting psychological goals—that only you know about— then it is of the utmost importance that you fully choose to implement the related goals or, of course, you will not make any progress in this arena.

Let's consider the core aspects of goals working through the acronym, SMARTY. The components consist of the following:

Specific: An essential starting point of goal setting is to start from the end. We need to know what is most important for you to achieve. The wonderful thing about getting ready for a performance is that the long-term goal is pretty clear—you'd like to achieve some clear mark of success (win, be selected, or be evaluated by others as having some mark of an excellent performance). Specific goals clearly state what you would like to achieve. Wanting to get a bit better at playing the guitar is not nearly as specific as, say, "I will learn 20 new songs so I can play a paid two-hour gig." The more specific the goal, the more likely you will be able create a plan to achieve it. What is your long-term goal?

Knowing what you want to achieve in the future is clearly important. You've got to know what your future target is. Take a moment to note this in Exercise 11.1.

How about specific psychological goals? It is equally important to be specific about the psychological-emotional shift that you would like to make—on a daily basis—to help yourself achieve your long-term goal. What will it take—psychologically—for you to achieve your goal beyond the many hours of training that you are already putting in? What needs to happen in your next practice session? It is not enough to say, for example, that you would like to have a "good attitude," that you'd like to give "full effort" each day to training. The daily strategy must be specific enough for you to know whether or not you implemented something. A specific example of an effortful daily action—having a good attitude could be, "I'll remind myself that I still love playing each time I feel frustrated after making a mistake." Having a specified, pre-planned action or thought—that requires awareness and effort—are essential is setting a daily psychological action plan.

Exercise 11.1. Your goal

Your long-term goal (six months or more out)

Measurable: For goals to be measurable means that you can, well, literally measure your progress or success in some way. It is best to be able to measure where you are at the start (baseline) and where you'd like to be when you finish (your goal). Losing weight is a very clear example. Let's say you want to lose 10 pounds. That is clearly measurable. It is easy when the goal is objective and measurable, like the goals to make the starting line-up at the beginning of next season or win the national championship. There is a clear outcome, you either do or don't achieve the goal.

Making our daily goal psychological goals measurable takes a bit more thought. Consider the example above of bringing a good attitude to daily practice. You may use the strategy reminding yourself, "I still love playing." To make this measureable you could decide to say this to yourself at least three times in your next practice. You can simply measure this by counting the number of times you state this phrase to yourself.

Although we want them to be measurable, more often than not, our daily psychological goals can be quite subjective in nature. Some subjective goals are essential to us (e.g., the goal of wanting to "do your best," or "pay 100% attention to improving"). These are powerful, positive intentions. Yet, when it comes to goal setting, we also need to be able to measure them in some way so we can establish a baseline and know whether or not we ultimately have hit our target.

If you have a goal that is important to you, yet is not easily measured, I strongly encourage you to put the goal on a Likert scale (a sliding number scale). So if your goal is to enjoy your training or practice more (where 0 equals misery and 10 equals a nirvana state), then you can assess where you are today. And then you can set a goal at a higher point on the scale (for some date you determine in the future). Let's say that your enjoyment of practice is usually 3 out of 10. You could have a goal of hitting a 5 out of 10 for your next practice. (After this you'd need to come up with some strategy to bump up your enjoyment, like purposefully focusing on aspects of practice that bring you joy.)

By using the strategy of putting a number to your important subjective goals, you give yourself the power to assess and be aware of where you are now and what you would like to achieve. Using a Likert scale for assessing a mind state in a practice can also be helpful. You could say that on a scale of 0 to 10, that you'd like to be at an 8 or above in focusing on improving technique for a given day.

Adjustable: Being willing to adjust your goals is essential. I have found that one of the biggest challenges to working with high-level performers is their high level of discomfort with setting a goal and coming up short. This leads to frustration, embarrassment, and ultimately, not trying as hard. Setting a plan to help achieve a long-term goal and not following through on the plan can be quite embarrassing and can erode your confidence. But only if you let it!

Dutch triathlon champion Marijke Zeekant talks about what happens when she doesn't feel good in a training run. Though long daily training sessions are essential Marijke notes that sometimes her body is not up for it. She recalls, "As soon as I don't feel good, if I'm not capable of certain training, I say, OK, this feels really bad. I'll just turn around and go back home. I'll take a shower and relax." Marijke has learned how to adjust and feel good about making changes and not meeting a daily training goal (e.g., bike 40 miles and run 10). Though she is clearly highly committed to training, she knows that taking time off unexpectedly (adjusting) is far better than ultimately getting injured or burned out. She recalls her coach telling her, "If you miss out of training, if things change, then skip a training and pick up the rest of the schedule. Keep your rest day. If you miss it, just cross it off. Don't try to fit in an extra training that you missed." Whether our adjustment is due to soreness, exhaustion, or simply a blip in our determination and commitment, it is far better to get right back on track than to allow ourselves to get stuck in a downward spiral of negative thinking. We must be able to adjust. We can set a plan and then, if for some reason it doesn't work out, we must be able to learn from it and accept it.

Realistic: Long-term goals do not need to be logical or realistic. Any long-term goal is fine. Who knows what is possible for you! The key, though, is that the goal achievement strategies that you set for today, tomorrow, and the rest of the week must be realistic. The more you set yourself up for success in the short term, the quicker you and your confidence will improve. I worked with Lexi, a figure skater, who was committed to hitting a double-axle jump. It turned out that she was terrified of trying to land the double. She could not envision herself successfully landing the double. So each time she forced herself to try in practice, it only left her bruised and embarrassed. I strongly encouraged her to hang on to her long-term goal, but for the next week it was important to start visualizing hitting her doubles first. She also spent more time doing pre-jump drills to strengthen her physical abilities and skills to hit the double. With this change, her confidence began to strengthen.

It is just as important to set realistic psychological goals. It would be unreasonable to expect to experience a level 10 of enjoyment if you tend to be quite nervous for performance assessments or competition. If you usually are at a 2, you may set a psychological goal of being at a 4 or 5 for the next competition. And then create a reasonable, achievable psychological strategy to set yourself up for success (like visualize yourself performing at your best for a few seconds each time you feel a rush of fear through your system).

Time Sensitive: The key to a goal being time sensitive is that you need to set a date by which you will achieve your goal. If you say you are going to run a marathon someday, it sounds like a wistful want. However, if you determine you will run the San Francisco marathon in a particular year, it becomes much clearer what you want to do and, with the end in mind, you will have a better sense of what you need to do this week to start working toward the goal.

Setting a date and committing to achieve something throws us into action. I often think about the importance of goal setting when I hear someone is going to get married. What, typically, is the first question we ask a couple when they say that they just got engaged? We ask, "When are you getting married?" If there is a date set, we are pretty confident that they will get married. If there is no date set, we question whether or not the wedding will actually ever take place. It works the same way with goal setting. Once we set our goal and a date by which we will commit to making it happen, we generally get into action. We have committed to believing that it is possible to achieve.

In terms of making changes in what we think about, what our intentions are, or how we manage our emotions, the most effective way to begin is to decide to change how you approach what you are doing. It takes time to change a habit of thinking or responding. To be able to focus our energy on staying in the space of determined enjoyment takes practice. The time is now to shift our mental approach to allow ourselves to train and perform as much as possible in the sweet spot.

You: The idea of you (the Y of SMARTY) emphasizes the importance of making sure that whatever goal you set is aligned with your own personal values and interests. Making sure that the goal is aligned with what truly matters to you is essential. When you commit to self-chosen goals, you are asking yourself to carry through with the goal achievement strategies during both those moments when you do and don't want to do it. For those moments when you just don't feel like it, having a goal set that still aligns with what you intrinsically care about can help you get through.

And then when it comes to psychological goals, you believing in them, valuing them, and choosing to implement them is critical. With our physical goals, we get support. For example, a coach knows if we are physically lagging and a boss knows if we are not showing up on time for work. But when it comes to making psychological goals of shifting how we are thinking, how we are feeling, or what we are focusing on—it is totally up to each of us. There is no one in our heads checking on our thinking. Changing how you mentally approach things is powerful, but there is usually no one but you to keep yourself accountable. So of all types of goals, the *you* part of SMARTY is most important when choosing and implementing psychological goals

We all need to know what the end is, on what we are focusing our energy and time to create. Yet the real challenge with goal setting is not about understanding the basic, conceptual ideas of goal setting. The ideas are clear. With some thought we can figure out what exactly we want to achieve, by when and what actions to take each day. The real challenge is figuring out what will help you—starting today—to incorporate positive intentions, positive emotion and managing your negative emotions. What could you choose to focus on today to help get you there?

The challenge is figuring out what we can do today. What can we add to our daily plan that is achievable and will help us perform at a higher level? Figuring out what needs to psychologically change or improve that will fast track us to best performance can help make a quick, radical change. One of the tricks is figuring out a change that is not too overwhelming to take on. We want to stretch ourselves, not put ourselves into panic mode.

Now that we've had a chance to consider the SMARTY approach to goal setting, let's look at how you can specifically apply these toward determining which psychological goals would serve you best. For the remainder of the chapter consider what psychological goals would serve you best. In this book we've considered the value of positive emotions, shifting or accepting negative emotions, the value of considering your strengths, the power of gratitude and optimism, your precious resource of willpower, as well as the power of the thoughts that go through your head. From these concepts, you can identify the psychological goals that will serve you best.

As we've considered, though important, it usually is not enough to do all the physical work or practice necessary to reach our long-term goals. We must focus in on how we are doing it, as well. The process is key. And part of this *how* is about how we use our minds. It often takes self-awareness and commitment to making subtle changes in what we focus on and how we respond to the many demands made of us. The question at hand really is, what will it take to tip the psychological balance for your performance? What will nudge you back into your sweet spot so you are getting the most out of your training?

DAILY GOAL ACHIEVEMENT STRATEGIES

The goal setting conversation is only a mental exercise up to the point that we decide to take action. And, truly, the only day we can directly impact is today. I have found that it can feel like making a small change in what you focus on is a big effort with no gain. You may think, "Come on! Is thinking about how good it feels to play a musical verse really going to get me to play a two-hour set well? Is thinking about my strength of, say, determination really going to help me make that team?" or "Is eating more fruit and vegetables today really going to make a difference in my health?"

Can small changes in how I think or what I focus on really make a big difference in the end? The surprising answer is, yes. In fact, choosing small changes can make all the difference—it just takes time. It is like stretching. For example, you may be quite tight and if you stretch every day, you feel like you are making no progress. You just keep feeling tight. But if you pay attention, a few weeks into your stretching, you start to feel a little more open, a bit more flexible. The same goes for focusing on implementing changes in how you think, how you assess what is happening around you and where you focus your thoughts. Change requires daily effort. In an excellent applied sport psychology text, Tom Hanson and Ken Ravizza emphasize the importance of how what we do today affects our performance. They note that, "Today plus today plus today… equals achievement."

For many of the athletes with whom I've worked, I have helped them establish daily goals for one-week periods (in-between our weekly meetings). I've found that these daily goal achievement strategies are essential for change. I do keep them very specific and very simple. For example, I have recommended that an athlete practice a particular type of focused meditation five minutes per day at a certain time of the day. Another example is recommending that a football player practice a particular move successfully in his mind, through visualization, three times each day at a particular time of the day. The specific, simple, and planned psychological goals set you up for a better chance of attaining your long term goals, as long as they are thoughtfully tailored to you.

The question remains: "What small mental change(s) in your training can significantly contribute to your upcoming performance? Recall our discussion of the highest point of leverage from Peter Senge's book *The Fifth Discipline*. The highest point of leverage is the single change that would make the biggest, most positive impact on a system. He focused on actions that would most contribute to the success of an organization. When considered on the micro level, you can consider what would have the biggest impact on your system.

We can't upgrade all aspects of ourselves, all at once. We must choose. And if we choose wisely we may find some positive domino effect on our emotional-mental experience of training and performance. We need to consider the few changes that might make the biggest, most positive impact on our ability to perform when it counts.

There is a positive domino effect that can happen when you choose an effective point of change. Recently, I've been working with Peter, an aspiring junior hockey player. He was struggling with the fact that he was not on the starting line-up of his team. There were even games when he is demoted one level and had to play with the younger guys. He knew that where he was placed on the team could have an impact on collegiate recruiters' opinions of his abilities. The more he sat on the bench, the more frustrated he became. And the more nights when he had to play with the lower level guys, the more embarrassed and angry he would get. He broke one too many sticks and sat in the penalty box one too many times. He came to me to help him pull his psychological game back together. Peter's attitude and reputation were quickly and steadily declining.

After a few sessions, I asked him, "What do you like about playing, even though you are not playing at the level you want to be, and even though you don't respect your coach?" After a few moment of silence, he had a powerful moment of insight. He said, "It's still hockey!" His whole demeanor changed. He seemed to lighten up. He came up with this one statement that was true about what mattered to him most. Peter loved to play. He realized that no one could take away his love of playing, regardless of his level of play. He realized that if he got ice time, he still got to do his thing. He decided to bring up this phrase in his mind each time he began feeling frustrated.

The positive domino effect went into full effect. With Peter's shift in perspective, his entire experience shifted. His problems with his coach dissolved, Peter was no longer acting out in practice. His emotional outbursts on the ice dissolved. Instead of breaking sticks and sulking in the penalty box, he was in a space of appreciation for the game of hockey. He no longer felt like he was being constantly let down by his coach's misperceptions of his abilities. Peter's lack of effort in practice transformed into engaged workouts. His concern over not being a team captain dissolved. He was almost immediately the team leader again, albeit not in an official capacity.

Peter experienced a positive domino effect from one small change in attitude and conscious appreciation for the game. After he thought through what was important to him, he realized that what really mattered was his chance to play hockey. His go-to phrase when things were going poorly became, "It's still hockey." This allowed him to shift back into doing what he enjoyed with suspended self-judgment. And with this change, he now is able to play consistent, aggressive, passionate hockey. One small constructive change in the system can have a ripple effect in your ability to perform in many unexpected, positive ways. (I'll never know why, but Peter was moved up permanently to the highest level of junior hockey within two months of making this change.)

THERE'S NO COACHING ON THE PSYCHOLOGICAL *HOW* OF PRACTICE

I can distinctly recall a particular day when I was training for the Olympic team. Our coach decided that we were to keep our heart rate elevated to 150 beats per minute for three hours (yes, 180 minutes!). That day, much of this training was indoors on rowing machines and stationary bicycles. He would randomly grab our necks and check our pulse rate (by feeling for the pulse of the blood pounding in our necks). There was a very clear external goal for that practice: Keep your heart rate at 150 beats per minute or risk being humiliated.

There was no encouragement or help about *how* to psychologically get through that three-hour session. Or better yet, there was no help in the *how* of strengthening our psychology in that three-hour bout of training. There was no help in dealing with the intense fatigue or the negative thoughts. There was no encouragement to focus on what was going well, the good of the body rhythm in motion, or how our willpower was being strengthened through extreme stretch. Most coaches probably cannot help with all of this. But we, as performers, can radically change how we psychologically deal with our training bouts.

Your teachers or coaches help strengthen your strategies, technical skills, and physical abilities. These leaders set up training for their groups of students, athletes, or performers to help everyone in the group improve their physical and technical aspects of performance. We have become very good at following the instructions and plans of others, plans that were developed for the good of the group. Yet most of us have not developed the skill of being able to focus in on tailoring what we do or how we do it, psychologically, to give ourselves the best chance to do our best in key moments. We can leverage the best of what our mentors and teachers can give us and then take some time to determine what slight change in what we do or how we think could make the biggest difference.

I worked with Liz, an Olympic hopeful in the single scull (one person in a rowing boat). She was training twice per day, six days per week. She was following the grueling National Team training program. Liz was, as you'd expect, incredibly fit. She was one of the top rowers in the country. When she came to work with me, she wanted to figure out what would help her most in terms of preparing for the upcoming Olympic team selection. To get a sense of Liz's approach to training and competing, I asked her to tell me about a typical training row on the river.

Liz seemed surprised at this question. She wanted to focus on racing, not training. She reluctantly proceeded to tell me about how she approached practice. She said, "Well, I just get in the boat and look forward to when I get to a certain point in the river, and then I get to turn around and come in." I asked Liz to tell me about what she focuses on to improve her stroke, rhythm, and power application in her practice rows. Liz replied, "I don't think about it. I just try to get through it. I save that for my technical rows." There were a few moments of silence after this statement.

Liz realized that her complacent attitude in practice was a block to her ultimate success. Though she was diligently going for her 90-minute afternoon rows and maintaining her heart rate at 150 beats per minute, she realized that she was missing out on an obvious aspect of training that she had been completely ignoring. Liz realized that, though she was following the National Team training program physically, she was not making best use of her attention while training.

She had gotten into the habit of having a lazy mind. After her statement, a moment of insight occurred. Immediately, both Liz and I knew that her approach to training, her focus in training, was a critical place to start in helping her prepare for racing. The more she could improve her rowing efficiency and focus during training, the better equipped she would be for racing. Even though she trained about 30-plus hours per week, she needed to be more aware of where she purposefully focused her mind.

In our sessions, we discussed what an optimal row should feel like. From this, we created very small daily strategies of where she could more effectively focus. We developed an image (she would bring up an image of the best rower in the world and see herself rowing exactly the same way) and a cue word that would remind herself what would be best to focus on that week. As she passed particular landmarks (discussed in advance) in her row, she would remind herself to bring up the planned phrases and images. The image and cue words were developed to bring her attention back to *how* she was rowing. She worked on developing a habit of rowing as well as possible, at all times.

There is no magic, perfect, shared training focus for all of us. As human beings, we are complex and all of us are slightly different in what will help us most in our preparation for optimizing performance. The process that works best for each of us—that which is tailored to who we are, our skills, and how we mentally approach training—will vary.

WHAT YOU SHOULD FOCUS ON ("JUST DO . . . WHAT?")

Most coaches and teachers are not able to key into the one, specific mental-emotional point of focus that would most help you. Even the best of coaches are unable to determine how you can best successfully endure, psychologically, a rigorous training bout. Sure, they can yell and encourage. Great coaches and teachers are able to tell us how best to physically train and what to focus on in terms of skills and strategies—but the process of what is happening in our minds is up to us.

We have to learn where to focus our minds so that we can most efficiently improve our skills. We are the ones who have to deal with our own thoughts and emotions as we train and compete. We can develop this last aspect of training on our own. We can purposefully apply the powerful tool of goal setting toward what is happening in our minds as we train and perform.

What should you focus on when considering tailoring your program to best serve you? In the following chart, I've put some key points of consideration when thinking about how best to apply the powerful tools of goal setting to the psychological aspect of your training and performance. Take a moment to consider the answers to the questions Exercise 11.2.

PERFORMANCE PROFILING FOR EMOTIONS AND FOCUS

Now that you have a sense of what you already do to use your mind effectively for your focus and management of your emotions, let's move to what else you could do. If you were to strengthen your effort to train psychologically wisely, what might you try? What characteristics would you need to strengthen to leave you more satisfied in your efforts, regardless of how the upcoming performance may turn out? What upgrade to your mental approach might give you your best shot at achieving your longed-for goals and keep you in your sweet spot while training?

Exercise 11.2. Key questions to help tailor your daily training

Key questions	Your answers
1. What are your key points of focus for your thoughts before and during practice and performance?	
2. What do you think or do to influence your emotional reactions when they are getting in the way of performance?	
3. What would it take for you to pay more attention to the technical, tactical, and physical factors that will allow you to be most successful for your next big moment?	

It is important to consider the *how* of training. It is important to consider what you are focusing on and how you are feeling when you are doing your daily training. I'd like you to consider the intentions and qualities that are most important to you in your effort to be most fully prepared for the day of competition. In the sport psychology world, *performance profiling* is an intervention (created by Richard J. Butler and Lew Hardy) that helps you quickly hone in on tailoring what is most important for you to efficiently get ready for the big moments. In performance profiling, you ask yourself to consider the key qualities and characteristics that will help you to ultimately perform your best. Some terms that performers will include in their lists are things like confidence, focus, determination, physical strength, and emotional control.

I am encouraging you to think about the qualities and characteristics that are specific to helping you get, psychologically, best prepared. To get your ideas flowing, it can help to think of someone in your field or sport who you respect and is great at what they do. What psychological qualities (of managing their intentions, focus and emotions) do you sense that they have? They may love to train, exude a great sense of confidence, have a dog-with-a-bone type of focus when they perform, or are at ease speaking in front of 500 people. Chances are that if you are aware of these great qualities in them that you either possess them yourself or they are qualities that you know that you need to enhance. Just as in our conversations about strengths, it is important to consider the important qualities that you have already well-developed and others that you would you like to strengthen.

Try to come up with your top seven qualities or characteristics that would best serve you. You can include both qualities that are already quite strong in and others that need to be further developed. This is an important step. If you need to, take a few moments now to allow the ideas to emerge in your thinking. Once you've come up with these seven qualities, assess yourself on a scale of 1 to 10 as to where you are right now (1 being not at all, and 10 being you fully embody the given characteristic). Go ahead and evaluate where you are today for each quality that you list. Next, consider where you would want to be on game day. For example, if your emotional experience of pure joy when competing is a 2 out of 10 today, where could you reasonably be for your next big performance? How about your confidence? You could consider your ability to focus and block out distractions or to get into a positive and energized state. Consider, next, what you could do to make a positive change to help strengthen each quality (unless some are already at a 10!). What might you be willing to change and manifest?

The last column in this chart, *What I could do to make a positive change,* may be a great source of information for you in terms of what mini-daily plans could set you up to best prepare for game day. Awareness of what aspects of your ability to perform that need strengthening paired with a plan to make small, positive steps in improvement is the key to really making a change.

What small change now could make the biggest difference to strengthen your ability to perform? I have had hundreds of athletes at this point make a decision to think one different thought during a specific, planned-for moment in competition, which created a positive domino effect in the direction of

Exercise 11.3. Performance profiling for psychological readiness
(adapted from Butler and Hardy, 1992)

Psychological quality or characteristic that is key to being in my sweet spot	Where I am now (scale of 1–10)	Where I am committed to be for game day (scale of 1–10)	What I could do to make a positive change
1.			
2.			
3.			
4.			
5.			
6.			
7.			

confidence, present-focus, and excellent performance. And that is what they were looking for, a simple, clear way to significantly improve their ability to perform and compete.

To determine your highest point of leverage change, reconsider your list of seven characteristics or qualities that would most contribute to your ability to optimize performance. Choose the one area that you think would help you the most to make a constructive highest-point-of-leverage shift. (You may not know the right one to choose, but with some experimentation and persistence, I know that you can figure it out!) After you've chosen the quality to be shifted, what action in terms of behavior or thought might it take for you

Exercise 11.4. Your highest point of leverage in preparation for performance

Characteristic or quality	What needs to change?	Action to be taken	Thought or image to cue action
Perspective	Attitude, negative self-judgment	Go hard to the boards	Shift from negative thoughts to "It's still hockey!"
Your #1 option:			
Your #2 option:			

to make this positive shift? In the first row of Exercise 11.4, I've used Peter as an example. Consider one change that could make the biggest difference for you? I invite you to think about it and jot down your answers in Exercise 11.4.

There are many, many things which any of us could use a specific goal to help us change. We could adjust what we focus on, how we cope with our emotions, and how we'd like to optimally be thinking during big moments. We could make plans to shift particular points of focus for endless moments throughout a day of performance. Yet, changing any habit or focus in training and performance can take significant commitment and effort. We have to hone in on just one or two changes.

THE CHALLENGE

One practical approach to considering change is to consider what the one change will focus on and then to consider both the pros and cons of change before you get into action. We often think that making a constructive change is good. But, of course, there are real reasons why we have not made the change. It may be simply awareness or it may be that the cost is too high. For example, if one of your goals is to be fully focused in training, it is easy to see the upside. You would improve more quickly, you would gain more respect from those with whom you train or those near you, and your performances would be better, more consistent.

So why doesn't everyone commit to being fully focused in training? What could possibly be the downside? There are potentially many. Being fully focused takes more mental effort. Often being fully engaged means that you might experience more physical pain (like when running suicide drills or going for an hour-long fitness run). It also is a huge mental task to take on when we just don't want to be fully engaged. It is important to remember that the change doesn't have to be from 0 to 60. If you *practice well* about 25% of the time, then upping the good quality practice to 50% of the time would be great progress!

Another downside to really putting yourself out there is that you may still come up short in some performance. Of course, this can also be hard to take. To put out your best and still, for example, not be in the starting line-up is painful. We can easily become disappointed with ourselves (for many, it is easier on our egos to not try and fail than to try and fail). Yet, to improve (perhaps faster than those around us), we must put ourselves out there, whether it is imagining ourselves performing at our best in hard training bouts or reminding ourselves that we love it even if a coach yells at us.

We can change. We can create. Yet the truth remains that it will take effort on our part. Bronwyn Malicoat, a wise friend of mine, recently said, "If you want to change, you have a lot of work in front of you." Regardless of the challenge, if we want to change, to pursue something that is of value to us, we must be willing to stretch and change ourselves. Most of us have been trained well to push ourselves physically, technically, and tactically. But most of us still have quite a bit of room to improve in the emotional-mental realm of performance. It is hard work, but is wide open with possibilities.

Any change can be tough, especially when no one will really know or keep track of what you are up to. If you choose to change some aspect of your mental/psychological approach to training, it will be up to you to keep it on your radar screen and keep at it when old, habituated ways of thinking and behaving naturally arise. The good news is that the more consistent you are in practicing any shift of focus or emotion, the stronger you will reinforce that shift as a go-to experience when the pressure is on.

PART III
THE DAY OF PERFORMANCE

12

Empowered Thinking

Establishing Your Go-to Responses When it Counts

"I know it is race day and I'm ready.
My legs are shaking right before the
flag goes down—that means
I'm going to race well."
—Three-time Olympian

No one has consistent, effective, positive thinking all the time. The point isn't to be perfect in our thinking or always to be upbeat. The goal is to have and expand constructive internal thoughts for high-pressure moments and to rebound as quickly as possible from negative mental spins through the habit of empowered thinking. But first, what is empowered thinking? Empowered thinking is using your mind purposefully so you can most effectively cope with upset or focus on the good of what is occurring. Empowered thinking can help you achieve your goals and take joy in the good that surrounds you as much as possible. Empowered thinking begins with being aware of your thinking. It begins with noticing how you interpret what is going on around you. You can learn to notice your ways of thinking that contribute positively to the quality of your training and performance. And you can learn to pay attention to your ways of thinking that contribute negatively to your performance. With awareness you can learn to shift your thinking. And as we mentally move toward what empowers us and away from what is distracting, we perform better.

The idea of empowered thinking may sound vague and ephemeral to you. But you can actually learn to employ empowered thinking. That is how sport and positive psychology have made a difference. The rest of this chapter will show you how to do it. The first step is to become aware of how you interpret or assess what is happening in your performance environment. For example, if your coach screams or gives feedback with a harsh tone, how would you generally think about this? There are many ways to interpret or assess such experiences. Some ways of making sense of this would be to believe that:

1. Your coach is mean (and therefore you don't like him or her),

2. Your coach doesn't believe in you,

3. Your coach really wants to help you and just isn't compassionate or kind in the way that s/he relays information, or,

4. Your coach is sharing essential information with you to help you get better.

There are many ways to interpret such a situation. The key is to realize that any situation can be interpreted to genuinely mean a variety of very different truths. And even if you think some truths are, well, truer than others, it is essential to be able to get your mind to move toward interpretations that set you up to do your best when the pressure is on. Because with each interpretation comes an emotional response and ultimately affects what you focus on and what you do.

How do you know which thoughts will really help you? Sometimes you may find yourself feeling like your coach/teacher doesn't believe in you and you respond by performing great. Or other times you may find yourself feeling at ease and peaceful inside and feeling flat when the lights go on. So what thoughts generate the type of presence that you ideally want to create? It's not about just having nice thoughts. The goal is to know yourself and know what thoughts make you feel empowered—whatever gets you there.

When creating habits of empowered thinking, it is important to consider situations in which you feel empowered and others in which you feel out of control or hopeless. Both instances can give you insight. When you feel confident and focused, you probably are putting empowered thinking into practice. It is important to notice such instances so you can learn how to strengthen such responses. It is also important to notice what thoughts feed your fire of misery so you can consider how you may shift out of unhelpful patterns of thought. And one of the keys to strengthening the habit of empowered thinking is to notice when you are able to shift into the constructive.

Vanessa, lead singer for the band Vanessa Trien and The Jumping Monkeys, talks about how she feels before she gets on stage–and ultimately how she shifts into an empowered mental state. She freely notes that she has some recurring self-doubt right before she is ready to play. She said, "My insecurities flare up. (I ask myself)… 'will people like it? Will I perform well? Will people not come?' I worry more than I should." Though Vanessa has been playing in front of audiences for more than 20 years—first as a pianist, then folk singer, and now focused on children's music—she still feels the waves of anxiety that are so common before we get ready to perform or compete.

Yet, she has a strategy to get out of her own head. She focuses her thoughts and energy outside of herself. She mingles with her crowd as they begin to pour in. She purposefully focuses on interacting with her audience to bring her confidence up just before performing. She said,

> I get a wave of insecurity. But when people show up, I just start saying hi to them. I kick the social aspect of it in gear, and that gets rid of the nerves… I don't go back stage before like most musicians. I don't do that. Talking with my audience helps me get out of my own head and connect with the people that I'm there connect with. I play off of the kids' excitement for the show.

Though Vanessa does not report a specific word or phrase she thinks about to get herself into a constructive state of mind, she knows what she needs to do to get ready. Talking with those in her audience stops her from getting caught up in her recurring negative, fear-based thoughts. She believes that once she is on stage she will put on a good show. Go-to thoughts that she could consider saying to herself include, "I know I can put on a good show", or "I get joy out of playing in front of others."

THE DAY OF COMPETITION: GO-TO THOUGHTS FOR WHAT IS GOING RIGHT

The day of competition is the day to limit any critique of your strategy and skill and is the time to focus on what is going well, whenever possible. It is a time to notice what aspects of your physical movement feel right. It is time to notice who does support you and believes in you. It is time to recall what you do well, your strengths, and your gifts. It is time to recall times before when you performed just the way that you'd like to perform. It is a day to think about how you could perform to the best of your abilities in the upcoming minutes or hours of performance. How we think about all that surrounds us and what we focus on—the good or bad—generates our emotional responses. And our emotions, in turn, are strong forces in our desire to push ourselves to the limit or to withdraw mentally and simply to go through the motions.

It can be invaluable to create the habit of paying attention to the factors that will help keep you in an optimistic, constructive state of mind on the day of performance. Practicing this way of thinking every day will help prepare you to be able to shift to them when you truly need them. Again, what will help you stay focused on the key performance factors in the moment will vary. Part of being human is that we all have greatly different combinations of motivations, desires, and habits of thought. However, there are some excellent core reminders that can help most performers shift into a more empowered way of thinking, particularly when the pressure is on. Just like practicing your go-to thoughts each day is very helpful in creating positive habits of thinking.

It is also invaluable to learn to notice the good in your training, performance, and life on a daily basis. The daily focus on the good will also help you create habits of positive, empowered thinking. And then when you need it most in performance, when the pressure is mounting, you will know just where to take your mind. Or at best, it will move to the good automatically.

What you love about it: One of the first places I start when working with athletes and performers, to strengthen their passion and confidence, is to have them consider what they love most about their sport or performance realm. For some, they have to go back far in time and in their memory to recall what it is about their sport that they loved. For others, the love of what they do is still quite present and palpable. For just a moment, consider what it is that you love about your sport or performance realm. If you can, try thinking of the aspects that have nothing to do with winning or losing. What is it about the movement, the people, the activity itself, or even the environment that is truly compelling to you?

Your strengths: Though we have talked about strengths, it is important to remember what it is that you can fully rely upon from yourself. When things are tough, what can you count on? What aspects of your personality, skills, strategies, and abilities can you lean on when you are up against a wall, physically or psychologically? In the following list I'll ask you some questions that I hope will eventually lead to you developing one or two go-to thoughts to use in both daily practice and game day. Here are a few questions to consider:

- If I were my own best friend, what would I say was my top strength as a performer?
- When I have been under great pressure before, what did I rely upon to overcome the challenge?
- When I'm really honest with myself, what do I admire or respect about myself in my performance world?

I encourage you to notice your strengths in a very quiet way. Focus on internal, intra-personal recognition. Though it may be a quiet, quick exercise, it is can be very helpful to maintain an awareness of your strengths, what you can rely upon. When you are behind, or the lactic acid levels are rising, it is important to be able to recall what it is about you that will help you get through the toughest moments. And noticing your strengths on a daily basis will contribute to your habit of having empowered thinking, instead of saying to youself, *"I just can't do it. I don't match up. I'm just not as quick, big, strong, small, or as smart as they are."* This way of thinking can be transformed into thoughts such as, *"I know that this is going to be tough, but I am determined, I'll keep trying or I can accept what comes."*

Perspective: Maintaining perspective when under pressure is a tough demand, yet it is possible with practice. One of the hardest mental challenges is to believe that your life will be OK, regardless of what happens. Whether you bomb or have a peak performance, it is possible to believe that you will still survive and your life will still have meaning. A peak performance doesn't have to mean that you a better person. And a poor performance doesn't have to mean that you a worse person.

The other dimension of perspective is that once one is just preparing for performance, there is absolutely nothing that you can do to prepare better or more in that pivotal moment. All that you can do, which is the all-important thing to do in that moment, is to become and remain totally present. The best that you can do is to engage in exactly what you are doing each moment. Thinking about the *what ifs* only serves to distract you from what will help you the most in the present moment. For the musician, it will be merging with her instrument, expressing the music, and fully connecting to the audience. For the athlete, it will be remaining fully present to the movement of the body, the full focus on strategy and skill. There is no space for other considerations at this time.

Understanding and believing that any consideration or focus on what has happened or what will happen doesn't help you perform well. Believing that your life has meaning outside of your performance realm can help you thrive under the demands of pressured performances. It is easy to suggest that having perspective is essential, yet believing it and having it can be so hard when you have been preparing for months or years for a particular event. However, I have found in my sport psychology practice, and certainly as a performer myself, that without a sense of perspective, without a belief that you will be OK and survive at the end of a performance, you set yourself up for unnecessarily high levels of dread and anxiety prior to performance. And, at once, such a mindset can easily distract you from your most effective mental approach to performance. It can be helpful to consider what is important to you, regardless of what happens, and at once to remind yourself that being present, moment to moment, will serve you best when your performance counts. (And maintaining perspective makes performance significantly more enjoyable to experience!)

In Exercise 12.1, I encourage you to come up with a go-to thought for each area, a word or phrase that will remind you of what it is about doing your thing that you love, a strength of yours that you value, and a word or phrase that will help create some perspective when you are under pressure to do your thing well. Though you may not choose to put these phrases into practice, it can be very helpful to simply acknowledge a thought that confirms what you love about what you are doing, what you bring to the dance, and why your life is worth living, regardless of how you do on the next big performance day.

THE DAY OF: GO-TO THOUGHTS FOR WHAT MIGHT GO WRONG

Even the most seasoned and successful performers are sometimes challenged by how they think about training and performance. The times when we are often most challenged by unhelpful thoughts are when faced with a performance that holds meaning for our performance standings. Whenever we put ourselves on the line, be it an end-of-the-season championship, a public speech for which you've been preparing for months, or a solo performance, it can generate feelings of doubt, fear, and sometimes pure terror.

In one of my studies, Joe, a two-time silver medalist and three-time Olympic athlete, recalled feeling surges of self-doubt on the morning of his third

Exercise 12.1. Your go-to empowered thoughts to strengthen the positive

The good in your sport/ performance domain	Go-to empowered thought: Strengthen the positive
My love for...	e.g., "I love the power I feel when I cut through the water." YOURS:
My strengths	e.g., "I can count on myself to give everything that I have." YOURS:
My perspective	e.g., "I am lucky to have a chance to be here. I can take whatever comes." YOURS:

and last round of Olympic racing finals. He recalled fearfully wondering, "Have I stretched enough? Have I eaten right? Am I rested well enough?... Am I really ready?" He was used to feeling confident, but recalled feeling quite uncomfortable emotionally. He knew that he had to put a stop to this line of thinking. Joe's ability to notice this is quite similar to the example of Vanessa above. Going into an Olympic final riddled with doubt would adversely impact his ability to perform his best. Joe was lucky, though. He had created the habit of quickly shifting out of the doubt when it occurred. He recalled that his mind answered each of these questions directly and honestly, and based in reality, "Yes, I have stretched. Yes, I did eat right, and I slept as well as can be expected. Yes, I'm ready." Joe clearly had created a habit of mind such that he could quickly rebound from unwelcome thoughts of fear, self-doubt, or other forms of negative thinking into empowered habits of thinking. How we think on game day—and on any day for that matter—has a significant impact on our emotions, our motivations, and, ultimately, our behavior.

We've all probably experienced times when we felt unbeatable and times when we were washed over with unreasonable and unwelcome surges of fear. When we become afraid or our confidence is shaken, we typically get bombarded by negative thoughts. It is invaluable to learn how to develop the ability to influence how you think or assess the challenges around you in more effective ways. We all interpret what is happening around us all of the time, automatically. Sometimes we can handle our response to challenge with good instincts, and such instances require no purposeful, careful thinking. Yet, other times, we can get overcome up by our negative thoughts.

I know that I used to believe that I just thought the way that I thought. I believed that to change your thinking about how you perceived a situation or challenge was merely being a fake. I believed that whatever I was dealing with was just the way that it was and that there was only one true way of looking at things. But, thankfully, I was wrong. We can change how we see situations in authentic ways that empower our ability to perform.

I didn't understand that we actually have the choice to see the same thing from many different perspectives. And the many different perspectives can all be quite different and true at the same time. The skill is learning how to focus in on authentic perspectives that serve you. For example, if you begin to lose confidence in yourself after coming up short in a practice or performance, you may have thoughts like, "What is the matter with me? Why can't I be more consistent in thinking in a stronger way?" With the exact same challenge of shaken confidence, you also could think, "This is normal; everyone gets a little shaky inside, sometimes." We can remind ourselves of our strengths. We can choose to remind ourselves of what we can do well, what we have been able to produce, even when we don't feel our best inside. It is a matter of choosing to think in a more productive way. We don't have to let the influx of negative thinking get the better of us.

We have a choice in how we appraise or interpret our experiences. And when we become aware of thoughts or thought patterns that do not serve us, we have the choice to change them. It can be very hard. Changing habits of thought can be one of the hardest challenges any performer may face. And shifting to more empowered thoughts may be the most powerful tool we have to nudge ourselves back into being able to live and perform in the sweet spot.

Honesty with our feelings and thoughts is essential, especially the thoughts and feelings that seem weak, ugly, and even pathetic at times. We have to face thoughts like, "Maybe I just am not as gifted as my competitors"; "Maybe when it really counts, I just don't have the courage to pull through"; or "I am just not good enough, strong enough, gifted enough, or good-looking enough." Once we become aware of the destructive patterns of thought, we create a chance to shift into more empowered ways of thinking.

Having one main go-to thought when going into competition can be an invaluable mental weapon. Anyone can get thrown off their mental game. It is good to have a very simple go-to thought. Such a plan can help you get focused on performing instead of worrying about outcome or how others may evaluate you. Recently, I worked with Emily, an all-star collegiate female soccer player. She was easily able to recount times when she was under great pressure and was able to regain her composure. Emily recalled that after missing a key shot in the game when her team was down by one at the half that she felt quite disheartened. She felt distracted and angry. She recalled going to the side of the field and "talking [myself] back into the game."

I asked her what she was saying to herself. I asked the question about that one particular instance because I wanted to help her come up with a go-to phrase for future games when she might get caught in the same negative mind state. She smiled and said, "I just kept telling myself that I was better than that." At this point I knew that she could use this phrase in future, challenging moments of competition. I said, "There it is. There is your go-to phrase. When you are down, just remind yourself, 'I'm better than this.'" Even though talking herself out of that hard moment had worked, she did not recognize the power of that phrase for future games when she wasn't playing well. Though the strategy of repeating a powerful phrase had worked beautifully for her, she did not realize that she could take this phrase with her to future tough moments in competition.

It is about learning to more quickly gain control and shift to an effective pattern of thought. You can learn to control or influence the instances when your mind suddenly gives way to terror and I-need-to-escape mode. Whatever the high expectation moment of challenge, even the most expert performer will, at times, be challenged with thoughts that reflect fear, doubt, or an unexpected lag in self-confidence.

Part of creating empowered thinking on game days comes from practicing empowered thinking every day. I recall that shortly after I retired from elite sport, I was able to do fewer pull-ups and ran slower with each passing day of exercising one or two hours per day. During my years training for the Olympics, we had built up to five or six hours per day of fitness and strength training. It was truly disheartening to put the effort into daily exercising and finding myself becoming weaker and slower. When I allowed in negative thoughts, while exercising, such as "This is pathetic"; "This is a waste of my time"; "I'm just getting slower"; "Why bother!" I became progressively less inspired to exercise. I realized that if I didn't do something about how I was thinking, I would simply stop exercising. Yet I just couldn't tolerate the wash of negative emotions that were triggered by my negative thinking.

In desperation, I tried to come up with a different way of thinking about my exercise. I came up with the phrase, "At least I'm moving." It was the most positive thought that I could come up with. It was true and it put some value on my effort to continue to exercise (even though I was becoming slower and weaker with each passing day). This experience was transformative. Unknowingly, I created a go-to thought. This means when I was feeling down or negative about my effort, I was able to go to a pre-planned thought that helped me acknowledge the truth of what was going on, but in a way that was slightly humorous and encouraging. It kept me running, lifting, rollerblading, biking, and stretching when otherwise I would have become sedentary.

It was the first time I had used a pre-developed phrase to help me get through an expected, future tough moment. And there were many moments of self-doubt and frustration as my power dwindled and my speed diminished. Many times, I felt badly about becoming less fit, but the go-to thought helped me stay focused and motivated countless times. This strategy of purposefully creating a go-to empowered thought has been one of the most helpful interventions in my work as a sport psychologist with highly competitive athletes and performers. Go-to thoughts can have great power in return for a small effort.

Habituating this strategy—using empowered thoughts—to key moments in performance can help make the difference between giving up and pushing harder in the crucial performance moments. But it takes practicing the skill in daily training so that when the pressure is on, you have developed the habit of going to empowered thoughts that will best serve you for the big moments. I like to think about the go-to thoughts as planned empowered thinking, because the thoughts you go to are not always positive or nice. What matters is that the pre-planned thought or phrase (it can also be an image) facilitates you getting your mind back to paying full attention to what you are doing or thinking about in a situation in a manner that is most helpful to you in the moment.

Learning to create go-to thoughts in training is also a great strategy to help you build the habit of using empowered, purposeful thinking for moments when you might begin to feel flustered, fearful, or uninspired. We generally have a few consistent red flags that indicate when it is time to shift to a go-to empowered thought (e.g., "I hate this"; "I can't"; or "I'm humiliated"). Clearly, there can be many variations of distractions. The majority of distractions I have seen as a performance psychologist include overcoming a loss, coping with physical pain, feeling fearf/doubt, and being distracted by social factors (such as a coach, teammates, a teacher, family, or the media).

Consider the moment that is generally most challenging for you. When do you feel like giving up or feel like you just can't do it? Or when do you find yourself so distracted by other people or things that you find that your attention on what you are doing is less than 50% or 25% of your energy? Once you have the challenge selected, the next step is to figure out a go-to thought that would work for you. The key to this is to select a word or phrase that you believe would, in this quiet, reflective moment, work for you. The expected Pollyanna phrases like, "I can do it," often don't work. You've got to pick something that rings true for you and something that you feel or instinctively know would work for you in those seemingly overwhelming and awful moments. (But if "I can do it" will work, great!)

Recently, I worked with a group of classical musicians to help them mentally prepare for performance. One of the musicians, Greg, reported that he always felt terrified before he walked out onto the stage. He was unable to come up with any go-to statement. Even after the group shared a range of wonderful options that worked for them before they went on stage—which included, "I love this," "I've worked hard for this," and "It isn't about me, it's about sharing the music"—Greg could find nothing that would work for him.

After some discussion and seemingly coming to a point where he might not find an authentic go-to thought, he unexpectedly blurted out, "At least my mother loves me," and exploded with laughter. In that moment, both Greg and I knew that this would work for him. It was a phrase that he knew to be true, and somehow focusing on his mom's love—even as an adult—was both comforting and humorous. It was just what he needed to shift himself out of the fear and into the presence of doing his thing. Though saying this phrase to himself did not mitigate all of his fear, it did allow him to lighten the mood internally just enough that he was again able to reclaim his ability to be more focused on what he was doing as opposed to feeing fully controlled by his fear.

How about you? What are expected psychological red flags for you. Try creating one or two go-to empowered thoughts that you could try before you get too pressed to the wall and log them in Exercise 12.2.

There is a range of distractions that get in the way of performance. It can be helpful to consider developing a go-to phrase for each of the key challenges that you may face in high-pressure moments.

Exercise 12.2. Typical mental challenges

Challenge e.g., "I hate this."	Go-to empowered thought e.g., "If I push through now, I'll be able to do it again."
1.	1.
2.	2.

Physical: A great example of a physical distraction is one presented by Eliza, one of the most gifted collegiate rowers I have ever worked with. She was six feet tall and had dense, strong muscles. She came to me because her coach thought that she was not living up to her potential. She had an upcoming indoor rowing championship, and she wanted to go faster on her 2,000-meter race. As I talked with her about what she typically felt and thought about during a race, she said something that I thought was quite striking. She talked about how her legs would feel like they were on fire. She said that with each stroke, she experienced "more fire" in her legs. As you can imagine, this was quite a painful experience for Eliza.

I am certain that she felt significant physiological discomfort. And I'm certain that it did indeed feel like her legs were on fire. But I invited her to look at the exact same situation a little differently. Though there were many instances just before and during her race that we could have worked on, it was clear that her biggest distraction from focusing on racing to the best of her ability was her unrelenting focus on the burning sensation in her legs.

I asked her to consider how she could also think about her legs in a way that would be more empowering. I encouraged her to only choose a thought that she believed would work for her even when she was alone, racing, with the building, burning sensation in her legs. After much deliberation, she decided that she would try thinking, "My legs are getting warmer and warmer."

Two weeks after this session, she went on to earn one of the fastest collegiate times in the national 2000-meter ergometer (rowing machine) competition. She was willing to shift her automatic thought during a key performance moment. This only worked for her because she planned it in advance and she practiced saying this phrase to herself every day during the two weeks in practice as she was preparing for the big event. She did not wait until the day of the race to shift to the thought, "My legs are getting warmer and warmer." Every day, she practiced using this phrase. She was able to make a radical change in her actual performance (she cut over 20 seconds off her time) because of her well-rehearsed go-to thought.

Mistakes: Our emotional upset over a failure or disappointment in our performance can be a major block to optimizing performance, as well. It can be so easy to get quickly discouraged by one mistake. Though we all understand, rationally, that getting upset after a mistake and losing our focus will typically hurt our ability to perform—we all still do it! We all can still suffer from the sting of letting the ball get by us, making a mistake on a musical passage, or being just too far off in a pass. Regardless, in the performance realm, we all come up short, sometimes. The question really isn't how to stop making mistakes or failing, because we all will continue to face this reality. The question is, how are we going to respond to it so we can continue to perform at our best?

Fear: Thoughts associated with fear are the most common challenges at any big competitive event or performance moment. For most of us, the question isn't whether or not you will have fear, but how you will best cope with it—coming up with a go-to thought that would feel soothing and supportive is a great option for many performers. The challenge is coming up with the go-to thought that will work best for you. Unfortunately, there is not a magical go-to phrase that will work for all of us. But with some serious consideration, you can come up with a phrase that would authentically resonate within your soul. Often, it takes some experimenting to figure out what will work best for you.

What will work for each of us is unpredictable and varied. Over the past decade, there have been some typical areas of focus that have been helpful to hundreds of performers. Some performers are able to thrive when they go to a phrase that reminds them that they will survive the outcome of the performance, win or lose. For others reminding themselves of how hard they've worked, what they love about what they do, or that only this moment matters can also all be helpful.

What really matters most is what feels right to you. Sometimes a go-to thought can help you refocus and reduce your experience of fear. And for some of us, a go-to thought could simply remind us that the awful feeling might just have to be there, like "Here the feeling comes again," to "OK, now what do I need to focus on?" In such instances, this is time to focus on doing what we need to do to perform. Sometimes, our phrases help us to better tolerate the onslaught of energized, fearful anticipation.

Others' Expectations: Feeling pressured by others is also a typical challenge on performance day. Whether it is a coach, teacher, teammate, colleague, or a member of the media, our minds can become quite attached to what others may think or how we guess others evaluate our abilities or our specific performance. I have had clients who have had powerfully negative reactions to having certain people at their competitions.

One all-star ninth grade starter on a girls' varsity high school soccer team would literally pass out when her dad showed up to watch a game. I've had Olympic athletes report that having their parents show up to an Olympic event was very unsettling and that they had a very hard time bringing their attention back to what they were doing. A more typical concern is guessing and worrying about how a coach may evaluate one's performance. Regardless of the source of the social pressure, having others around on performance day and having concerns about their evaluation of both your actual performance and, then, the meaning they draw from this about your future potential as a performer can feel daunting. Even the best of competitors can break under such pressure.

In fact, in my studies of the Olympic level rowers—in a sample of 38 athletes—over half reported wanting to quit in the middle of a race in which they were competing to make the U.S. team or in an actual World Championship or Olympic race. Almost all of us will experience a heightened sense of pressure when it comes to the day of competition. The question, again, is what will we do with such intensified feelings of wanting to prove ourselves?

I have found that helping performers prepare a place to go within their thoughts that are both empowering and supportive can be invaluable. In the following table, consider negative thoughts that you may have on days of performance. There are a few main categories and examples of each to think about in your effort to create a possible go-to phrase that might be helpful to you. You may not find all of these categories relevant or helpful to your plan. For many of us, we really only need one or two go-to thoughts at the anticipated critical points in performance. If, for example, you have no challenge when pushing yourself physically, than there is no need for a go-to thought in this category for you. However, if you are in a sport or performance arena that requires long bouts of tolerating high levels of lactic acid (like running, biking, or swimming) or long lulls between needing to focus, it may be very helpful for you to create such a go-to phrase.

YOUR PERFORMANCE DAY: GO-TO THOUGHT(S)

In an effort to help strengthen your habit of empowered thinking, we've considered the areas that can frequently generate negative thoughts (physical discomfort, fear, mistakes, and the judgment of others) and the areas that can generate positive ones (what you love about it, perspective, and your strengths). It is helpful to practice addressing both in training (and in life) as you prepare for a significant upcoming performance. As you strengthen your habit to mentally move to more constructive go-to thoughts, you will increase the likelihood that these mental pathways are available when the pressure is on.

I encourage you to choose one phrase to enhance the positive and one phrase to shift out of the negative. What word or phrase could you use to

Exercise 12.3. Go-to thoughts: Dealing with day-of negatives

Challenge	Go-to empowered thought
Physical *e.g.,* "I can't keep going." YOURS:	*e.g.,* "I feel my power."
Overcoming mistakes *e.g.,* "I can't believe I just missed!" YOURS:	*e.g.,* "It's OK. Next play." YOURS:
Fear *e.g.,* "I feel totally terrified." YOURS:	*e.g.,* "It is OK to feel this, I just need to focus on what I'm doing." YOURS:
People *e.g.,* "What will they think?!" YOURS:	*e.g.,* "I decide what I do." YOURS:

remind yourself of your commitment, ability, effort, or intention that would help buoy you in the most difficult moment? And when you are feeling good, what word or phrase might help you the most to get fully, 100% focused, on each moment of performance? What would remind you that with a full effort and focus on the actual physical and mental activity of what you are doing—in each moment—you will be able to perform your best?

In the chart in Exercise 12.4, consider these questions and take a moment to jot down your answers. Better yet, get out an index card and write down these two phrases—one for hard moments and one to strengthen your focus

Exercise 12.4. Your main go-to empowered thought for the big moment

Specific challenge	Go-to empowered thoughts for game day
Negative: e.g. "Pull you out of negative spiral" YOURS:	**Positive:** e.g., "I'm better than this." YOURS:
The good:	e.g., "The power of right now." YOURS:

on the good. Use your card as a bookmark, or put it somewhere that you will see it to remind you of where you want your mind to go when it counts.

When it comes to performance day, choosing one or two go-to phrases can be essential to getting or keeping yourself in a constructive state of mind. It can be helpful to choose phrases that you know are true and ones that you can believe could be pivotal in maintaining your empowered state of mind. If you want to use these during performance, it is key begin experiment using go-to phrases right away. When emotions are high and your performance demands almost every bit of your attention, go-to phrases will only surface with some previous thought and implementation. Using a phrase that resonates with you and helps keep you focused on doing your thing well can make all of the difference. Such a phrase can serve as a nudge to keep you performing in the sweet spot and bypassing the unnecessary mental spirals downward.

I encourage you, for today, to practice using one go-to phrase. Right now you could imagine yourself in training and pulling up one of your go-to phrases. Plan for your next training bout: pick a particular moment in practice when you will call up the thought. If it feels right and empowering, keep using it. If not, experiment with using another word or phrase. Look back at the phrases that you developed in the various exercises in this chapter. Only with effort and practice will you be able to hone in on the focus or thought that will best serve you to maintain empowered thinking for performance.

13

Emotions on the Day of Performance

Getting the Most out of Your Emotional Engine

"I am nervous before the race, but once my hand is on the oar handle I can relax. There is nothing else that I can do."
—C.B. Sands, two-time U.S. World Rowing champion

There are times when important days of performance arrive, and we are confident and washed over with a great sense of knowing that we will do well. Sometimes we simply feel fully prepared and at ease. We can imagine being fully present to performance and can savor how well we will do. And, sometimes, this great sense of positive anticipation transfers directly into our performance, and we actually become fully engaged in what we are doing. We are so intensely engaged with and enjoying what we are doing that there is nothing to contemplate but the intense joy of the moment. We all have had at least one performance that has gone this magically.

And now, back to reality. Game day can also make momentary cowards of any of us. Most of us (OK, let's be honest—all of us) at some point before or during some performance have experienced intensified surges of unwelcome, distracting emotions. In fact, game day is notorious for conjuring such intense emotions. On the positive side, game day can increase our sense of hope and excitement. On the negative side, game day can also elicit doubt, dread, and unwelcome anxiety. It is not bad that these surges of emotions occur. In fact, wild surges of emotions are common when the pressure mounts. There is something we can do with this. We can learn to be

- fully aware of potential negative emotional spirals, so that we can re-bound into a constructive focus as soon as possible, and

- fully aware of positive emotional spirals, so we can capitalize on them.

The more prepared we are and the more quickly we can shift our focus, our thoughts, our behaviors, and effectively cope with unwelcome intense emotions, the better we will be able to perform, more consistently. And the more we can leverage the constructive emotional surges, the better off we are, as well.

When I was training for the U.S. National and Olympic teams, I almost always felt terrified before I raced. The fears were not rational—I was very fit and strong. I had highly-practiced technical skills. In my sport, it seems pretty simple. Just put the oar in the water and pull, like I did every day for years prior.

Yet I would get overwhelmed with an intense feeling of dread. I worried about who might be able to beat me. I wondered how I would be able to get through the physical pain, which always hit about mid-way through every race. The surges of panic seemed impossible to deal with. And in my sport, like most, it was not socially acceptable to talk about your fears. We were all supposed to be tough-minded. We were supposed to be able to handle anything that came at us. Yet, for those of us who are human, what do we do with these intense emotions? I felt like I was a victim to them. I had no idea of how to deal with them. No one talked about it. I often wondered what might have become of my athletic career had I had the psychological skills to deal with such surges of emotion.

Clearly, we do not have to buy into the fact that the fear means that we are not ready, are not competent, or are not worthy. The fear does come for most of us. The important issue is what you do with it. There are very real answers to make the surges of fear secondary to what we are doing.

WE CAN LEARN TO MAKE USE OF OUR INTENSE EMOTIONS

There is no question that game day intensifies our emotional states. The question is, "How will these intensified emotions impact our performance?" And if the intensified emotions are problematic, what do we do with them? Two of the top sport psychology researchers, Sheldon Hanton and Graham Jones, conducted a study with U.S. swimmers that shed light on these important questions. The athletes in their study were all top-10, nationally ranked swimmers. All of the swimmers recalled that when they were young they had many negative thoughts and emotions before and during racing. They experienced doubt, negativity, and physical symptoms that reflected anxiety, such as stomachaches and exhaustion. The feelings that they reported are similar to feelings that I have heard athletes report for over a decade in my private sport psychology practice. Muscle tension, sweaty palms, and even shaky limbs are typical. Having thoughts of doubt about physical and technical preparation are also common.

In this study of the top swimmers, all athletes reported having "early unwanted negative (emotional and mental) experience[s]." These experiences reported in the study were not surprising. However, the next set of findings from the study were. The results from this swimming study indicated that these top-level competitors reported that they learned to do two things: they had learned to accept the negative emotions and they had learned to channel these negative emotions, and physical sensations into energy for racing. They were not natural-born superstars in terms of emotional control. They struggled from the start, as all humans do. They reported that they could not totally get rid of their intense negative emotions even at the height of their athletic careers. Yet many of the athletes had learned to equate the anxiety-driven sensations with feeling ready to race!

Some of the racers consciously realized the actual importance of having these surges of negative, fear-generated emotions. These same sensations that used to mark fear began to mark readiness and a form of energy that was necessary to optimize performance. These are the same swimmers who had been crippled by fear and dread at the start of their careers. Through mental discipline, they had learned to manage and use these exact same emotions. We can all learn how to cope with wild game day emotions. It is a matter of awareness and determination to change our habitual responses to the moments that we put ourselves on the proverbial line.

The remarkable point about the swimming study is that the data indicates that these athletes were not just born with mentally tough mindsets. Usually, we think of our elite athletes as those who are natural-born winners. We might just assume that these elite athletes are naturally tough minded, also. We might think, "Of course they would be able to be mentally tough because that is just the way they are." We might be fooled into believing the myth of the born winner. These athletes certainly represent mental toughness, but their minds of steel are probably not an intrinsic gift. They worked hard for these tough mindsets. We, too, can continue to strengthen our own strong responses to our game day emotions with clear intentions and mental hard work. The bulk of this chapter deals with the specifics of how to do this.

Being mentally tough and able to deal with the pressure of competition is a learned habit. It has become very clear to me over the many years of applied practice as a sport psychologist that athletes and performers can learn effective habits of thinking and responding that serve them well in both practice and performance.

The athletes in the swimming study were lucky in some way. At young ages, they had adults who helped them learn how to work with their fears. Many of the participants in the study reported that their coaches and parents were instrumental in their learning to cope effectively with the anxiety and fear. The swimmers in Sheldon Hanton's studies were taught to believe and understand that intensified emotional states were normal, important, and even to be valued. They learned that the manifestation of nerves could actually be positive and help prepare them to swim their fastest.

It is important to note, though, that even when some reached the elite status of being one of the top ten in their events, they were still unable to stop their anxiety from showing up on race day. However, they learned to accept these sensations. They learned to label and to evaluate the experience differently. This acceptance of *nerves* is not automatic or easy to attain. In fact, these athletes continued to lean on a variety of strategies while competing at the elite level to enable them to either refocus or accept the emotions and physical sensations so that they could still perform their best.

To prepare for performances, these top swimmers use imagery and goal setting, as we discussed in previous chapters. For the actual day of performance, they rely heavily on purposefully redirecting their thoughts when thoughts of doubts or fear arise. They use positive imagery, relaxation skills, and purposefully focus their attention on factors that they can control (regardless of what their competitors are doing) and sometimes purposefully distract themselves or purposefully discount the importance of the given event. From a young age, these swimmers developed many strategies to help them, ultimately, focus on their swimming, as opposed to being distracted by the fears of not living up to their own or others' expectations.

In my research study of elite rowers, I also found many instances of athletes experiencing what many would consider negative physical signs of anxiety. Yet these top U.S. athletes (rowers in this instance), would also interpret the physical signs in a way that helped them race well. For example, one of the athletes in my study—I'll call her Laura—would experience extreme trembling in her legs before she raced. In one session of a research interview, she recalled the positive thought which she typically had going through her mind just before racing. She also casually noted the concurrent, chronic physical trembling which she also experienced just before racing. As she approached the start line for the finals' race of her second Olympics, she recalled thinking and feeling: "I know we can do it. We have done it. We have done it when we were exhausted, so we are not exhausted now, we can do it. And we went up to the line, my fingers were shaking, my knees were shaking. My knees and hands always shake before I race."

When I commented on how hard it must have been to have her body shaking, Laura laughed. She noted that if she wasn't shaking then she would have been concerned. To her, physical shaking meant that she was ready to race. Another study participant consistently vomited just before he raced. He interpreted this extreme physical manifestation of stress in a positive way. He reported, "I always hurl before I race. It just means that I'm ready to go!" An expert public speaker and teacher I know reported to me that about six hours before she has to give a big presentation, she feels horribly anxious and bursts into tears and cries for several minutes. Then she knows she's ready to give the big talk, and her emotions return to excited readiness.

The truth is that when the pressure is on, we all feel it in some way. Most of us have already developed some strategies to help us use this energy and focus on what we need to think about. The remainder of this chapter will focus on helping you handle—versus falling victim to—intense emotions that will show up for big moments. A lot of preparing for the negative emotions is knowing that they will come and then having a plan for dealing with them. Through the use of pre-planned thoughts and responses to the expected surges of emotion, you too can strengthen your ability to deal with them. When they are negative, you can learn to change what you are experiencing emotionally or learn to accept the intensified emotions and still get on with manifesting the very best performance within your ability. When they are positive, you can learn to capitalize on the energy and focus.

MINDFUL ACCEPTANCE OF INTENSIFIED EMOTIONS

Intensified emotions will show up for almost all performers the few hours before a big performance. (And if they don't, we are often quite concerned. We need to care enough to elicit such a surge of energy.) The question isn't whether or not the emotions show up. Rather, the question is, "How you will choose to develop your habitual responses to your energized state?" Some athletes have learned how to shift into a positive, accepting state. A great example of this is C.B. Sands, a two-time world champion. When I asked her how she typically feels before racing, she reported that she always feels anxious when she is coming down to the racecourse. Yes, like all of us. No surprise.

Yet, the surprising report of C.B. is that she has figured out how to become filled with a sense of being at ease—and almost relief—before the race begins! She says that once she touches her oars, she is fine. She, in fact, likes to brings her oars down to the river herself before a race, so that she can she feel at ease more quickly. At this point before the race starts, she feels that the pressure is gone. She is able to be totally present and accept whatever may come. This is how she feels before she races:

> Before I get to the racecourse, I feel nervous…. My stomach is upset, I feel shaky, though I'm not physically shaky. But as soon as I touch the oars, I feel much calmer. I know that there's nothing else that I can do in terms of preparation, because I am here. This is the moment. From that point on, I enjoy the walk, bringing the oars down. I think, 'It is over. The work is all done.' The training is harder than the actual race. Those days, weeks, and sometimes years… you've done all the work. I think, 'I can relax and enjoy everything.' By the time I shove off the dock, I think that this is what I love to do. There is a huge diminishment [of anxiety] for me …. All that work you do before you sit down and do the race—it is so much bigger. They are choices, not sacrifices, to achieve your goals. If it is a sacrifice, why do it? You do your workout and go to bed early. That is so much more stressful, day in and day out. At the national team level, it was every day [that I asked myself the questions], 'Can I get through

the day? Can I stay in control of everything?' When you get to the racecourse, you can sigh a breath of relief."

Whether it is putting ourselves on the line; comparing ourselves to others; seeing how well we can perform after months or years of competition; or determining how our performance will impact our options for making a team, earning a promotion, or getting the coveted spot; we are in a highly energized state.

The questions remain: "Where can you put your mind? What can you focus on that will help generate the most constructive state of mind?" For C.B., it was habituating herself to a particular thought: she practiced experiencing a great sense of perspective. She believes and focuses on the fact that racing is much easier than the long, grueling workouts. She also has habituated herself to being fully mindful and present before racing. In that particular span of time, there is absolutely nothing else that she can do to prepare. All that she can do is be fully present and do her best, stroke by stroke, moment by moment. The truth, of course, is that this is all that any of us can truly do to do our very best.

When we are fully focused on the moment of racing, competing, and performing, our fears dissolve and we are able to allow our bodies, minds, and souls to create their magic. C.B. is lucky (or more likely, she worked very hard) to be able to create such a sense of emotional ease and presence before she races. There are many strategies that we all can hone to help us get there, or at least closer, with some determination and a lot of practice.

When might you have a surge of negative emotion that you would like to simply accept? What is the moment in your performance day? Is it walking up to the stage? Is it right before the first game whistle blows? Is it an hour before the gun goes off? Consider a time that you can predictably expect a surge of negative emotions on the day of performance. What could you think about that would help you create some perspective or a shot of courage while, at the same time, feeling the unwelcome shot of emotion? Note below the situation and the expected negative emotions, and then try to come up with a word,

Exercise 13.1. Accepting negative emotions on game day

Situation	Challenging negative emotion	Word/phrase/image of acceptance

phrase, or image that would help you accept the emotion that is occurring and allow you to regain your focus on doing your thing.

DON'T SCRATCH THE ITCH (OF NEGATIVE EMOTIONS)

There are times when we can shift our emotional state toward the positive by thinking about our strengths or the good of having the opportunity to compete. However, on some days, regardless of what we say to ourselves, we may still begin our warm-up while filled by an awful, negative emotional state. At such times, the negative, anxiety-ridden emotions must simply be tolerated. Sometimes, it is possible to feel the normal pre-game jitters and then be able to naturally transition our focus to the task at hand and be fully ready to go, like C.B. described, above, before racing.

But there are certainly times that we have all experienced pre-performance emotions that are more overwhelming than the normal pre-race jitters. We all have fully dreaded an upcoming performance. We wish we could dissolve and reappear in a different lifetime or just be someone else. The last thing on the planet we want to do is to compete. But we must. We have been preparing for months or years and we are forced to put ourselves on the line against all the conflicting desires of our soul. In such instances, what do we do?

Psychologist Carolyn Youren, an expert in helping people cope with anxiety, often uses the metaphor "don't scratch the itch" when she teaches people how to manage intense, harmful anxiety. She equates the desire to focus on the negative emotion with the desire to scratch poison ivy. If you have ever had poison ivy, you know that the more you scratch the intensely irritating itch, the more you itch!

The same is true for our focusing on aversive negative emotions that we somehow cannot transform. Sometimes we are just plain anxious, self-doubting, or feel totally off. During these times, we can't allow ourselves to focus on how scared we feel, how bad it will be if we do poorly, how much we are sweating or shaking, or how tight certain muscles are becoming. When we focus on these negative emotions and negative sensations we are actually strengthening the aversive negative experience.

The basic idea is what you focus on grows. If you focus on how emotionally uncomfortable you are, you will tend to get progressively more irritated or fearful. The more we allow our minds to dwell on the bad of how we are feeling physically and what we are thinking, the more we strengthen the aversive negative emotional response. For example, when we think how badly we will do, we might begin to breathe harder. When we notice our short breath patterns, we might think, "Oh God, this is going to be a bad one!" With such thoughts, we might begin to feel our stomach tightening or our face turning red. When we notice these physical signs, we might determine that we now have evidence that we don't feel right and that our performance is going to go poorly. In one of my studies, a U.S. Team athlete described it as, "Everything is … totally spiraling out of control."

We will have times that we just can't turn off the angst, the fear, the embarrassment, the guilt, or the social discomfort. But if you have ever been seized by the fear of failing or intense dread of having to perform, you know how hard it is to tolerate such emotions. At such times, we instinctively feel an intense urge to flee. But running away in such instances is not conducive to becoming a great performer. In such instances, we must learn to be accepting that the unwelcome emotional experience is happening and, then, just to continue on knowing that we will have to tolerate the discomfort to give ourselves the best shot at performing our best.

But what do we do when the resistant, negative, destructive emotions continue to wash over us? These are the times when the only thing we can do is accept that the feelings are there and then refocus on what we can do each moment to get ready for performance. We must remind ourselves that such bouts of extreme anxiety are normal in highly competitive situations and that to do our best, learning to tolerate these feelings will truly serve us.

The biggest mistake we can make is to believe that these emotions mean anything about our upcoming performance (unless we let them!). As an athlete myself, I mistakenly learned to believe that intense negative emotions before my most important performance moments meant something. I believed that they were a signal that I would fail. The feelings meant that I wasn't as fast as, as strong as, as competent as, or as skilled as my competitors. And the only data that I was relying on was my panicked and terror-ridden state. In truth, all that my sensations indicated was that my physical body was in a highly energized state. The meaning I took from this physical state was a choice. Unfortunately, I didn't know that I had a choice. I didn't know that we have a choice about whether or not we allow ourselves to fall victim to our fears.

For the many years leading up to my Olympic trials, I didn't know that it was possible to be aware of such feelings and still perform well. I didn't know how to purposefully shift my focus and use my available energy to row effectively. Positive feelings or not, I always had the opportunity to focus on what would make me move the boat fastest—like thinking about the rhythm, connecting with the water, or applying the pressure as efficiently as possible so I could last as long as possible when racing. However, when my mind was in terror-mode, I didn't know how to shift it to help me row well anyway. I intermittently teetered on the brink of quitting mentally.

THE DANGERS OF MENTALLY GIVING UP

Mentally giving up is something that all performers have been tempted by. Most of us actually have given up a few times while training, racing, or competing. It is important to consider, in a non-emotional, quiet moment, the pros and cons of mentally giving up in a race. What I mean by this is when, for example, a swimmer is racing and just as they get passed, their intensity, effort, and focus slip a little, and the distance quickly grows between themselves and the swimmer that just passed them. The body is still moving and the physical system is still working hard, but the one that just got passed has decided that they will not be able to win the race. The one that was just passed decided that fighting to the end just wasn't worth it.

The moment of mentally giving up is brutal. The experience itself is difficult to even make yourself recall, much less having to experience it. In my study of 38 elite U.S. National Team rowers, more than 50% acknowledged in one-on-one interviews with me that they had given up in high stakes competition (racing for the U.S. team or competing in an Olympic or World Championship race). Here is one example of an athlete recalling that awful moments of giving up: "I just want to get the hell out of this boat and I don't want to be here…. There was nothing I could have done that could have got me out of that boat faster and just on the plane and out of there…. Physically I was still rowing and finishing the race, but mentally I couldn't care less."

A second elite athlete reported what he experienced while in such a race: "Yeah, and [I recall] I am starting to fade. I am seeing people make moves and, pretty much, I don't feel like I am going to be able to respond. So I kind of packed my suitcase and just finished the race."

We are all challenged in such moments. We go into a performance with significant expectations of what we want to accomplish. The pressure comes from many sources. We may have spent years training for this moment of competition. We may have coaches and/or teachers who believe in our great abilities. Or we may have just decided that if we don't hit a particular level of performance, we, as human beings, are not worthy of being.

The problem is not just that moment of giving up. It gets worse. When we give up we begin creating a default, a potential automatic go-to response when things get tough. We are creatures of habit. Each time we act in a particular way in a particular circumstance, we are more likely to respond in the same way when the same circumstance arises again. Especially when the pressure is on and we have time constraints, we will feel an emotion and default to a particular behavior (e.g., if you are getting passed, you stop trying as hard without making a conscious decision to do so). Yet, with awareness and planning, we can choose a different approach in such moments. Giving into the urge to quit creates habits, which no one wants.

I interviewed champion triathlete Marijke Zeekant and asked her about the times in competition when she has negative thoughts and how she deals with them. There was a long pause in our conversation and she said that she didn't have them. I pressed her: "Oh, come on. Are you saying that in every race you feel good and you only have constructive thoughts?" She paused again and said, "I never think about quitting. As soon as you start quitting the race mentally [thinking thoughts such as]… this is not my day, [you say] I quit and I'll do it another [day]." Up until this point in the interview, I was not surprised. Yes, what she describes was parallel to what the many other athletes with whom I have talked have said. When you have negative thoughts and decide to quit, you set yourself up for a poor performance on that day. However, the long-term implications are something that we don't often think about. Marijke went on to point out:

> As soon as you give into that thought, it will be negative for the next race. You take it with you in[to] another race. Even if the result is not that good, it is better to finish the race and say I'm proud of myself for finishing the race. Even in bad situations, it is better to finish it and take the experience with you. You trained… take it for extra training. You learned from that one and you can take it with you.

The truth is that however you decide to respond, you will take it with you. When you mentally quit, you take the slightly strengthened habit of giving up when it is not going your way. So the next time you have the urge to quit, your habit is slightly strengthened to give into this tempting urge. On the other hand, when you learn to continue fighting through a race, competition, or performance, especially when it is not going well, you create a habit of doing your best, regardless of the circumstances. And the next time you feel yourself resistant to pushing through, even when you wildly don't want to, you are more likely to find the courage to do what is right for your training and development as opposed to giving into the momentary negative urge.

SO WHAT DO YOU FOCUS ON WHEN A PERFORMANCE ISN'T GOING WELL?

When you are overwhelmed with the desire to quit, where do you take your mind? What can you focus on? This, of course, is not a topic that you want to spend much time on, but it can be invaluable if you honestly consider where you could focus your mind if your performance day goes awry. You might think, "Yeah, OK. But can you expect me to shift my thoughts in such hard moments? When I have the feeling of wanting to quit, I don't want to try any more!" I asked Dutch athlete Marijke a similar question. I pushed her to consider the times when it was really not going well. She conceded and talked about the few times when her racing didn't go well: "And sometimes when it is not going well, I think to myself, 'Well, this is not going well, but that is the way it is. Just make the best of it.' You have to accept it. I try to make the best of it for that time."

In such poor racing moments, she accepts how she is racing. She accepts the state of her physical body. Yet, while accepting that she is not racing up to her expected level, she still looks to what she could think about to help her get through the difficulty by distracting herself with the good that surrounds her. Her core strategy seems to consist of an effort toward two things. She *accepts* what is happening and is *positively present*—she looks and thinks about what is good around her.

After describing how she thinks about those difficult moments while racing in a triathlon, she went on to explain this mindset of being present and accepting.

> You try to make your mindset a bit different…. You must try to get your mind off of the negative part and focus on the positive things… like people who are on the side who are there for you. Or you see what others are doing in the race. Or you consider, 'This is a nice area for a race. This is nice scenery.'

In this description, Marijke emphasizes the importance of purposefully switching her mindset. We have to move from being distracted by our negative emotions to being fully accepting of what is happening and being OK with it. With the ability to be accepting of such hard emotional moments, you put the brakes on spiraling out of control, emotionally and mentally. When you can distract yourself with the good around you, the positives of being where you are geographically, or of the energy that surrounds you, you then can put a stop to the potentially devastating impact of creating the all or nothing mindset that leads to giving up.

In Exercise 13.2 consider a time during performance when you might typically feel frustrated or disappointed. Consider what you could possibly focus on that would shift your focus to what is good about being where you are. It could also be helpful to think of a past performance when you had surges of negative emotions. If you could have that moment back to change, what could

Exercise 13.2. Shifting from the negative to the good

Situation	Challenging negative emotion	Word/phrase/image that represents the good in that moment

you have focused on that was good or positive about being in that moment? I encourage you to take a few moments to consider these questions and write down your answers. This may be a key point for you. It is easy to perform well when things are going well. But it is essential to have a plan when things are not. One shift of focus to acceptance or the positive could have a significant impact on your ability to create the habit of being determined and focused when it most counts.

HOPE AND EXCITEMENT: USING THE POWER OF YOUR ENERGIZED STATE

Game day is not always about tolerating negative, out-of-control emotions. There are times when we do feel good; we feel prepared and we experience surges of confidence and anticipation at having the chance to do our thing. Sometimes when it is going well, athletes and other performers don't purpose-fully tune into this good. And when we don't, it is a missed opportunity to expand on the positive or good.

We have not been taught to intentionally expand on the good energy and focus that can emerge on game day. Simply noticing what is good and what is working can be a great way to expand on what already is going well. Notice the quality of the air or the strength in your physical body. If your performance includes movement, enjoy the good qualities of the movement of your body. Notice those around you who believe in you and want the best for you. Consider the incredible opportunity to get to be doing what you are doing. Bring to your attention the aspects of what you are doing that you unequivocally love. Bring to your attention the moments of the upcoming performance that you will be able to do well. Notice positive reactions of others to your presence, to your warm up, and to your performance.

The more you bring to your attention what is good, what you love, and your skills and strengths, the more you will be able to build on what is good and right on game day. And with this attention, your experience of constructive, positive emotions may grow. In Exercise 13.3, consider a recent time

Exercise 13.3. Expanding on the good on game day

Situation	Empowering positive emotion	Word/phrase/image that represents the good in that moment

when you were performing to the best of your ability. Consider creating a word, phrase, or image that you can bring up that will help you expand and extend the empowering, positive emotion. You may consider using phrases like, "I've earned this," "This is just how I want it to feel," or "I love it when it feels like this." Consider a word, phrase, or image that will help you notice and strengthen the good when it occurs. Take the time to write down the phrase. Make a mental note to call up this constructive phrase the next time things are going well when you are performing.

I have found that there are a few ways to be able to consistently help performers get into a constructive state of mind for the day of performance. These areas of focus also work well when we are looking for ways to get ourselves into a positive energy state. Essentially, I have looked to help performers find points of focus that both get their minds on what is right and also help them free up their minds to do their thing for performance. Simply, and obviously, the more you are focused on what you are actually doing, the better you will perform. That means letting go of things like general performance fears, comparisons with others, or perceived judgments from others.

But how do you move away from these distractions? First, it is critical to focus on factors that you can control. One of the clearest ways to channel our good, confident energy on game day is to have a few specific points of focus that both block out potential distractions and help us perform well. The specific points of focus will vary greatly among performance realms, but it is critical to have your few go-to points of focus. A swimmer might think, "Cut powerfully through the water." A musician might think, "Just be with the music." Whatever it is, the key is to think about aspects of performance that you can directly affect, regardless what your competitors are doing. Second, hold onto your perspective. It is important to hold onto the fact that you'll be OK, no matter what happens. Have a specific go-to thought planned that reminds you that you will be fine no matter the outcome of the performance. As long as you can maintain perspective, you often are able to remain in a constructive, positive energy space. And finally, try using positive imagery. Preparing an image of how you'd like to perform, and how you'd like to look and feel just at the end of your performance, can be a great source of positive motivation and energy. Even when you are feeling great and on top of your game, it can be helpful to take a moment or two to envision just what you'd like to have happen. Practicing in your mind performing exactly as you'd like to and feeling just the way that you'd like to be feeling can help set you up for best performance. These three basic strategies are very helpful when you are trying to create or strengthen a positive emotional state when the pressure is on.

EXPECTING TO PERFORM AS YOU PRACTICE

Our expectations have a huge impact on our emotional state on game day. We often hope for an extraordinary out of body experience. We can want to be able to have skills, fitness, and strength that we have not yet achieved. When we try to perform outside of our current abilities and skills, we can set ourselves up for a significant amount of emotional discomfort. However, when we can fully accept where we are currently, we then can stretch from this point. When we can accept our fitness level, our strength, and our abilities, we can make a plan to work from this as our base.

Recently, I had to face this challenge. I raced in the Head of the Charles, an international rowing event. I had been exercising and was in good enough shape to make it up the three-mile course without fearing for my life. I knew I could make it. But then I found out that four of my boatmates were still train-ing many hours per day! I was momentarily seized with fear. I thought about how much better I'd have to row and how much more power I should be able to generate to keep up.

The day before I raced, I had a daydream of getting about one fourth through the race and literally collapsing. At this point, I knew that I had a big mental task in front of me. I had to fully accept my level of fitness. If I was going to try to produce power like I did 16 years ago, when I was an Olympic athlete, I was sure to fly and die. I would never make it through the race. But it was so hard to make myself pull at a level that I could actually sustain. I made the commitment to accept my current abilities. It turned out that I had one of the best races of my life. I pushed my edge—I didn't jump off of it. I stayed within the limits of my physical capabilities. And from there, I pushed as hard as I could.

When we can accept just where we are, we, in fact, can free ourselves up to perform to the best of our abilities. One point of comfort that we can give ourselves going into high stakes competition is that we cannot practically expect ourselves to be able to perform better on game day than we do on our days of practice.

In one of my research interviews, an eight-time U.S. Rowing Team mem-ber commented, "It doesn't matter if it is Sunday morning racing alone in the rain or if it is the World Championships' final, I race the same." When we expect ourselves to do the best that we can each practice and each training session, we need to do no more than that come race day. This perspective can take the dread out of race day emotions and allow us to create or remain in a state of mind that is most conducive to optimizing performance. We all can learn to accept where we are, tolerate the sometimes negative emotions, and, mostly, enjoy and expand a constructive state of mind.

14

Motivational Flexibility

Drawing on the Motivational Sources that Serve You

> *"I might think, 'We really have to win this race!" But then you think, you have to win every race! But then you must clear your head of everything.... You must focus strictly (back) on the moment and what you're doing.'"*
>
> —Dawn Riley, 5-time America's Cup sailor

Performing well under pressure takes either some good luck or some good awareness and planning. Our motivation controls our energy, our attention, and what we do. Many things can motivate us: the desire to beat a teammate, the love of doing our thing, the need to get approval from others, the fear of failing, or the desire to win. It is essential that we are clear on what is motivating us when we perform under stress. The point of this chapter is to explain and demonstrate how we can learn to shift our motivation from a less effective motivator to a more effective motivator. With awareness and effort, we actually can shift the direction and intensity of our efforts.

The weekend before my final round of races to make the Olympic team was one of the worst periods of my life. I was motivated only by fear. I could not stop thinking about how bad my life would be if I choked during my last round of races to make a boat to race in the 1992 Summer Olympic Games. I was living with an intense level of fear. I knew that I was terrified. I knew that I had no confidence. But I really had absolutely no idea of how to shift out of that hellish state. I had nowhere to turn. I had no wise guide to tell me what to think or what to do. I fully believed that I was just experiencing what I was experiencing and that there was no other option.

What is the wrong motivation at the wrong time? Certainly being highly energized by fear was not serving me. We all have experienced the wrong motivation at the wrong time. It doesn't have to be as dramatic as my experience. Any point of focus that draws our attention away from doing our best at the moment is a wrong motivation at the wrong time. For example, thinking about losing a race right before the gun goes off creates a strong urge to escape arising from the surge of fear. This surge of energy might distract us to the point that we either jump the start or have a slow start. Another example of wrong motivation at the wrong time is to feel highly energized about a recent mistake when a fly ball is coming right toward us. Our attention may be drawn toward thinking about how to avoid that past mistake, and with this in mind, we may be distracted and drop the ball coming right at us. When performing or getting ready to perform, we are essentially pulled by two strong attention grabbers. We think in terms of either success/failure, or we think in terms of being present to what we are doing—moment to moment:

- *Success/Failure:* We think (a lot) about trying to hit some mark of success, trying to make the team, the orchestra, or the cut. We want to win, to be the best, and to dominate. Alternatively (or maybe at the same time) we think about not failing, not being humiliated, not losing.

- *Doing our thing:* We also think about, regardless of who is watching, wanting to be great at what we do. We want to be excellent. We love to be fully absorbed in doing our thing. We love to run, jump, and create beautiful emotions or unusual rhythms. We love creating and manifesting moment to moment.

When we are honest with ourselves and the pressure is off, most of us tend to really like to do what we do. And often our attention is drawn to what we are doing in the moment as we prepare and compete. This is good.

However, when we are training, performing, and competing, our attention is also drawn toward thinking about our powerful desires to be successful—as compared to others. This can be good, too. It can help us, for example, push through when we are exhausted. However, focusing solely on the outcome while practicing and performing can also be a great source of distraction. Thinking about the results can be devastating, as it was for me when preparing for my last round of races to make the Olympic team. Both motivations are very powerful. To consistently perform well we must understand these powerful motivators that draw our attention, and we must know how to manage or direct them when they are not productive.

Simply stated, our motivations can lead us to success or drive us into the ground. If we are not careful, our desire for success can spin us into a state of fear, worry, or dread that can be devastating. But with self-awareness and a better understanding of the powers and directions of our motivations, we can learn to harness our attention and energy toward what serves us best. We tend to oscillate between thinking about how to do our thing and thinking about how important it is to us to be successful. We can't help it—that is how we are wired. Yet we can learn the essentials of choosing and consciously controlling the direction and source of our motivation. We can learn to use the energy.

Where is it best to keep our attention when performing? Should we just keep our attention on the moment and ignore our desires to achieve some external mark of success? Is this even possible? Much of the current literature would point toward focusing on the present—and *only* the present. You are encouraged to just stay with the moment of preparing to swing your golf club, or in the rhythmic moment of the fifth mile of a 26.3 mile marathon. Theoretically, the push to focus on the moment is supported by the concept of *flow*. If you recall Chapter 7, flow is when you are totally engaged in the moment-to-moment of performance—and experiencing flow is often synonymous with the best performance. Indeed, this is the ideal state while practicing or performing. You are fully present, stretching yourself to the best of your abilities, and attentive to the current activity in this state of flow.

Yet research also suggests that it is impossible to be in a chronic state of flow. It is impossible to always love what you are doing without a care in the world for the outcome of whatever it is that you are doing. Never did I race in an international competition or World Championship devoid of consideration for the outcome. I've never met a performer who had no care for the results of what they were doing. All performers must care, to some degree, about the ultimate result and evaluation of their performance. We are not able to put our competitive selves, in which we compare ourself with others, aside. Part of what drives most of us is to hit marks of external success.

In my final report to the U.S. Olympic Committee (USOC) for a study I conducted of National Team and Olympic-level rowers, I reported that these athletes were highly energized to do the best that they could, compared to others, in competition. They cared very much about medaling in national and international competition. Though this may seem like an obvious result for research on Olympic athletes and what they value, I was strongly criticized for reporting these results. The USOC did not like the fact that I was reporting that the Olympic athletes were motivated by this extrinsic factor. They didn't like me reporting that these athletes cared very much about winning and that they intensely wanted to win medals. They wanted me to report that the athletes were motivated by their intrinsic motivation, by the desire to do their best moment to moment (100% of the time). They didn't want me to report that the athletes were highly focused on winning. Clearly, there is a tension between what theory suggests we should ideally focus on and what we actually focus on while getting ready for a high-stakes performance, and during the actual performance.

So what really works? The truth is that when we are performing and competing, we need to be able to focus on both the outcome and on our love for the activity itself. And the ratio that works for you may be slightly different than what works for others. We need to be able to focus on what it takes to perform our best, moment to moment. And we sometimes need the carrot of potential success to push us when nothing else can. When you are in your last lap of a mile run and the lactic acid is burning your body, you need something to push you to keep going. Yet, holding both the desire to be present to our performance and desiring external success is tough to do well.

Many times, competitors will get so caught up in the desire to do well that they lose focus on the factors that will actually help them become successful. In one of my research studies, one four-time U.S. team member and Olympic athlete reflected on the complexity of values associated with competing. She highlighted the tension between wanting to win and doing one's best. In one part of her interview, this athlete reflected on the importance of beating others: "We [elite athletes] love to win, but not everybody can win…. The goal is to win. You can't deny it. Yeah, it is participation. It is being around it. But [winning] is the purpose, the end-all-be-all. You would be a fool if you didn't admit that."

However, in another part of the same interview, when asked directly about whether she would choose between realizing [her] potential 100% and losing, or not maximizing [her] potential and winning, she stated,

> My goal is to find my own potential…. I think that everyone is given a certain gift and if you don't fulfill it, if you don't find your potential in that gift, then you've let yourself down and other people, too…. And in that process [of finding my potential], I believe that a lot of the time I can be successful in terms of winning.

These brief comments shine a light on the complexity of the values performers face. We have the desire to do our best and the desire to beat others and win. We know that we think about both. The question is how to guide our minds wisely to optimize our mental performance when it counts. To address this challenge, I have coined the term *motivational flexibility* to explain what we practically need to be able to do when the pressure is turned up.

WHAT IS MOTIVATIONAL FLEXIBILITY?

The idea of motivational flexibility has been developing in my mind as I've worked with highly competitive athletes and top musicians. I've seen too many performers get stuck in negative motivational states (e.g., fearing failure). And, to be honest, I got stuck there one too many times myself! I've observed, over and over again, that when an athlete is able to control what they focus on and is authentically energized by this focus, they tend to perform better and they tend to be performing in the sweet spot as well. I think of this combination of focus and energy as motivational flexibility.

> Motivational flexibility is the ability to purposefully execute shifts in energy and direction of focus between intrinsic (because you like it) and extrinsic (because you want to achieve some outcome) motivations. These shifts are executed for the purpose of optimizing performance when in situations of high pressure and high expectations.

Essentially, motivational flexibility is being able to wisely shift between an in-the-moment focus and the desire to succeed. Practically, when we are performing at our best, we do execute motivational flexibility—we are able to move in our minds between being fully engaged with what we are doing and having flashes of the desire to be successful.

Researchers who study motivation sometimes categorize it into two main types: intrinsic and extrinsic motivation. The concept of intrinsic motivation reflects the times when you are doing your thing for the sheer joy of doing it. This could be when you are running and you just love the feel of it, or when you are lifting weights and you authentically enjoy the burn of the muscles maxing out. In contrast, the extrinsic motivation reflects when you are engaged in a behavior because it will produce some outcome that is important to you. You are doing something, not for the love of it in the moment, but for what you'll ultimately get out of the effort. Yes, you can have both motivations at the same time. But the issue is what is on your conscious level of attention, (e.g., I love this or I will succeed).

Now I'm going to get specific. The idea of motivational flexibility only includes a portion of extrinsic motivation (thanks to the theory of self-determination put forward by Richard Ryan and Edward Deci, we now have this distinction). The next bit of discussion may sound technical, but it is very important to clarify that extrinsic motivation—being motivated to achieve some outcome in the future—can be driven by two very different sources of motivation. There is a type that is constructive and a type that is destructive to our performance. The unsavory type of extrinsic motivation occurs when you feel coerced or guilted into action. This is the kind we want to stay away from, as much as possible.

The other type of extrinsic motivations is self-determined. We want this type of extrinsic motivation in our motivational flexibility equation. These self-chosen motivators are ones that resonate with our values even though they are not necessarily enjoyable in the moment. For example, you might run stadium stairs to become more fit. The process itself might be very painful and grueling, but you do it anyway because you value the extra fitness and strength that you gain from this activity. You may not enjoy it, but you choose to run the stadiums because it supports you striving toward an important self-chosen goal. As a musician, you may spend an extra fourth or fifth hour in the practice studio. You may be tired and hungry, yet you stay because you trust that the extra practice time will help you properly prepare for the upcoming audition.

The key to motivational flexibility is that you are able to flexibly, in your mind, shift between doing something because you are authentically motivated to do for the joy of it and doing something because it will help you achieve some extrinsic goal that you value. The trick is to know when to focus on the moment-to-moment of what you are doing and when to focus on the carrot to help inspire you to keep pushing. When I was going into the last round of races for the Olympic Games, I was so riveted by the carrot that I didn't have the capacity to do my thing in the boat. I totally choked. (I did make the team, but as an alternate—I rode the bench.) The model in Figure 14.1 presents a simple way of thinking about motivational flexibility. It is about being able to shift your authentic motivations, consciously, to best serve your purposes.

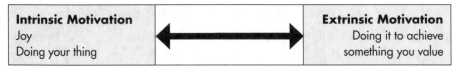

Intrinsic Motivation		**Extrinsic Motivation**
Joy		Doing it to achieve
Doing your thing		something you value

Figure 14.1: Motivational flexibility

I began to develop the idea of motivational flexibility after my own athletic experiences and my training as a sport psychologist. It more fully emerged after I started analyzing the data of two studies I conducted which focused on elite rowers. I explored how the athletes coped with competitive pressures. When they coped poorly, almost all of them were terrified just prior to racing in high-stakes competition, from the final round of selection for the U.S. team to World Championship or Olympic racing. In these events, the athletes had a powerful desire to win and, put simply, they couldn't stop worrying about the results of the race. They wanted so completely to win and be successful that their thinking became paralyzed.

They were stuck with inflexible, obsessive thoughts of how the race might go poorly. They were terrified of failure. Their motivation was about success—more specifically, the fear of not having it—and their motivation remained stuck there temporarily. Here are a few things that one athlete said about when she was stuck in the desire to perform coupled with fear that she would not be able to live up to expectations:

> It just kept kind of snowballing and I was getting really frantic about it [racing], and I didn't know how to pull myself back from it and take this overall look at it—like, 'OK, relax, and do what you know how to do.' I felt like things were kind of slipping away from me.... I mean, now I think I can see the things that I did wrong. But at that point, when I was doing it, I was just really caught up in it and had no idea about how to pull myself out and felt myself getting sucked in further and further [into the fear].

This athlete did not know how to shift out of the worry over her race results into the controllable factors that could actually help her perform. Instead of fearing that she might lose, she could have focused on thinking about body swing, power application, feeling the oar in her hand or matching her teammates while racing. Unfortunately, most athletes find themselves in similar situations. Perhaps not to this extreme, but most of us have had moments when we so badly wanted to do well that we forgot about the obvious in-the-moment simple strategy of getting our minds back to factors that we can control that will most help us with our immediate ability to perform.

Where does your mind get trapped when you begin thinking only of the outcome of a performance? What are some or your typical thoughts in these moments? I'll provide a few and then I encourage you can come up with yours. Usually, this is the easiest exercise in the book to do (it tends to be easiest to remember your negative thoughts and feelings—it is easy to put on our 2% blinders).

If you've read this far, keeping reading—this is definitely NOT where you want to stop. Awareness is important: being aware of when you might be inflexible in your thinking, your attention, and your energy usage is incredibly important. But if you just gain awareness of your thoughts and emotions that get in your way and stop there, you can actually make things harder for

Exercise 14.1. Motivational INflexibility:
Where does your mind get stuck?

e.g., "I am out of control," "If I don't win than the last 10 years of my life have been wasted," or "I'll be so embarrassed if I don't win."
1.
2.
3.

yourself. Awareness with no option for change is a tough spot to be in. So then what do you do?

The next step is to consider what being more flexible looks like. And the final step is to practice and expand your motivational flexibility in training and performance. You can practice how you want to think and respond. You will, ultimately, become aware of which motivation best serves you and strengthen your ability to draw on the motivational source that best serves you in high-pressure moments—moment to moment.

WHAT DOES MOTIVATIONAL FLEXIBILITY LOOK LIKE?

So now we know what motivational flexibility doesn't look like: being stuck with a fear of losing. In the next example, a six-time U.S. National Team member and two-time Olympian talks about how she developed the conscious ability to shift her motivation, energy, and attention. Unfortunately for her, this occurred just at the end of her career. In the following section, she discusses how, early in her elite-rowing career, she wasn't able to shift her thinking while racing. In one race, she recounted, "I felt myself totally just giving up [in a key race].... Deep down in my gut, I didn't believe in any of that suck it up, go ahead and do it." In her reflection, it is clear that she had learned to push her body, but had not yet learned to tap the potential of changing how she was thinking to shift the intensity and direction of her energy. She recalled,

> Racing... is a physical demand. There's not much you can do to change your physical ability in the midst of a race. So I was pushing myself, but mentally, I wasn't doing very well... so I was pushing myself harder into a wall [physically]. Once I hit the wall, then, mentally, I wasn't prepared to deal with it because I didn't have a plan for it.... I gave up.

Having a plan to shift your motivation before you hit your mental wall is the key. Sometimes, we can just magically shift into a better attitude—we may be triggered by a comment by someone or some random occurrence. But we don't want to leave it to chance. It is important to come up with a plan so that you know how to shift into productive ways of thinking, feeling, and acting. This same athlete had an inspired moment of clarity where she finally discovered how to purposefully shift her thinking. This insight happened in the warm-ups for her last Olympic race. Her warm-ups were going very poorly and she was initially tied up by the intense desire to do well, paired with a great fear of her race not going well. She stated,

> We were each so nervous; we were not rowing well together at all. When we got up to the top [of the course and near the start line]…, I was almost on the verge of tears. I just thought that this is horrible! Here I am, the last race of my rowing career and we are at the Olympics…. We were going to come in last…. My parents were in the stands and the world was watching…. This is going to be seven minutes of torture, pain, physical torture."

This line of thinking is not unlike that of many athletes when they are under a great pressure to perform, particularly when the event or competition is a once or twice in a lifetime event. With the pressure to perform intensified, we are more easily thrown off our game. We are more easily distracted by fears and by small mistakes or bobbles in warm-ups. Athletes will tend to doubt their abilities and consider the downside of how they would feel if they fail.

Yet, what happened next to this two-time Olympian is an excellent example of the thought process that represents fluidly and purposefully shifting one's motivational orientation. She was able to confront her line of thinking and realize that it was not serving her. Next, she was able to shift from her fear of the consequences to that focus that, in the moment, would help her race well. "And really in my mind, I thought, that's bullshit. We have rowed in this boat for four months; I have been rowing for 10 years…. There is no way that we are not going to do it…. Being doubtful about it is not going to help me, I mean, I know we can do it. We have done it."

Not only was she able to make the shift, but she was also aware that she was doing so deliberately. She reflected, "It was the best race of my life, really. Because, in the past, I may have had some successes, but I don't feel like it was as deliberate. I think they were, maybe in a way, flukes, a little bit—like I was lucky. I had the luck of a beginner, not realizing what's happening."

So, prior to the race, she became determined to shift from the fear of doing poorly to being determined to focus on what she could control to do the best that she could. She also had another shift while she raced. Though she clearly wanted to perform to the best of her abilities, she was able to focus on the present moment, stroke by stroke. She reflected, "I really made the effort not to make the effort. It was very much in the moment, right from the beginning, and everything seemed to flow. I had a sense of what was going on around me. I was really in tune with my body and with my boat."

So, though still conscious that she was racing in an Olympic final, her primary, conscious focus was not on that. She was thinking about how to row effectively, in the moment. Her final comments about the race indicated a significant sense of satisfaction with being able to shift her motivational orientation in a way that allowed her to race to the best of her abilities. She stated, "I felt, in the end, very satisfied because I came away from the experience doing what it is, ultimately, I always wanted to do. I faced that challenge and those fears."

This athlete seems almost lucky to have had the insight to shift focus just before her last round of Olympic level races.

The next athlete, also a subject in one of my studies, talks about being aware of his need to shift away from fear-based and outcome-focused thinking months before an important round of races. He practiced bringing his attention back to what he was doing, moment to moment, as he knew he was likely to get pulled into obsessive thoughts about his intense desire to make the next US Team while racing. The worry was that his thinking could get stuck on his overwhelming desire for success. He discussed purposefully preparing himself to cope with unwanted, negative emotions, which he anticipated would direct his attention to fear if he didn't do something about it. He used mental rehearsal for months prior to his big race in an effort to practice shifting his motivational orientation when it counted. He said, "I went through my race plan, focused and relaxed. I did some visualization of trying to think of what it actually would feel like to actually be in the situation and letting those emotions develop and then trying to deal with [them], at least mentally."I asked him what he actually practiced visualizing. He said,

> Hurting. In that moment... I'm trying to actually feel it. The mind is a very powerful thing, so maybe not so much fatigue that I would feel, but I can feel the anxiety of not being in the lead or things that I don't need to be thinking about. I put those out of my mind [and saw myself] sticking to my plan. [I asked myself] 'Can I go faster?'

The athlete in this instance reported on practicing in advance to purposefully, consciously exercise motivational shifts while racing. He practiced shifting from the macro focus, on winning, to the micro focus, on how to race efficiently within the framework of his significant desire to win.

By experiencing the negative, anxious feelings during his imagery practice, he created a learning opportunity about how to practice shifting his motivational approach when those anticipated negative motivational sources surfaced while racing. Though he clearly wanted to win, what was most helpful to his ultimate success was his learning to bring his focus back to a moment-to moment focus on what would help him race his best.

These two athletes talked about *the shift* as part of their discussion of coping with competitive pressure. After hearing what they had to say, I began interviewing other performers to get a sense of how others have learned to purposefully shift their attention and what they are energized by.

One of the athletes I had the chance to interview was Dawn Riley, the five-time America's Cup sailor. I asked her if she also uses this purposeful, conscious shifting of her motivation when racing. She stated that she understands the importance of focusing on what she can control, but she reported the challenges of her mind wandering and intermittently worrying about the outcome (while racing) and her conscious effort to shift her motivational orientation when necessary. Dawn recalled, "Under high-pressure, you just focus on what you can control. Yet you might think, 'We really have to win this race!' But then I think you have to win every race! You must clear your head of everything. You don't think, 'We have to win this race or the media will scour us.'... You must focus strictly on the moment and what you're doing."

Dawn was very aware of the pull to focus on the desire to win, but was also aware that a constant focus on outcome could be a big distraction. Her strategy is to pull attention back to the present as much as she can. When I asked if she consciously, purposefully does shift her attention, she said,

> I do it all the time. Of course, in sailing, there are slower moments; your mind has time to wander. You have to mentally slap yourself on the face and say, 'Come on!' I literally kick-start myself [physically]. I give myself a big surge of energy, a push.... It is a deep breath, an exhale, and (saying to myself) 'Let's go!' On the boat, you don't want people to think that you are psychotic. I shake it [the worry of wanting to win] off physically, I tense my thighs and generally I exhale.

Dawn is aware of the need to stay present. Yet her mind wanders to the finish line. She has strategies that help shift her energy back to the present, to the moment of competition. The question now is, "What works for you to shift your motivational source when you need to?"

MOTIVATIONAL FLEXIBILITY: WHAT STRATEGIES WORK FOR YOU?

Over the past decade in my work as a sport psychologist, I have come to the conclusion that to perform well—and to demonstrate motivational flexibility—requires an understanding of three basic things. We need to know:

- What can bring you back to the moment-to-moment of performance;

- What can get you highly motivated to keep your attention on what is occurring moment-to-moment; and

- What it is about achieving external success that is important to you.

Being aware of the factors that will help energize your motivational flexibility is essential. Though often we are more aware of our motivations about winning than of the motivations that keep up focused on the moment-to-moment of performance.

What is most helpful for you to pay attention to, moment to moment, when performing—especially when in the temporary grip of feeling fearful about the outcome? Just for a moment, think about what you are doing, what your mind is focusing on, what you are thinking about, and/or what your body is actually doing when you perform well. Consider a few key physical, mental, and emotional experiences that represent you doing your thing well. This segment is about considering what could pull your attention back here.

In Exercise 14.2, consider what you could think about to help you perform your best. Is it a physical movement? Is it a physical sensation? Do you have a particular go-to thought that makes you aware of what is occurring? What helps you to come back to being fully present to what you are doing? I invite you to think about and come up with words or phrases that represent you doing your thing while training or performing (e.g., flow, power, swing, the

Exercise 14.2. Motivational flexibility—
Shifting focus back on doing my thing

| **Bringing myself back to ny moment-to-moment focus:** |
| E.g., *"Just right here, right now."* |
| 1. |
| 2. |
| 3. |

movement, the emotions to be shared musically) In the chart, jot down a few phrases that could bring you back to being fully present to doing your thing, in moments when your concerns about the outcome could soon take over.

We all know that on some level, we need to focus on what we are doing to be successful. But sometimes, it is hard to get our attention there. We need some compelling reasons to get ourselves to become present. Why be in the moment? Why pay attention to what you are doing? For this next section, I ask that you think about what is in it for you when you are fully engaged in the moment of what you are doing. What is personally satisfying to you about the good that comes simply from running, competing, giving a speech, or playing a beautiful piece of music? Consider what is good about doing your thing—in the moment—when you are competing or performing. The key here is to avoid answers that are about the outcome, the end, and the result. Consider what is of value to you to just have the opportunity to be doing your thing. For the basketball player, it could be the feeling of being totally in synch with teammates, for the public speaker, it could be experiencing full engagement and connection with a large group of people, and for the swimmer, it could be the experience of feeling strong and powerful while cutting through the water. I invite you to consider your motivation for the process of performing. It could be the fun or good that comes from being engaged in what you're doing, the joy of doing the activity itself, or the positive feeling that comes from being really good at what you do. (e.g., "I love doing this; this is my time; I'm good enough to be here.")

And the last aspect to consider is, what is in it for you when you enjoy some external success? Why do you want to be successful? What is in it for you if you are able to hit the mark of success that you aspire to hit? It is important that the reason is important to you, not about what others around you want. Sometimes we need a carrot—we need a reason, a *why*. For example, for the marathon runner the first 20 miles can be grueling. What can push that athlete beyond the notion that running is joyful, because the truth is sometimes what we are doing is the opposite of joyful. Any high level performance can require grueling training or moments of performance. Sometimes

Exercise 14.3. Sources of my motivational flexibility—
why I like doing my thing

What energizes me to focus moment to moment? *What energizes you?*
1.
2.
3.

we need an extrinsic motivation beyond the moment. The key to this one is to consider why you want to be successful for your own reasons beyond the expectations of a teacher, coach, parent, or the media (e.g., "I've earned this; I want to achieve my potential; I want to honor my sport or my world"). It is easy to want to achieve success. Sometimes it takes some effort to consider why the success is personally important to you. I encourage you to take the time to think about your answers.

Now you have a sense of the effective points of focus when you are training and performing. Your motivation may shift between performing based upon your enjoyment and performing in an effort to achieve a level of success. Essentially, motivational flexibility is about getting yourself to be present to what you are doing and occasionally being inspired by the carrot of success; these are the poles between which we want our motivation to flexibly move between. These go-to points of focus are essential, particularly when you find yourself in the inflexible state of fear of wondering how your upcoming

Exercise 14.4. Sources of my motivational flexibility—
why I want to be successful

Why performing well is important to me:
1.
2.
3.

performance might go (badly). When this occurs, you can remind yourself with cue words or images of "shifting my focus back to doing my thing," and "why I like to do my thing." The more you practice bringing yourself back to authentically energizing sources of inspiration and motivation, the better you will be able to consistently perform.

What are the types of focus, thoughts, and actions that best serve you when competing in particular moments throughout important events? You may not know for sure, but you can experiment with these ideas to see which is the best match for you. What we do know is that remaining inflexibly stuck in fear or dread of the outcome will not serve you well in performance.

To bring this all together, I'd like to leave you with two phrases—one that will get you focused on your moment-to-moment performance, and a second one that will help remind you why pushing through the hard moments is important to you. Take one more moment to consider what a glimpse of you being successful will look and feel like. Write down a few words or phrases to represent this moment—what will most motivate you to be engaged in doing your thing and what will most motivate you for reasons of external success. After you've written these down, I encourage you to try out these thoughts in practice. Practice shifting between your love of your endeavor and positive intentions to achieve particular marks of success.

Exercise 14.5. Go-to motivational sources

Where?	Your go-to outcome-focused thought	Your go-to in the moment focused engagement
Practice	(e.g., "I can feel the joy!")	(e.g., "I'm part of my instrument.")
Performance		

By creating and practicing these go-to words and phrases, you can learn to strengthen your ability to be flexible in your motivations and learn to more quickly pull yourself out of potential mud holes of fear. We must have a plan for where we want our minds to go. Such a plan can be your key to shifting into the freedom to do your thing in the midst of a high-pressure situation or in practice. Even a few seconds of shifted focus can be all it takes to give you a very different performance experience. We all can learn to shift to the motivational source that best serves us. But all of these ideas take practice and commitment. The good news is that it might just be one word or phrase that you need to go to in your mind to leverage yourself into your best performance of your life.

15

Your Plan for Game Day

Tailoring the Ideas to Work for You

"I see in my mind a picture of how I'd like it to be right when I landed the jet— when I trap (on an aircraft carrier in the ocean when there is heavy rain and fog)."

—Carrie Dunai Lohrenz, a female U.S. military fighter pilot pioneer

With pre-planning we can make good use of our heightened state of energy on game day. Because we often also experience some fear, even with the effort of expanding on the positive and maintaining awareness of our competencies in daily training. The question isn't whether you will have moments of intensified energy. Everyone does. The question is, "How can you make good use of your intensified energy from the start?"

In one of my studies, I asked a three-time Olympian and multiple-time World Champion how he generally feels before racing. I asked, "What are your typical emotions?" He answered, "Always in the morning I am nervous. You always get out of bed wondering if you got enough sleep, if you ate enough that night, if you had enough breakfast. So it is always a little bit of nervous [ness], uneasiness. Or almost like being nervous and your mind [was] playing tricks on you... [asking] 'Can I do this?'

Even an athlete who dominated internationally for many years experiences doubts along with his excitement for game day. We all face it.

Part of learning to prepare for game day is to be honest with yourself and consider how you tend to feel and think. Though no one likes to talk about it or admit it, the duality of intensified energy and self-doubt on game day is common. The doubt part makes us look weak, psychologically, to our teammates and coaches if we admit such thoughts. So we've learned to keep quiet about these naturally arising emotions. We like to pretend that they don't exist. (And it is generally a good idea to not talk about your fears with your teammates or those with whom you perform because you don't want to appear psychologically weak to them.)

Yet we need to be aware of when the intensified energy, and sometimes accompanying fear, is emerging so that we can use it to our advantage. If we don't we may be sorely surprised and spin mentally out of control. The key is to prepare for such feelings so you can channel the energy in a good way and avoid mental meltdowns and subsequent disappointing performances.

The time to make a plan for coping effectively with the overall intensity of game day is when we are feeling at ease and can use our confident minds to figure out the best approach for ourselves (in the future) when the doubt hits. Sometimes with my clients, I ask them to give full voice to the fearful parts of themselves. I like to refer to it as the devil on their shoulder. In the same round of conversation I like to have them give full voice to their strong, confident parts as well. Parallel to the devil, I like to refer to this as an angel on their shoulder. It generally goes something like this:

> Consider how you might be thinking or feeling on the morning of the big day. I'd like you to think of it in two ways. First, think about times when you've felt a lot of pressure to do well and you were in a confident and strong state of mind. If only that

part of you was in charge, how would you be thinking and feeling the morning of your next big competition? Let's think of this as the "angel on your shoulder." Now, let's go to the part of you that gets really afraid and worries about how badly it could go. If you were only going to give this part of you full power, what would this part of you be thinking and feeling the morning of your next big competition? I'll refer to this as the "devil on your other shoulder." The truth is you can choose to give either of them power. You need to focus on the perspective that most empowers you.

The remainder of this chapter will give you ideas about how you can access the angel on your shoulder. We will consider the most powerful strategies that can help you to stay focused on the moment-to-moment of performance while using the energy of being determined to perform your best—regardless of pressure on game day.

Consider a moment in performance when you have felt out of control or in a deep fear state. We have thought of this before. But for now, focus in only on the part of your mind that is being directed by fear (the devil on your shoulder). How does this devil evaluate your ability to handle that moment in performance? Have you ever thought, "I can't do this!" or "I just want this to end?" What does the devil on your shoulder believe about your abilities? Your potential for success?

Next, consider the most confident part of yourself that loves doing your thing. Consider the angel on your shoulder. What does this part of you believe about your potential? How does this part of you view your past training, your readiness and your ability to focus in and do your thing well (and shine!)? How does your angel respond to the very same moment? Maybe with, "It's OK, this will make me stronger"; "If I push through this, I can push through anything"; or "I really still love having a chance to be here, right now." Take a few minutes to consider your answers.

When we admit that the fear will show up, then we make a plan to handle it. And with the plan in hand, we do not have to succumb to the doubt or fear.

Exercise 15.1. Game day awareness: The devil and the angel

Challenge: Self-assessment on game day	My fearful response (devil)	My confident response (angel)

We can turn it around. We can change how we habitually respond, when we are feeling mentally off, to the challenge of game day. Some people have learned to turn it around without having to purposefully engage mentally. They have learned how to respond to the fear and doubt through the guidance of wise parents or coaches, or have just luckily had a genetic predisposition to rise above. Some may have stumbled onto responses that work and they were lucky enough to develop effective mental-emotional habits of how to effectively cope with the emotional challenge of putting oneself on the line. But we all have the capacity to learn how to effectively cope with the wild emotions that often accompany big performance days. You can key into your angel on your shoulder any time. It is a choice and a habit of mind.

FOCUS ON THIS MOMENT (REGARDLESS OF MISTAKES)

In many ways, this book is giving you many strategies and many ways to think about how to become present. The simple truth in performance psychology is that the more we can focus on what we are doing moment to moment—courageously, with or without fear—the more we set ourselves up to improve the most and perform our best. The more we practice being present to the opportunity of what we can do each moment, the stronger this habit becomes.

The most typical challenges for all performers are the monsters of doubt and fear—about what happened or what might happen. We can become highly focused on what will happen until we finally cross the line or when the last game whistle is blown. We can be lulled into thinking about what will happen instead of thinking of what is happening in the moment, both in our bodies and around ourselves.

Jessica is another Olympic athlete whom I interviewed for one of my studies. She was filled with the fear of what might happen:

> I knew that I had all this pressure on me and I was just so worried about performing well, so worried about messing up. I can remember very distinctively being afraid of messing up as opposed to what to do to make myself faster, what to do to be on for every piece.... I was pretty tense. I was having a hard time getting over it. I just remember being in a little pity party. I couldn't get over myself, couldn't get over my own bad attitude.... I was dwelling on each thing and letting it snowball into a ball of tension.

Jessica remembered this moment as a wake-up call. She realized that to make the Olympic team, she had to gain more control over her attitude and perspective when racing. She noted that she had to develop optimism about the next moment. She had to focus on what she could do, not what mistakes she had made or could make. Jessica sums it up by saying, "Instead of dwelling on a mistake, you make a mistake and you go on to the next stroke, it is just one stroke at a time. You keep looking ahead instead of dwelling on something that was negative." Jessica had learned to focus on the positive, focus on what she would like to make happen and what she hoped she could make happen.

It is possible to shift yourself into a confident, focused, constructive state of mind. You can give yourself your best chance of creating an optimal performance. But how do you do this? We'll start with some key questions that will help you formulate and tailor a game day plan that will work for you. These questions are designed to help you plan how you would like to be throughout your next big performance. The following essential questions will help you think about where to focus your mind and energy:

- What will it take for you to minimize distractions that show up on game day?

- What will it take for you to feel centered and in control while performing?

- What will it take for you to be fully focused on doing your thing (focusing on the task at hand) when it counts?

Unfortunately, there is no universal, perfect way to prepare for game day. However, there are some strategies that can help you move away from the fears or doubts on game day toward getting yourself in a mindset that will facilitate you getting the most out of your current abilities and skills. Some of these ideas have been considered in previous chapters. It can be helpful to consider them all together while focusing on making a plan for game day.

EXPAND ON THE GOOD

As we've discussed, one successful approach to get us into a constructive state of mind is to purposefully focus on what is going right moment to moment. We can begin this focus the day of, or even the day before, competition. Instead of forcing ourselves to be tough, another option is to create an empowered mindset on game day by focusing on what is good and what is going right. We can begin to notice what is going right by simply focusing on any good that surrounds us. As we focus on what feels good and what is good about ourselves, we set a foundation for the day to expand on the good that is occurring.

We also can recall when previous races or performances went well. If even for a few seconds at a time, using ourselves as models of how well we could perform is a great way to both build your confidence for the day but also build a sense of positive emotion in your system. Often, there is a lot of good happening during a performance, but we may not even notice it. (We have been so habituated to notice what is wrong.) And if we don't notice it, it is impossible to recall in memory when it would serve us to get psychologically ready for performance.

For example, I worked with Rachel, a marathon runner, who recently had one of the best runs of her life. I asked what had happened. Rachel said that she was running to qualify for the Boston Marathon. She said that during a late stage in the race, she was running so fast that she knew that without watching her time she would definitely qualify. "At mile 17, I ripped the watch off of my wrist and threw it to my father who was there to cheer me on." I asked her what happened over the last nine miles. Rachel simply smiled. She had greatly enjoyed her timed run, but hadn't made the effort to put to words all the good that had occurred.

She had never considered the importance of replaying in her mind what had happened meta-cognitively (thinking about her thinking) over the good portions of her races. I asked her if she, in any way, purposefully focused on and sustained the good emotions and attitude that were surging through her body after the pivotal moment of removing the watch from her wrist. After a few more minutes of discussion, Rachel recalled that she had, in fact, kept her mind focused on the good as she raced her last nine miles. Even though she said that the pain intensified over the last five miles, she kept reminding herself of how fast she was running, how well her body was doing, and how wonderful it felt to be so ahead of her target. She kept her mind on the good. But afterward she had forgotten that is what she did. But with the new awareness she could begin noticing the good moments in training and racing. As she approached a next race, she could remember what had gone well last time. She could think about how she wants to include this good in her next race.

Keeping your mind on what is going right is, of course, easier to do when the performance day is unfolding in a positive way. However, focusing on what is right is available to us at all times. It is a matter of choice. Though we may more habitually go to what is wrong, from our caveman days of keeping ourselves safe through visceral responses to potential fears, it is possible to purposefully shift to what is right. This is especially true during game day, when we probably cannot improve in terms of tactics, technique, or fitness. The only thing we can most powerfully change is our attitude, our focus, and energy use. Focusing on the good is a great way to increase the likelihood of performing your best when it counts.

Take a moment to consider a recent performance. What good did you notice on your performance day? What other good was occurring that you could have noticed that day? Take a moment to think about it and write down your ideas using Exericse 15.2. With a heightened awareness of what is good, you will begin to notice it more and more, even during high stakes competition days. There are many things from which you can choose. You could notice how good it is to have the chance to compete or the good in those with whom you are competing. You could consider the energy in the environment. You could notice the strengths and skills that you have developed. There is no right answer except for looking to any good that is within you or surrounds you, that is considered authentically good to you. Internal signs of good are valuable, as well, to notice. This could range from having moments of great ease to swells of confidence and hope.

Exercise 15.2. The good on a recent performance day

My good on performance day
1.
2.
3.

When trying to focus on the good, you don't need to spend too much time on it. You can let it arise naturally as long as you keep the intention of noticing what is good and right. Also, it is key that you focus on the good that resonates with you as opposed to thinking about what you "should" pay attention to. Focusing on the good around you can be a powerful source of good energy and a way to positively change perspective in a sometimes fear-inducing circumstance.

YOUR PERFORMANCE DAY PERSPECTIVE

You can also prepare yourself to get into an optimal mindset for game day by clarifying your performance day perspective before you get to a big game day. What do I mean by perspective? I mean how you make meaning of the upcoming competition. Without a plan in place, you can get stuck in the belief that your value as a human being hangs by the luck of having a good round of performance or not. The most typical set up for emotional disaster goes something like this: "If I don't win, I'm worthless, or I've wasted the last years of my life, or I'll feel humiliated." This mindset is a total set up for anxiety and distraction. Of course we all want success. But obsessing about it doesn't get us there. So we do know that expecting ourselves to be perfect doesn't work. We do know that expecting ourselves to manifest a best performance doesn't work. This line of thinking gets us caught up in worrying about things that we cannot control.

So what does work? Part of living and performing in the sweet spot requires that we maintain perspective. We have to develop a game day perspective that, at a conscious level, will allow us to focus on the things that we can control like our effort, engaging with the moment to moment demands of bouncing our ball, hitting a musical note, or being present to our audience. One way to help get ourselves to focus on what we can control is through accepting, in advance, the outcome. When we accept what will come, we free ourselves to dig in and get present to increase our changes for best performance that day.

What will work for you? You know yourself better than anyone else knows you. You need to draw on your self-wisdom to determine the performance perspective that will most empower you and be most real for you. How can you think about your performance that will allow you to accept that you cannot control the (ultimate) outcome of your efforts, but that you do have control over what you do and think each moment?

A place to start is to consider a few of your best performances and then consider how you were feeling and what you were focusing on both a few hours and just before you began your performance. From these moments, you will be able to mine a performance approach that will work best for you. What perspective could you go into your game day with? How could you frame your day? It can be helpful to have one go-to thought or phrase that represents how you would like to frame your day. The thought could be about your level of preparation, your love for your performance realm, or a cue word to remind yourself that focusing on the task at hand will most empower you to perform. The challenge is that there is not one right performance perspective. It can be invaluable to name your own, it will help you to focus on what best serves you just before your next performance begins. I encourage you to complete all of the following three phrases or sentences in Exercise 15.3.

VISUALIZE THE END

Visualizing a successful end to your performance or competition is a powerful strategy. Imagining yourself feeling just how you would ideally feel and look just after a great performance can help you set the intention of creating such an ending. Also, when you start from the finish, you know what you need to focus on to enable yourself to achieve such success. Seeing the end can also serve to strengthen your belief in your ability to manifest the type of performance you would like to create. Imaging or visualizing our future success can be a great step in helping us get there. We must know what we are working toward. With a clear and vivid image of just what we'd like to achieve, we clarify what it will take to get there.

Exercise 15.3. Your performance day perspective

In terms of my effort, what matters to me most is to…
I will be proud of myself no matter what, because…
I love _____ _____ about actually doing my thing.

I've had a chance to talk with Carey Lohrenz, one of the first female fighter pilots in the U.S. military. As part of her job as a Navy fighter pilot, Carey would take off from and land on aircraft carriers out at sea. She has successfully completed more than 160 such landings in her career. I asked her how she prepares herself mentally for the landings. Please note that she faced the reality of having to land on a surface that was just over 600 feet long with an approach speed of 150 miles per hour. At touchdown, if all goes well, the arresting hook snags a wire stretched across the deck and the aircraft is yanked to a halt. This is considered a controlled crash, stopping the aircraft from 150 miles per hour to 0 in less than 400 feet. Aircraft carrier landing decks are angled about nine degrees off the centerline so that when pilots fail to trap a wire, you don't run into other aircraft but fly off the front end of the deck. Carey recalls, "This is why on every landing we slam the throttles to full power in case one of those wires breaks or we fail to catch the hook." If she missed, or bolstered, too many times (she had a limited amount of tries due to fuel limitations) she could crash many miles out to sea. She recalled,

Landing a fighter jet on an aircraft carrier at night is the most harrowing thing to do in all of military aviation. Night landings are really intense, a lot of adrenaline is involved—frankly, sometimes you want to and sometimes you don't want to land. But that isn't an option! It is hardest when there is a thick fog and you know the deck is pitching and rolling… But you have to rely on your training and continually visualize where you want to be and focus intently on what matters.

How will you be feeling just after you nail your upcoming performance? How would you like to be feeling and thinking just as you finish? Just after you've finished? How would you like those who see your performance to respond to what you've just accomplished? Take a moment to jot down your intention for the end of your upcoming performance.

Exercise 15.4. Intending the end of your performance

Your performance	Experience *just before* your performance ends	Experience *when* your performance ends
Physically?		
Emotionally?		
Satisfaction level?		
Joy level?		

PREPARE FOR A MINI-MIND

When we are performing, our full moment-to-moment attention is required to give us the best chance of optimizing performance. The need to be fully focused and engaged is consistent with the concept of *flow,* a concept coined by Mihaly Csikszentmihaly and discussed at length in Chapter 7. To be fully engaged, we must be fully committed while stretching our capacity. When we remain focused in the moment and engaged with the activity itself, there are no problems. We tend to perform at our absolute best.

However, when thoughts of fear or doubt arise unexpectedly, performance troubles may follow. Our performance can be thwarted by random, involuntary thoughts. We can experience surges of pain and doubt. Because when we are competing so much of our attention is absorbed by the task at hand, we don't have our normal capacity to notice and manage debilitating thoughts and emotions. I like to think of it as having a *mini-mind.*

What do I mean by mini-mind? I think of this as having access to only a small portion of our mind power when performing. In many types of performance domains, we have minimal access to our logical, thoughtful responses because we are so engaged in the moment with what we are doing. If things are going well, there is no problem. But if we hit a difficult challenge without a plan, we can't expect much from our deep thinking abilities. For example, a runner in the last lap of a mile race when they are feeling intense physical pain may not have the ability to figure out how to be responding to their self-doubt, in that moment. Because of the potential debilitative experience of a mini-mind, we must prepare for it. If mini-mind hits without preparation, we can blow our chances of optimizing performance. Unless we prepare in advance, we can't handle the mental challenges while competing because our minds are already so tapped.

In almost any realm of performance, there are a few predictable moments that can throw us off. The key is to prepare for such moments. An example of having reduced access to one's mind and being able to rebound is exampled by the experience of triathlete Marijke. She recalls that in her last Ironman race, after swimming 2.4 miles and biking 112 miles, she was in the middle of her marathon when she mentally hit a wall. She felt like she had nothing left. She purposefully looked up to see when the next kilometer mark was and began calculating how many kilometers she would have to keep racing.

Marijke recalls that she was just in the decision-making process if she would "agree with herself... that she didn't care if she was passed by anyone." Out of nowhere, a spectator on the side of the road began speaking to her and said, "You are running great. You just look great. If you are able to keep up with this pace, you will for sure be able to move into third place [from fifth]." With these words, Marijke felt a powerful shift in her attitude and in her physical body. All of a sudden, her calculations radically shifted: She began counting how many kilometers that she had left to calculate how much time she had to pass the athletes currently in third and fourth places. She had few mental resources in that moment. Thanks to the comments of a stranger, though, she was greatly helped to shift how she was thinking. She, in fact, did pass them and ended finishing third in the triathlon.

Even with her list of athletic accomplishments, Marijke was unable to overcome that moment of doubt. It took an unexpected voice from the crowd to help her make her mental shift in this particular instance. The only change that occurred was in her thinking. Though her body was probably exhausted, the shift in thinking reenergized and recommitted her to fully engaging in her determination to do her best in that given race. It would be expected that in such a grueling race, there would potentially be a moment when the performer wants to give up.

In fact, in two studies that I conducted with 38 elite and U.S. Team rowers, I found that over 50% reported that in their worst coping experience in competitive sport that during an Olympic trials, World Championship race, or Olympic race, they had mentally given up. Though they did not literally stop rowing, they did stop fighting. One of the athletes from the study recalled a time when she was racing in the World Championships. Her team and coach expected a gold medal. They went into the race with a high level of confidence, but totally lacked a plan about how to handle things if the race did not unfold as planned. Her boat had started out in first place, but was passed and another crew was moving on them (it looked they would pass her boat as well). The athlete recalled thinking in the middle of this World Championship finals race,

> I just want to get the hell out of this boat and I don't want to be here. I just want to go home.... There was nothing I could have done that could have got me out of that boat faster and just on the plane and out of there. I just wanted to leave. I didn't give up, but mentally I gave up. Physically, I was still rowing and finishing the race, but mentally I couldn't care less. I just remember thinking, 'I don't care what happens.'

It was astounding to me at the time of these studies that so many elite athletes reported having given up mentally in races, races that many of them had been hoping and preparing to participate in for years. It was hard to believe that they really did not care in the moment about the results of the race. They were racing in one of the most important races of their careers and were giving into their fears.

The truth is that they felt totally helpless in the moment. They were either unexpectedly losing to someone who they thought that they could beat or performing below their standards. They had no plan. They had no resources to draw on to bounce back and fight. I have come to the conclusion after considering this research and having practiced performance psychology for the past decade that if U.S. and Olympic team athletes give up during key international competitions, when they don't have a mental plan, most athletes and performers will also give up at some point. It is therefore important to plan for such moments.

No matter how confident, how competent, or how mentally tough we are, we all need a plan to fall back on during key performance moments when our confidence is shaken or mini-mind sets in. We need a plan to deal with our mini-minds when we hit the hardest of performance challenges. We need to come up with a plan for the predictably hardest moments in our upcoming performances.

In Exercise 15.5, consider the moment(s) that could be hardest for you. The moment(s) may or may not arise, but it can be very helpful to have a plan, just in case. For endurance athletes, think about the time when you may be most highly challenged by a competitor or when you may not be coping well with the intense sensations associated with lactic acid build-up. For the musicians, you can consider how you will handle it if you make a mistake or are thrown off by the evaluation of some important other in the audience. You may consider the key moments of pressure when you are expected to win.

Consider the point in competition in which a change in your thinking, action, emotion, or motivation may have the biggest, most constructive impact on your performance. The goal is to come up with a simple, clear plan to focus on strengthening or changing your approach in this key performance moment. It can help you to develop both a go-to phrase and a go-to image of what might help you most in the mini-mind moments of competition. It is most helpful to have just one go-to thought and one go-to image. This is an instance where simplicity and clarity are most powerful. It is hard to ask much of your mind in such pained or weak moments. What might work best for you? I've given a few examples, below. This is when you can carefully tailor the plan to you. Only you know what image or phrase will empower you to recommit and reinvest in the performance.

Exercise 15.5. Planning for negative mini-mind moments

Your key moment:	Your planned thought (to invite the refocus)	Your planned image (to invite the refocus)
e.g.,	"I've earned this." "I belong here."	Seeing a rocket blast off. A star.

CHOOSE ONE THING

This book is filled with essential ideas about how to prepare for performance. There is no way that anyone could implement all of the ideas, all at once, in their preparation for performance. It can feel overwhelming to think about trying to notice your strengths, expand the good emotions, learn to effectively cope with negative emotions, and the many other core ideas in this book. The truth is that to make a significant change in your mental approach to training and performance, it is best to start with making one change. You know yourself better than any sport or performance psychologist ever could. As you read through the many exercises, some resonated with you and others may not have captured your interest. You have internal knowledge that will indicate which point of focus will help you the most.

Try one. When I send a client out of my office, the most I will ask them to do is to bring up one cue word (e.g., "I chose this, I love this") or one image (e.g., seeing themselves performing to the best of their ability while filled with joy and intense focus). I'll send them home with an index card with a few words written on it or a reminder word or two to help them recall the image that evokes the feeling and focus that will most help them in a particular and important moment of training or performing. I encourage you to take an index card and write down a few words that will help you work toward the one change that will be most pivotal in the next step to becoming an even better competitor and performer.

I hope that after reading *Living in the Sweet Spot* you can more fully enjoy your training and can take joy in all that you are and all that you can become. Celebrate each time you nurture your positive emotions and disarm your negative emotions, and remember that with daily, focused effort you can be living in the sweet spot.

References

CHAPTER 2

Aristotle. (1908). *Nichomachean ethics.* Ross, W. D. (Trans.). Oxford, UK: Clarendon Press.

Bandura, A. (1997). *Self-efficacy: The exercise of control.* New York: Worth Publishers.

Peterson, C. (2006). *A primer in positive psychology.* New York: Oxford Press.

Peterson, C., & Seligman, M. (2004). *Character strengths and virtues: A handbook and classification.* New York: Oxford University Press.

CHAPTER 3

Fredrickson, B. (2001). The role of positive emotions in positive psychology: The broaden-and-build theory of positive emotions. *American Psychologist, 56*(3), 218-226.

Fredrickson, B. (2009). *Positivity: Groundbreaking research reveals how to embrace the hidden strength of positive emotions, overcome negativity, and thrive.* New York: Random House.

CHAPTER 4

Baumeister, R. (2002). Ego depletion and self-control failure: An energy model of the self's executive function. *Self and Identity, 129-136.*

Baumeister, R., Bratslavsky, E., Muraven, M., & Tice, D. (1998). Ego depletion: Is the active self a limited resource? *Journal of personality and social psychology, 74*(5), 1252-1265.

Danner, D., Snowdon, D., & Friesen, W. (2001). Positive emotions in early life and longevity: Findings from the nun study. *Journal of personality and social psychology, 80,* 804-813.

Fredrickson, B., & Losada, M. (2005). Positive affect and the complex dynamics of human flourishing. *American Psychologist, 60*(7), 680.

Galliot, M., Baumeister, R., DeWall, C., Maner, J., Plant, A., Tice, D., Brewer, L., & Schmeichel, B. (2007). Self-control relies on glucose as a limited energy source: Willpower is more than a metaphor. *Journal of personality and social psychology, 92*(2), 325-336.

Orlick, T. (2000). *In pursuit of excellence* (3rd ed.). Champaign, IL: Human Kinetics.

Rozanski, A., & Kubzansky, L. D. (2005). Psychologic functioning and physical health: A paradigm of flexibility. *Psychosomatic Medicine, 67*(1) S47-S53.

Senge, P. (2006). *The fifth discipline: The art & practice of the learning organization.* New York: Random House.

CHAPTER 5

Baltzell, A. (2000). *Psychological factors and coping resources related to elite rowers' performance.* USOC Final Report: A USOC Science and Technology Grant Project Final Report.

Dweck, C. (2006). Mindset: The new psychology of success. New York: Random House.

CHAPTER 6

Carver, C. S., Scheier, M. F., & Segerstrom, S. C. (in press). *Optimism.* Clinical Psychology Review.

Emmons R., & Shelton, C. M. (2005). Gratitude and the science of positive psychology. In C. Snyder & S. Lopez (Eds.), *Handbook of positive psychology* (pp. 459-471). New York: Oxford University Press.

Maslow, A. (1970). *Motivation and personality.* New York: Harper and Row.

Peterson, C. (2006). *A primer in positive psychology.* New York: Oxford Press.

Snyder, C., & Lopez, S. (Eds.). (2002). *Handbook of positive psychology.* New York: Oxford University Press.

CHAPTER 7

Csikszentmihalyi, M. (1991, 2008). *Flow.* New York: Harper and Row.

Jackson, S. (1992). Athletes in flow: A qualitative investigation of flow states in elite figure skaters. *Journal of Applied Sport Psychology, 4,* 161-180.

Jackson, S. (1995). Factors influencing the occurrence of flow state in elite athletes. *Journal of Applied Sport Psychology, 7,* 138-166.

Jackson, S., & Csikszentmihalyi, M. (1999). *Flow in sports: The keys to optimal experiences and performances.* Champaign, IL: Human Kinetics.

CHAPTER 8

Fredrickson, B., & Losada, M. (2005). Positive affect and the complex dynamics of human flourishing. *American Psychologist, 60*(7), 678-686.

Gottman, J. M. (1994). *What predicts divorce? The relationship between marital processes and marital outcomes.* Hillsdale, NJ: Erlbaum.

Hanton, S., & Jones, G. (1999). The acquisition and development of cognitive skills and strategies: I. Making the butterflies fly in formation. *The Sport Psychologist, 13,* 1-21.

Kabat-Zinn, J. (2009). *Letting everything become your teacher: 100 lessons in mindfulness.* New York: Random House.

Lazarus, R. (2000). How emotions influence performance in competitive sports. *The Sport Psychologist, 14,* 229-252.

Nhat Hanh, T. (1999). *The miracle of mindfulness.* Boston: Beacon Press.

CHAPTER 9
Peterson, C. (2006). *A primer in positive psychology.* New York: Oxford Press.

CHAPTER 10
Deyer, W. (2001). *You'll see it when you believe I: The way to your personal transformation.* New York: HarperCollins Publisher.

Feltz, D. L., Landers, D. M., & Becker, B. J. (1988). A revised meta-analysis of the mental practice literature on motor skill learning. In D. Druckman & J. A. Swets (Eds.), *Enhancing human performance: Issues, theories, and techniques.* Washington, DC: National Academy Press.

Morris, T., Spittle, M., & Watt, A. (2005). Imagery in sport. Champaign, IL: Human Kinetics.

CHAPTER 11
Butler, R., & Hardy, L. (1992). The performance profile: Theory and application. *The Sport Psychologist,* 6253-264.

Hanson, T., & Ravizza, K. (1995). *Heads-up baseball: Playing the game one pitch at a time.* Emeryville, CA: McGraw Hill.

Senge, P. (2006). *The fifth discipline: The art & practice of the learning organization.* Sydney: Random House.

CHAPTER 13
Hanton, S., & Jones, G. (1999). The acquisition and development of cognitive skills and strategies: I. Making the butterflies fly in formation. *The Sport Psychologist, 13,* 1-21.

CHAPTER 15
Hanson, T., & Ravizza, K. (1995). *Heads-up baseball: Playing the game one pitch at a time.* Emeryville, CA: McGraw Hill.

Kok, B. E., Catalino, L. I., & Fredrickson, B. L. (2008). The broadening, building, buffering effects of positive emotions. In S. J. Lopez (Ed.), *Positive psychology: Exploring the best of people, Vol. 3: Capitalizing on emotional experiences* (pp. 1-19). Westport, CT: Greenwood Publishing Company.

Index

About the Author

Amy L. Baltzell

Amy L. Baltzell, EdD, directs the sport psychology program and is a professor in the School of Education at Boston University. Her academic credentials include a bachelor's degree in economics from Wesleyan University of Connecticut (1987), a master's in counseling (1996) from Boston University, and a doctorate in counseling psychology, specializing in sport psychology, from Boston University in 1999. Her research interests are in the areas of mindfulness, performance enhancement, and values in sport. She has presented a dozen academic papers and dozens of invited talks across the country.

As a licensed psychologist specializing in sport and performance, Baltzell works with professional, elite, collegiate, and high school athletes and professional musicians. She provides educational workshops to teams and organizations, keynote presentations, and coach education training sessions. She also has a private practice in which she provides one-on-one consulting to athletes and performers.

Prior to entering academia, Baltzell was an elite multi-sport athlete. She was a three-year member of the U.S. National Rowing Team, including the 1992 Olympic team and during that time won multiple national and international gold medals. She also was a member of the historic 1995 all-women's America's Cup sailing team, America. Additionally, she played basketball, lacrosse, field hockey, sailed, and ran the Boston Marathon. She also previously served as an athletic coach, notably as the head women's lightweight rowing coach at Harvard University.

This is Baltzell's third book. She is a co-author of *Whose Game is it Anyway, Parenting Your Athletic Child* and *Character and Coaching.*